International
Business
and Trade

Theory, Practice,
and Policy

Claude M. Jonnard

S^t_L

St. Lucie Press

Boca Raton   Boston   London   New York   Washington, D.C.

Library of Congress Cataloging-in-Publication Data

Catalog information may be obtained from the Library of Congress

This book contains information obtained from authentic and highly regarded sources. Reprinted material is quoted with permission, and sources are indicated. A wide variety of references are listed. Reasonable efforts have been made to publish reliable data and information, but the author and the publisher cannot assume responsibility for the validity of all materials or for the consequences of their use.

Neither this book nor any part may be reproduced or transmitted in any form or by any means, electronic or mechanical, including photocopying, microfilming, and recording, or by any information storage or retrieval system, without prior permission in writing from the publisher.

The consent of CRC Press LLC does not extend to copying for general distribution, for promotion, for creating new works, or for resale. Specific permission must be obtained in writing from CRC Press LLC for such copying.

Direct all inquiries to CRC Press LLC, 2000 Corporate Blvd., N.W., Boca Raton, Florida 33431.

Trademark Notice: Product or corporate names may be trademarks or registered trademarks, and are used only for identification and explanation, without intent to infringe.

© 1998 by CRC Press LLC
St. Lucie Press is an imprint of CRC Press LLC

No claim to original U.S. Government works
International Standard Book Number 1-57444-155-8
Printed in the United States of America 1 2 3 4 5 6 7 8 9 0
Printed on acid-free paper

Table of Contents

Preface v
Acknowledgments ix
About the Author x

PART I: INTERNATIONAL BUSINESS THEORIES AND CONCEPTS
1 Corporate Challenges 3
2 A Philosophy of Business for the Twenty-First Century 15
3 International Business Operations 27
4 The Monetary System 41
5 The Balance of Payments 55
6 Foreign Exchange and Foreign Exchange Management 67

PART II: INTERNATIONAL TRADE AND BUSINESS OPERATIONS
7 International Trade Practices: The Parties 83
8 The Legal Environment of International Business 91
9 Product Warranty and Product Liability Issues 99
10 Protection of Intellectual Assets 105
11 International Trade Logistics 113
12 Financing Trade: The Banking System 125
13 Financing Trade: Payments and Collections 137
14 International Letters of Credit 147
15 Foreign Manufacturing and Assembly 155
16 International Licensing and Franchising 163
17 Strategic Alliances 173
18 Foreign Investments 181

PART III: POLICY AND INSTITUTIONS
19 Trade Regulation and Restrictions 191
20 Investment Restrictions 199

21 U.S. Policies: Taxation and Related Programs 207
22 U.S. Trade and Investment Support Organizations 225
23 International Systems and Organizations 245

GLOSSARY 267

ABBREVIATIONS AND ACRONYMS 279

APPENDIX: THE U.S. BALANCE OF PAYMENTS 281

INDEX 287

Preface

Chapter 1. Corporate Challenges. Readers are introduced to the major changes that have taken place in the last two centuries. They are also introduced to the challenges that may be facing large, globally oriented businesses, acting as economic surrogates of society, in the twenty-first century.

Chapter 2. A Philosophy of Business for the Twenty-First Century. In this chapter, three major competing philosophies are reviewed in order to analyze which ideas may be best suited to the management of society in the new century. Some leading corporate philosophies are also analyzed to examine how the business community sees itself blending into the emerging world order.

Chapter 3. International Business Operations. In this chapter, the various forms of cross-border activities in which large multinational corporations, along with smaller companies, engage are reviewed in summary form.

Chapter 4. The Monetary System. The monetary system governing the short- and long-term financial management of trade and investments can be traced back to the early nineteenth century. It evolved from the monetization of gold as a nation's holder of value in due course and coincided with the increasing use of paper currency in the twentieth century. The themes of this chapter are to show how the current monetary system developed into its current form, how it affects all aspects of a company's global activities, and what shape the monetary system may have in the future.

Chapter 5. The Balance of Payments. In this chapter, international trade, business, and investments are analyzed from the perspective of the flow of cross-border exchange of debits, credits, and payments among nations. These exchanges are recorded in a country's national accounts statistics, called "the balance of payments."

Chapter 6. Foreign Exchange and Foreign Exchange Management. The understanding and management of foreign exchange has become a major preoccupation for multinational corporations. The concept and operation of the foreign exchange market and how companies manage their foreign currency assets to minimize the risk of sustaining foreign exchange losses are discussed in this chapter.

Chapter 7. International Trade Practices: The Parties. The parties involved in the practice of international trade and how they interface to create and complete an import–export transaction are reviewed in this chapter. Merchandise exports and imports are said to be the crankshaft of all international business operations, although they are no longer the primary reason for the pursuit of global enterprise.

Chapter 8. The Legal Environment of International Business. In this chapter, the legal environment of international business practices is examined. Questions concerning the rights and obligations of those participating in cross-border transactions are addressed.

Chapter 9. Product Warranty and Product Liability Issues. The various aspects of companies' rights and obligations in product warranty and liability situations are discussed in this chapter. Product warranties are promises by a manufacturer that its products will perform as stated in published literature. They can be explicit or implicit. Warranties are explicit when a manufacturer includes a written statement describing what guarantees it offers in the event of product performance failure and for how long a period of time those guarantees are good.

Chapter 10. Protection of Intellectual Assets. The nature of intellectual assets and their importance to companies doing business internationally are explored in this chapter. The protection of these assets is growing in importance as goods and services are being produced, marketed, and traded on a global scale. Intellectual assets and goodwill consist of patents, trade names, trademarks, and copyrights, the sum of which identify a company's goods and services as belonging to it.

Chapter 11. International Trade Logistics. Often ignored by business executives in planning international business strategies for their companies is the transportation environment. In this chapter, the specialized terminology used in international trade to define the rights and obligations of all parties to a transaction is reviewed. In-transit insurance, without which the physical distribution of goods internationally would be riskier than it is, is examined closely.

Chapter 12. Financing Trade: The Banking System. The international banking system and documentation that must be prepared by international traders as shipments proceed to their destination are described in this chapter. The paperwork, which includes the seller's commercial invoices, is commonly called "documentation." Its accurate and timely preparation and distribution (the collection process) enable importers to receive their goods and make it easier for exporters to receive on-time payment.

Chapter 13. Financing Trade: Payments and Collections. The focus of this chapter is the more popular payment terms used by companies in the export business. The role played by the international banking system in providing an operating environment that makes it easier for exporters to receive on-time payment for their shipments is also closely examined.

Chapter 14. International Letters of Credit. The focus of this chapter is payment risk minimization through the use of letters of credit. It will also be seen that these documents may be used to finance international trade.

Chapter 15. Foreign Manufacturing and Assembly. Turnkey systems, management contracts, and contract manufacturing agreements, used as means of introducing high-technology systems and/or goods produced in other countries expediently and without long-term foreign direct investments, are discussed in this chapter.

Chapter 16. International Licensing and Franchising. In this chapter, the international transfer of technology and know-how through arrangements called licensing and franchising agreements is explored. These agreements are contracts through which owners of intellectual properties such as patents, trademarks, trade names, and copyrights are able to temporarily rent, through a "lease" or "license," their rights to those assets to a licensee in return for a fee or royalty.

Chapter 17. Strategic Alliances. This chapter illustrates how businesses can use strategic alliances in an international environment to mutual advantage. Strategic alliances are intercorporate agreements between two or more companies designed to achieve various degrees of vertical and horizontal integration. This vertical/horizontal integration is also possible with wholly owned subsidiaries, where expansion takes place through merger, acquisition, and joint ventures.

Chapter 18. Foreign Investments. This chapter takes a close look at foreign direct investments in the form of joint ventures and wholly owned subsidiaries. Foreign direct investments are investments into other countries with the objective of owning partially or entirely an economic enterprise for the purpose of establishing market share and generating revenue and profits. Foreign portfolio investments are investments into financial instruments such as stocks and bonds, where the goal is not to engage in business but to generate dividend income, interest income, and capital gains.

Chapter 19. Trade Regulation and Restrictions. The regulatory environment of international trade and investments and the impact of restrictions on the conduct of international business transactions are examined in this chapter.

Chapter 20. Investment Restrictions. In this chapter, the regulatory environment of international investments and its impact on the conduct of international business transactions are examined. Beyond a government's responsibility to regulate trade is said to lie an obligation to guide investments into areas of economic activity seen as necessary to promote economic growth and development. Governments fulfill this obligation through a mix of fiscal (tax) and monetary (interest rate and foreign exchange manipulation) policies.

Chapter 21. U.S. Policies: Taxation and Related Programs. U.S. trade and investment policies have tended to encourage the nation to export, import, invest overseas, and invite investments from abroad. The general official attitude has been, from the country's beginnings, that trade and investments are good for the economy in an overall, long-term sense. U.S. government policies and programs embodied in a number of tax laws that specifically support private sector involvement in international trade and investments are analyzed in this chapter.

Chapter 22. U.S. Trade and Investment Support Organizations. In this chapter, the roles played by key U.S. government organizations in assisting business in doing business overseas are examined. The focus is on four support groups: the Overseas Private Investment Corporation, the Export-Import Bank of the United States, the U.S. Small Business Administration, and the United States Agency for International Development.

Chapter 23. International Systems and Organizations. The trend toward international economic cooperation through the creation of trade blocs, euphemistically called the "regionalization" of trade and investments, is reviewed in this chapter. The roles played by international organizations like the World Bank and the International Monetary Fund in assisting nations to grow their economies through international trade and investments are also examined.

Acknowledgments

The author is privileged to acknowledge the contributions of those who have made this book possible. A word of thanks goes to my family for their patience, along with a special expression of gratitude to Professor J. Griffith for much of the research and writing that went into completing this work. Most of the information contained in the book was obtained either from hard copy references or through the Internet, from publications by the U.S. Department of Commerce, the U.S. Department of State, the Small Business Administration, the United States Agency for International Development, the Export-Import Bank of the United States, the Overseas Private Investment Corporation, the U.S. Internal Revenue Service, the International Monetary Fund, the World Bank, Chemical Bank (now Chase Manhattan Bank), and Dun & Bradstreet Information Services.

About the Author

Claude M. Jonnard is a professor of economics and international business at Fairleigh Dickinson University, Madison, New Jersey. He is also vice president of The Horizon Trading Company, a family-owned securities and equipment sales and financing business. He has a master's degree from New York University and is a member of the National Association for Business Economics.

PART I

International Business Theories and Concepts

CHAPTER 1

Corporate Challenges

INTRODUCTION

The major changes that have taken place in the last two centuries are introduced, as are the challenges that will be facing globally oriented businesses functioning as economic surrogates of society in the twenty-first century.

DIFFERENCES BETWEEN TODAY AND YESTERDAY

How the world has changed. Were one to ask how many changes have occurred in the past 200 years, it would be possible to list an almost endless number, beginning with the invention of the telephone and combustible engine and ending at the end of this millennium with the computer, space travel, genetic engineering, and artificial intelligence. At a very personal level, the world has come a long way since the days of the fan and wood-burning stove as means of climate control and flags, smoke signals, and the pony express as means of communication.

There have also been macro changes in the past century. Demographic patterns of growth and development have forged a path from rural life barely touched by urban communities to the point where the populations of most societies live and work within an urban–suburban environment and surrounding rural communities either provide complementary services or sink to the status of economic backwaters.

An evolution in behavioral ideologies. Major political, social, and economic philosophies have emerged in that same time frame to postulate the key theories of human organization and behavior that order society today. Most belief systems regarding resource development and allocation, wealth and income creation and distribution, political structures, and social interaction stem from ancient ideas articulated into working theories in the nineteenth and twentieth centuries.

Technology and control over resources. It can probably be argued that two factors can be given credit for bringing about many of the changes, constructive as well as destructive, that have affected humanity. The first factor is a long-term movement toward the concentration of resource development and use and the organization and conduct of economic activity in the hands of monolithic, globally oriented private sector businesses known as multinational or transnational corporations. The second factor is the accelerating pace of technological change. It is reasonable to suspect in this connection that the momentum of technological change is being increasingly fueled by market-driven corporate entrepreneurial initiatives, with infrastructure support provided by governments.

The force of private enterprise and the state as surrogate of society. The channeling of effort in most areas of the world to achieve market-driven goals is accelerating economic growth and development in many societies which a few years ago might have been consigned to perpetual underdevelopment.

It is also altering traditional ideas about relationships between the individual, the community, the corporate business, and the sovereign state. The concern is whether there will be room for the state to continue, as it has in the past century, as the surrogate of society if private business becomes responsible by fiat for operating an economy and its competitiveness on a global scale.

BUSINESS IN A CHANGING WORLD

Fuzzy distinctions between domestic and international businesses. Separating business into domestic and international components for discussion purposes is largely irrelevant today. Businesses become large and prosperous when they adopt a global vision and strategy in matters ranging from the allocation of resources to the production and marketing of their goods and services.

The option of staying small and thinking "local" can be fatal. Even the smallest community-oriented enterprises, like the neighborhood pizza parlor, the local clothing store, the village cleaner, the corner market, and the independently owned pharmacy, wittingly or unwittingly rely on the global sourcing of the goods and services they sell. Knowledgeable local retailers and wholesalers will routinely attend the major trade shows where their industries are featured in order to remain current and competitive. Those who attempt to move forward wearing blinders usually go out of business in short order. There is very little sold in the United States or in any other country that is not at least partially made elsewhere.

Big business is a relatively new phenomenon. There were few large privately owned businesses in the United States or in the world before the American Revolution or before the Industrial Revolution in Europe. The few large commercial entities that did flourish did so under close government control or ownership. Interestingly, among the first enterprises to operate fairly autonomously of government control were financial institutions, perhaps because many of them started as offshoots of powerful and aristocratic titled families who acted as moneylenders to their royal overlords.

Private ownership is a contemporary idea. The concept of private ownership also was not clearly established, even in land ownership, until the nineteenth century. Acceptance of the idea that the factors of production could be owned by private stockholders and could be worked by private citizens hired and supervised by professional managers on behalf of those stockholders became rooted in the United States after 1800 and then spread to other areas. Even in Adam Smith's England, the ancestral home of the Industrial Revolution, the concept of private ownership of large enterprises that stretched out across national borders was not well recognized. It was generally accepted that the government (crown) owned all the factors of production (especially land and its resources) and that while those factors could be managed by private individuals, a temporary license or franchise first had to be granted by the state.

Privatization is a trend. The trend today, following the dynamic growth of private enterprise in the nineteenth and twentieth centuries, is to encourage even more privately owned and controlled business. This is a response to observations that a government does not have the wherewithal to micromanage society. It is also a response to a general feeling that the management of human resources enjoys greater efficiency when left in private hands.

The global vision thing. Even the smallest business establishments in the smallest towns are directly impacted by world events influenced by multinational businesses and governments. The time when a growth-oriented enterprise could base itself and operate within the borders of a single country and prosper is probably over. Corporate growth and survival today require a global perspective and strategy. The principles of business behavior in a global environment are as important to master today as economics, accounting, and mathematics if managers of economic enterprise are to succeed in this new arena of global competition, interaction, and interdependence.

DEMOGRAPHICS AND THE ENVIRONMENT

Six billion and growing. More than 6 billion people inhabit the planet today (1998) compared with about 1.5 billion 100 years ago or about 4.4 billion in 1980. This makes the world a more crowded place in which to live, work, and play. Until this decade, total world population had been growing at an increasing annual rate until it peaked in the 1980s at about 2%. The current annual rate of population growth is 1.7%.*

World population will grow, decline, or stay the same? There is a division of opinion as to whether or not global population growth has peaked. An extreme-case scenario at a 2% annual growth rate would mean a doubling to more than 12 billion people by the mid-2030s. More conservative scenarios see the world's population peaking at less than 9 billion people by the mid-2050s. There is also a doomsday scenario that suggests the start of a precipitous decline as societies industrialize and families bear fewer children. One may indeed observe among those countries that have high-income populations, or are moving rapidly to become high-income societies, a real consistent decline in their birth rates.

Population pressure on resources and facilities. Whatever direction population will take, any change must be anticipated by government and the private sector to enable societies to maintain and improve the living standards of their constituencies. A stationary or expanding population will call for more efficient utilization of resources and considerable investments in education, technology development, and expansion of business and employment. A declining population will require serious planning to provide social services for greater numbers of the aged and infirm while still maintaining economic growth and development momentum.

---

* World Bank, *World Development Report, 1996*, Table 4, pp. 194–195, Oxford University Press, New York, 1996.

The major challenge for the next 50 years. The major challenge for the twenty-first century will probably be to support large and increasing populations with enough resources and infrastructures to sustain economic growth and development without destroying the environment. This can be translated into "people" issues such as food and energy, shelter, healthcare, education, welfare and social services, transportation and communications, production and distribution, money and banking, and income and employment.

The smallest and largest countries of the world. The World Bank, in its 1996 publication *World Development Report,* lists 209 countries. Some are tiny, like Grenada with a population over slightly more than 92,000. Some have large populations, like China and India (1.2 billion and 914 million, respectively, in 1997).*

A few countries cover vast territories and are demographically sparse (Mongolia with 2.4 million), and a few countries (Indonesia with 190.4 million and the Netherlands with 15.4 million) occupy small land masses and support very large populations. With the exception of the Netherlands, whose population growth is relatively static (0.7%), most countries have significantly increased their numbers since 1994. For example, as of this writing, China has over two billion people, while India has reached the one billion mark. It is probable that these two nations now account for about 50% of the world's population.*

Who is growing and who is not. Popular literature still talks about "industrial" societies and "developing" countries. The *World Development Report* classifies countries as low-income, middle-income, and high-income economies. All areas with an annual per capita gross national product (GNP) of more than $9,000 are included among the high-income countries.

These societies account for about 20% of the world's population and are growing at an average of 0.5% annually. All other non-high-income countries account for 80% and are growing at an average of 2 to 3% annually, depending on the region. It is estimated that if current trends persist, 90% of all people will be living in developing areas.

There is another dimension to high rates of population growth. In many countries, over half of the total population is under 21 years of age. If demographic trends continue, over half of the population of these countries will be under the age of 16.

---

* World Bank, *World Development Report, 1996,* Tables 1 and 1a, pp. 188, 189, 222, Oxford University Press, New York, 1996.

The richest and the poorest. The five richest industrial countries in terms of annual per capita GNP are (1997 figures) Switzerland ($40,000), Japan ($36,000), Denmark ($29,000), Norway ($28,000), and the United States ($27,000).

The five poorest countries are Rwanda ($80), Mozambique ($90), Ethiopia ($100), Tanzania ($140), and Burundi ($160).

THE INCOME GAP

Part of the world is developing rapidly. Many developing nations are rapidly moving their economies ahead and are catching up with high-income societies, many of which are themselves surging ahead. In many areas, people are better off today than ever before and have been enjoying the fruits of sustained economic growth and development for several decades.

Part of the world remains an economic backwater. Unfortunately, the level of material affluence seen in parts of the world has not spread to many countries in Asia, Africa, Latin America, and the Caribbean. There has even been some economic regression in parts of Eastern Europe and in the new republics of the former Soviet Union. With incomes rising rapidly in so many countries, the gap between the so-called "haves" and "have-nots" remains glaring.

In short, everyone in the world may be getting richer, but the rich are becoming richer faster! One tends to observe this situation when making cross-border comparisons. However, the phenomenon of growing income disparity is a problem within highly industrial and technology-intensive societies such as the United States.

Two-class societies. The trend in income distribution patterns in many parts of the world is toward greater inequality. Globally, an average of 30% of all populations accounts for 70% or more of earned income. Income inequality is more askew among poorer countries and least askew in the higher income Scandinavian nations. Some countries, such as Cuba, have achieved income equality but nevertheless remain poor.

Changes in the income gap over time. It is interesting that the ratio of "rich to poor" societies has not really changed over the years. Some areas have indeed become developed, but they tend to be geographically and demographically small units like Singapore. Somewhat larger nations, like Taiwan and South Korea, have developed, to be sure, but mainly by virtue of their special relationship with the United States. In most other cases, the distance between the affluence of a small part of the global village and the relative poverty of many of its parts remains great.

GLOBAL CHALLENGES

Corporate Responsibility

The charge to multinational corporations in this era seems to have evolved to include three areas of responsibility that are much broader and complex than their nineteenth century focus on economic power and domination for the sole benefit of their owners. John Rockefeller and Henry Flagler grew their oil, real estate, and railroad empires without much regard for the constituencies they served and the environments they affected.

The Three-Cornered Hat Concept

Things are different today. A large corporation today can be said to wear a three-cornered hat that shelters all its constituencies. Each corner reflects an area of critical responsibility.

Obligation to the stockholders. The first area of corporate endeavor is to protect the interests of its stockholder owners by making its best efforts to generate reasonably expected returns on their investment. This is an important activity because not only must earnings be created to meet stockholder expectations, but additional earnings must be forthcoming to help keep the business going and growing and to meet its two other significant obligations or responsibilities.

Obligation to the human resources. The second area of responsibility is to the employees, the human resources without which the enterprise cannot exist. It is now generally recognized that companies have an obligation to provide a safe and wholesome working environment, with equal pay for equal work along with a compensation package that allows human resources a commonly acceptable standard of living and a fair opportunity for advancement.

Obligation to the community. The third area of responsibility is to the communities that corporations serve through the production and sale of their goods and services and in which they operate. The idea that businesses can pollute environments and physically harm people is rapidly becoming universally unacceptable. No argument is made for banning noxious processes and driving under companies that produce important products. The argument is that these processes must be changed through new technologies to eliminate environmental and human damage and that private enterprise must be held accountable for making the necessary changes.

People Issues

The continued success of private multinational enterprise may depend upon how well these nerve centers of economic activity address the basic needs of all societies. Global business's big challenge will be to successfully meet those needs and still be able to turn a profit. The fundamental problems that directly affect the individual, the community, and society at large (to name a few constituencies) are education, food and energy, healthcare, income and employment, money and banking, shelter, transportation and communications, and welfare and social services.

Education. The great majority of the world remains undereducated and functionally illiterate. Existence of and access to college- and university-level programs are limited. On average, in most developing areas, less than 5% of young people between the ages of 19 and 23 attend college/university programs. By contrast, participation rates range from 30 to 70% in developed areas.*

Food and energy. The industrialization of food production coupled with advances in the agricultural sciences has enabled supplies to keep pace with population growth. Yet food distribution and availability remain problems in many areas where low-income societies are unable to meet local demand through domestic production and cannot afford foreign imports. Daily caloric intake remains under 2,000 calories in many areas, compared to over 3,500 calories among the richer countries.**

Energy resource allocation also suffers uneven distribution. A full 75% of all energy resources produced in any given year is consumed by that 25% of the world's population which inhabits industrialized areas.

Healthcare. This remains an eyesore in many countries. Human longevity in the richer areas reaches an average of 80 years in comparison to 40 to 50 years in the poorest societies. Average life span is 39 years in Guinea-Bissau, 42 years in Sierra Leone, and 48 years in Ethiopia. Availability of physicians to the general population is also a good indi-

---

* World Bank, *World Development Report, 1996*, Table 7, p. 200, Oxford University Press, New York, 1996.
* World Bank, *World Development Report, 1992*, Table 28, pp. 272, 273, Oxford University Press, New York, 1992.

cator of the status of healthcare. Among industrial countries, the range is from 200 to 500 inhabitants per physician. In Third World areas, the lack of physicians becomes acute. There is one physician for every 32,000 people in Ethiopia, and the situation is even worse in other countries.*

Income and employment. It is estimated that unemployment rates for industrial countries range from 2 to 15%, depending on the country and the state of its economy. In many developing areas, the combined unemployment and underemployment rate is over 50%. This means that in much of the Third World, although people toil extremely hard in subsistence economic activities to stay alive, there is little permanent full-time, value-adding work for most of the teenage and adult population. It is estimated that a full 40% of the world's adult labor force works for menial wages and/or produces its own sustenance.**

Money and banking. The world of credit and finance, as it is known in many high-income countries, is beginning to expand its ground in the rest of the world. The pace of expansion will have to quicken if demand is to be stimulated to encourage investments to spread faster to developing areas. A comprehensive technology-intensive financial sector that can be continually tapped as a resource for investment funding is critical to accelerating the economic growth and development of countries. It is estimated, as this century draws to a close, that over 50% of the world's adult population engages in barter and functions outside of the money economy. It is also estimated that only 20% of this same group uses a checkbook.

Shelter. It is estimated that over 50% of people in developing areas live without permanent shelter. In terms of solid numbers, this means that two billion people sleep in makeshift dwellings without running water or heating, cooking, and sanitary facilities.

Transportation and communications. Mass transit and intercity transit for goods and people are well established in developed countries, but they are woefully lacking in the Third World. In Haiti, for example, a drive from Port-au-Prince to Cape Haitian, some 130 miles to the north, can take up to 12 hours. That same distance between Newark Airport and Atlantic City can be covered in less than three hours. In the United States, there are probably more telephones than people. In most countries, the average is one phone per hundred people.

---

* World Bank, *World Development Report, 1992,* Table 28, pp. 272, 273, Oxford University Press, New York, 1992.
* World Bank, *World Development Report, 1994,* p. 6, Oxford University Press, New York, 1994.

Welfare and social services. Social security insurance and all sorts of other social services and annuities which have been taken for granted for so long among industrial nations barely exist in many developing areas. There, the extended family is the major source of welfare and social service for non-self-supporting individuals such the very young, the aged, and the infirm. In the villages of many countries, such as India and Bangladesh, for example, a young couple entering marriage learns that they must rear as many as eight children or more if there are to be two surviving offspring as the couple approaches old age. Each surviving offspring would then be able to accept an aging parent into his or her extended family.

Corporate Challenges

Turning problems into opportunities. Multinational businesses might, at first blush, take the position that problems faced by much of the world are too great to be resolved by the private sector and that they should stick to the traditional bread-and-butter markets of the industrial countries. However, the rush by large corporations to tap Third World markets anywhere they may exist testifies to the fact that a potential exists for both market share and profits.

Taking the long view. Investors and professional managers are taking the long view that these new markets will some day be industrialized and prosperous. It is therefore the responsibility of the multinationals to maintain a presence in and to participate in the economic growth and development of all emerging regions.

The environmental challenge. It is clear that the processes of economic change impact the environment. How long the planet can continue to endure the battering of its infrastructure is a matter of argument. There is nevertheless general agreement that technologies must be developed and brought into play that will minimize environmental damage and perhaps even repair damage already done. Hence, corporate actions will have to balance stockholder enthusiasm and financial viability with the need to operate environmentally friendly businesses.

The resource and technology challenge. There is a school of thought that maintains that resources are finite. That may not be the case however. The material resources employed in the distant past are no longer utilized in the same manner today. Ships were once made of wood and used human labor for locomotion. Today, they are made of plastic and steel and are propelled by diesel fuel or nuclear energy. The plastics industry itself is a testament to the creation of synthetic resources as a function of the development of new technologies. Developing and then implementing these new technologies to meet the needs of a changing world is probably one of the more daunting tasks faced by the multinationals. Successfully accomplishing those tasks will require the cultivation of a critical mass of skilled and educated human resources.

CONCLUSION AND SUMMARY

The inadequacy of the food supply in many parts of the world perpetuates chronic hunger, malnutrition, and diseases that slow both mind and body and eventually reduces human productivity. The lack of permanent shelter dims the promise of sanctuary at the end of a day's labor. Limited access to energy means limited or no power and light at home or at work. Poor healthcare means more untreated diseases and ailments, which also saps human productivity and shortens life. Poor education hinders a society's ability to have a critical mass of skilled workers to compete in the global marketplace. Poor transportation and telecommunications systems slow down the movement of goods and services. Finally, high unemployment coupled with large numbers of undereducated young people and a generally unequal distribution of income threatens political stability. Unless these challenges are successfully met, development in many areas will remain stunted and threaten the survival of the rest of the world.

KEY TERMS AND CONCEPTS

Developed countries. Nations whose economies are expanding more slowly and whose incomes are significantly higher than those of other countries. Examples would be the United States and Japan.

Developing countries. Nations whose economies are expanding faster than those of their more mature, industrialized partners. They are sometimes called newly industrializing countries. An example would be Malaysia. Most of the world's developing countries are classified by the World Bank as "low-income," "lower middle-income," and "high middle-income" states.

Globalization. A process of corporate enterprise that involves the procurement of resources from the best available source worldwide and the production and sale of goods and services in the widest possible markets.

Key people issues. Education, food, energy, healthcare, income, employment, money and banking, shelter, social services and welfare, transportation and communications, a pollution-free environment.

Know-how. The application of technology to effectively produce goods and services.

Macro changes. Changes that affect an entire society.

Micro changes. Changes that affect a part of society (e.g., a single family, community, or business enterprise).

Multinational company. A corporation that produces and sells its goods and services in many countries simultaneously.

Private ownership. Legitimate possession of assets by individuals and their representative corporations as a basic right of life and social existence.

Privatization. A process of transferring the ownership of assets and the factors of production from the state to the private sector.

Technology. Ideas brought together into applications to create new goods and services or to improve on existing goods and services.

Three-cornered hat. A corporation's three basic areas of responsibility: an obligation to reasonably maximize stockholder returns, an obligation to provide its human resources with an adequate standard of living, and an obligation to behave for the common good of the communities it serves.

QUESTIONS

1.1 Describe and explain the ways in which the world has changed since the end of the eighteenth century.

1.2 Describe and explain the ways in which the world has remained basically unchanged since the end of the eighteenth century.

1.3 Explain the state as the "surrogate of society." Will that change? if so, to what? If not, why?

1.4 Explain what corporations, the state, and communities must do if the private sector is to effectively wear its three-cornered hat.

1.5 Describe and explain some of the challenges presented by a growing population.

1.6 Describe and explain some of the challenges presented by a declining population.

CHAPTER 2

A Philosophy of Business for the Twenty-First Century

INTRODUCTION

It is generally agreed that the main challenge of the twenty-first century will be to develop the infrastructures and economic enterprises necessary to maintain large numbers of people in political order at acceptable living standards without destroying the environment. Business, as society's surrogate for economic progress, has a central role to play in meeting this challenge. This is irrespective of whether it is envisioned as an arm of government, seen as an independent force, or sandwiched somewhere between state and private ownership. Three major competing philosophies are reviewed in this chapter to see which ideas are best suited to the management of society in the new century. Some leading corporate philosophies are also analyzed to examine how the business community sees itself blending into the emerging world order.

THREE COMPETING PHILOSOPHIES

Three competing philosophies have captured the imaginations of policymakers and thinkers in the twentieth century: capitalism, communism, and the mixed economy.

Capitalism

This philosophy posits that societies should be less macro- and micromanaged by governments. It suggests that more faith and reliance should be placed in less regulated and controlled approaches to human affairs. The conceptual basis of capitalist thinking can be traced from the seventeenth and eighteenth century physiocrats and mercantilists through Adam Smith, Thomas Malthus, and David Ricardo in the late 1700s and early 1800s to John Stuart Mill in the mid-1800s and finally to Keynes in the 1900s. These ideas call for a fundamental freedom of entrepreneurial action in which the role of government is minimized except to encourage and protect private sector economic activity.

Several neo-Malthusian and Darwinesque theories have emerged in recent decades. They suggest that the key to organized and continued economic growth and development may be through more "laissez-faire" non-interventionist public policies in which the private sector is given maximum latitude in determining the course of economic affairs. This could even be at the expense of pulling away support systems from less fortunate populations. Societies would self-manage their populations. Only the best, the strongest, and the ablest would survive the bloodied and bared fangs of this new economic liberalism.

Communism

Often called socialism, this philosophy perceives the tasks of economic growth and development as the obligatory domain of government in representing the state in discharging its responsibilities to the people living within its borders. The factors of production are to be owned and managed by the state through special government agencies to reach prescribed goals such as full employment at a given standard of living.

Communist ideology is as old as capitalist philosophy. Karl Marx and Friedrich Engels were its cardinal advocates in the nineteenth century, although its ideas can be traced back through Hegel, Kant, and Hobbes to Plato. It remains today a doctrine of sociopolitical order in many parts of the world. The private sector may exist and indeed prosper, but only in a manner subordinate to state policy.

The Mixed Economy

A more pragmatic and balanced philosophy has evolved in the last 30 years. It seeks to synthesize the extreme positions of capitalism and communism. It accepts the socialist proposition that larger and more interdependent population groupings need more comprehensive and interactive central planning to harmonize human affairs for the good of everyone. Hence, a certain amount of central government planning, intervention, and even ownership of productive assets may be essential. However, it also embraces the capitalist notion that the productive capability and capacity of society are best stimulated when left in the hands of private entrepreneurs who know best how to manage risk and wrestle with unpredictable market forces.

The mixed economy calls for more public and private sector cooperation. It allows for a balance between public and private policy. Government is charged with the responsibility of macromanaging the economy to reduce the friction and discord that result from totally unregulated activity. Private capital would be charged with the obligation of micromanagement by generating market-inspired and profit-oriented enterprises.

CORPORATE BUSINESS ORGANIZATION AND PHILOSOPHY

Large corporate enterprises among the world's high-income countries tend to classify themselves as multinational in the sense that they function in many countries simultaneously. It is not unusual for their annual reports to indicate that they have plant and office locations in 30 or 40 countries and distributorship arrangements in many more. Many of these companies call themselves "global" businesses.

Despite the very wide scope of their activities, most large enterprises organize their affairs along three overlapping modes. Companies function as ethnocentric, polycentric, or geocentric (global) organizations. Each system involves a set of attitudes that impact a company's management of human resources, research and development, production and purchasing, marketing and sales, and finance and accounting.

Ethnocentric Corporations

These are large businesses whose equity base is usually concentrated in a given geographic area (e.g., the United States). Corporate stockholders and stockholder groups are mostly of a single national origin. Corporate boards of directors also tend to reflect a particular national ethos. This creates a strong inclination for top management to develop and implement policies and programs that are skewed to the needs and wants of the national community hosting the corporate center without giving the same equal weight to international markets and opportunities.

Human Resource Development and Management

Ethnocentric corporations tend to depend on home nationals for most executive positions in both domestic and foreign markets. Implicit in this approach is the belief system that home nationals are best qualified to reflect the special culture and interest of the corporate center and the society in which it is situated. The same ideas and practices that work so well domestically are transported with investments overseas through the widespread use of expatriates, employees from the home office who are assigned to duty tours with the company's foreign affiliates.

Thus, it would be considered natural for the chief executive officer of Company A in the United States to be an American. It would also be seen as natural for the CEO of Company B, Company A's Belgian subsidiary, to also be an American, transplanted to Europe with spouse and family for a two- or three-year assignment. This would ensure that policies, programs, and strategies carefully crafted in the home country will be effectively executed in the host society.

Research and Development

Ethnocentric organizations tend to jealously guard their research and development facilities and efforts by concentrating all work in the domestic market. The R&D effort is geared to generating new technologies to create new products geared to meeting home market demand. Products found suitable for and successful in the domestic market may then be marketed overseas.

This "over-the-shoulder" approach to managing R&D output was standard practice for most U.S. multinational corporations until the last few decades. It can be credited for many marketing successes in the 1960s and 1970s. Procter & Gamble's Pampers, which captured the U.S. market before establishing significant market share in the rest of the world, is a good example of that success. But the company also endured difficulties in the late 1970s and 1980s when other of its toiletry and soap products were introduced in Germany and Eastern Europe.

Production and Purchasing

The classical view of managing these functions has been to centralize them in the home country to avoid logistic problems. There was, and there still remains, a generalized feeling that the domestic resource base is large and diverse enough to accommodate most material needs. Sourcing materials from within therefore makes good sense, good politics, and good economics.

This "buy American" attitude evolved out of World War II, when economic self-sufficiency was a military necessity. It became more entrenched in the decades following the war, when it was obvious that most of the world, because of the generalized chaos as a result of the war, did not have the production and technological capacity to supply the United States with the mix of industrial and consumer goods it required.

Many of the industrial nations had been reduced to rubble, while new countries, emerging from colonial status, were still far from achieving any competitive economic potential. The United States, by process of military triumph, became the world's supplier of goods, services, technology, and financial capital.

Ethnocentricity in production and purchasing is not an exclusively American experience. Its practice was common in European societies impacted by the Industrial Revolution and their quest for world empire through the processes of colonization. Countries like England and France had passed laws encouraging the manufacture of finished and semi-finished goods in exchange for raw materials from vassal states (colonies) that were forbidden to engage in value-added production.

The emerging political independence of most national societies after 1945 made it only a matter of time before technology and know-how that were confined to a few industrial states became available to all. With political independence came economic emancipation for many people who have come to develop and manage their resources effectively in competition with the United States and other market leaders.

Hence, the practice of single-source purchasing and single-nation production quickly became obsolete. Corporations came to realize that productivity, followed by enhanced competitive positioning, led to greater profits. It was noted that productivity always seemed to rise as enterprises engaged in multiple-source purchasing, outsourcing, and by having multinational production facilities.

Marketing and Sales

The classical ethnocentric organization relied on domestic brand and product managers to develop the plans and budgets that would be executed by highly trained sales forces primarily in the domestic market. Whatever worked at home would then be replicated in overseas markets through a network of import distributors, import agents, contract manufacturers, licensees, and a few joint venture arrangements and wholly owned subsidiaries.

Finance and Accounting

An ethnocentric attitude can also be detected in financial and accounting practices. U.S. rules and procedures vary in concept and substance from those practiced in many other countries. The GAAP (General Accepted Accounting Procedures), a standard in North America, requires modification or reconciliation with systems used in other societies. Definitions of financial agency, assets and liabilities, appropriate debt–equity relationships, and the nature and use of interest, to name a few, are ideas not universally shared. Difficulties in achieving cross-border corporate cooperation arise when managers insist upon having affiliate financials mirror home office methodologies.

There is also a tendency to require all foreign-source earnings to be repatriated as rapidly as possible. More often than not, an ethnocentric company regards foreign markets as cash cows that can be fed technology and know-how already in use at home and then milked for sheer profit.

Polycentric Corporations

These companies tend to organize themselves in a conglomerate mold with far-flung and diversified operations in many different parts of the world. The focus of effort is less upon the development of core businesses to achieve overall market share and earnings and more on allocating bottom line responsibility to regional affiliates, whatever their particular enterprise might be. The classic example is ITT (International Telephone & Telegraph), which at one time simultaneously was in telecommunications, baked goods, the car rental business, and hotels. Management control therefore tends to be more decentralized. Often, equity ownership is spread out over several or many countries, as in the cases of Royal Dutch Shell and Unilever.

Human Resource Development and Management

Polycentric corporations tend to depend on host country nationals for most executive positions in foreign markets. Senior positions may or may not be reserved for home country expatriates. Implicit in this approach is the belief that host country nationals are more qualified to reflect the needs of the local culture and are better connected with their society's power structure. While some home office training and indoctrination are usually provided, the foreign affiliate is usually left to its own devices as long as it continues to generate prescribed financial returns and reaches its announced goals.

Thus, it would be considered natural for the chief executive officer of Company A in the United States to be an American. It would also be considered natural for the CEO of Company B, Company A's Belgian subsidiary, to be a Belgian. The subsidiary's policies, programs, and strategies would be drafted in Belgium for final approval by the U.S. "parent" and then returned for execution by the Belgian cohort. The plans would not be initiated in the United States.

Research and Development

Polycentric organizations tend to establish technology and research and development facilities in many countries in order to tailor their efforts to the needs of the local market. The R&D effort is geared to generate new technologies to create new products geared to meet individual national market demand. Products found suitable for and successful in one market may then be introduced elsewhere, although that usually happens on an ad hoc basis and does not follow a given policy. This is the approach taken by Colgate-Palmolive in the development of its technology centers in key areas of the world.

Production and Purchasing

The polycentric approach is to decentralize these functions down to the local level, with an emphasis on local sourcing and with little control or oversight from the home office. It is only in recent years that practice has shifted to global sourcing (best-source purchasing). The idea of local sourcing differs little from its ethnocentric partner, home country sourcing, where the goal is to avoid logistic problems. As in home country sourcing, buying materials locally makes good sense, good politics, and good economics.

Marketing and Sales

A polycentric organization allows for a diversity of marketing strategies, each suited to a particular area. A home country marketing plan might be used, but it often has been altered beyond recognition to suit the local environment. Reliance is less on home country brand and product managers to develop and implement plans and budgets than on host country marketing executives.

Finance and Accounting

Polycentric companies typically shift responsibility for financial accountability to their foreign affiliates. Local standards may be applied if bottom line performance can be translated back into a meaningful earnings picture for the parent company.

The need to require all foreign-source earnings to be repatriated as rapidly as possible is not as urgent for polycentric corporations. This may in a sense reflect the greater national diversity of their major stockholder groups, whose residency may not be concentrated in any one country.

Geocentric Corporations

These companies tend to organize themselves around a single decision-making center that regards the world as a single market to be approached with a unified strategy that does not necessarily reflect the interest or the image of a single national group or perspective.

The spirit of the geocentric executive is perhaps best captured by the worlds of two people two centuries apart. Thomas Jefferson was reputed to have said in 1806, "Merchants have no country. The mere spot they stand on does not constitute so strong an attachment as that from which they draw their gain." In 1989, Gilbert Williamson, then president of the National Cash Register Company, was quoted as saying, "I was asked the other day about United States competitiveness and I replied that I don't think about it at all. We at NCR think of ourselves as a globally competitive company that happens to be headquartered in the United States."

Human Resource Development and Management

Geocentric corporations tend to seek, develop, and then manage the most qualified human resources available from anywhere in the world.

They are not committed to either home or host country nationals for any particular position within their operations.

Thus, senior positions may or may not be reserved for home country or host country nationals. It would not be unusual for the manager of a U.S. geocentric corporation's Singapore office to be a third-country expatriate, say from Brazil. Implicit in this approach is the objective of global best-source procurement. As in the case of polycentric companies, home office training and indoctrination are provided. Being no fools, geocentric companies also rely on key host country employees who are qualified to reflect the needs of the local culture and are better connected with their society's power structure.

Research and Development

Geocentric organizations tend to establish technology and research and development facilities in many countries of the world to meet global objectives. The R&D effort is geared to generate new technologies to create new products geared to meet specific market demand that may exist in many countries simultaneously. Products like wireless communication devices (cellular telephones) are developed to attract buyers and users in a global setting based upon a commonality of demand.

Production and Purchasing

The geocentric approach is to centralize decision making in these functions to maximize global sourcing opportunities, referred to above as "global best-source procurement." Host and home country sourcing is de-emphasized except when it becomes politically necessary or when it can be shown that local sourcing makes the most sense on a cost–benefit analysis basis.

Marketing and Sales

A geocentric organization encourages the development of a single global strategy designed to achieve a worldwide target and market share. The single-strategy approach might still allow for different marketing strategies spun off from the master plan, each suited to a particular area. A home country marketing plan might be used, but it often will be altered beyond recognition to suit the global perspective. Reliance is less on home or host country brand and product managers and more on managers with global profit-and-loss responsibility to develop and implement plans and budgets.

Finance and Accounting

Geocentric companies typically shift responsibility for financial accountability to the decision-making center, wherever that might be. Criteria for financial performance are how well disparate parts of the enterprise throughout the world contribute synergistically to the well-being of the whole. It might be acceptable, for example, for the U.S. affiliate to lose money in order that the Mexican affiliate show a profit, hence encouraging some transfer pricing policies, if, in the final analysis, the overall after-tax profitability of the entire geocentric enterprise is enhanced. The need to require all foreign-source earnings to be repatriated quickly to the U.S. parent is not paramount in such instances.

CONCLUSION AND SUMMARY

Corporate executives do not suddenly awake in the morning, stare into a mirror, and declare their companies to be polycentric or geocentric effective immediately. Nor are companies wholly one way or another. It is probably also unwarranted for any corporation to puritanically seek a particular operating philosophy. The successful multinational companies are what they are and where they are often because of a mixture of happenstance and design. They are successful in achieving objectives by virtue of smart and flexible management. It is entirely possible for an ethnocentric company to operate in a geocentric fashion in some areas and in a polycentric or geocentric manner in others. The key is what works best for the company in the wearing of its three-cornered hat and in achieving its specific objectives. A mix-and-match philosophy can often be the best approach.

The same approach can apply to the particular "ism" that dominates the macro environment. Choices need not be made between socialism or capitalism or something in between the two. Multinational companies have proven remarkably adaptable to working with both centrally planned societies with totalitarian governments as well as countries with little government control and interference. Again, the versatility of corporate management, adaptability to change, and the effective harnessing of key competencies and technologies to utilize resources and penetrate markets wherever they are may be the real ingredients of global success.

KEY TERMS AND CONCEPTS

Capitalism. The private ownership and management of economic enterprise with minimum or no government involvement.

Communism. Government ownership and/or control of economic enterprise and all factors of production.

Ethnocentric corporations. Large businesses whose equity base is usually concentrated in a given geographic area (e.g., the United States). Corporate stockholders and stockholder groups are mostly of a single national origin. Corporate boards of directors also tend to reflect a particular national ethos. This creates a strong inclination for top management to develop and implement policies and programs that are skewed to the needs and wants of the national community hosting the corporate center without giving the same equal weight to international markets and opportunities.

Geocentric corporations. These companies tend to organize themselves around a single decision-making center that regards the world as a single market to be approached with a unified strategy that does not necessarily reflect the interest or the image of a single national group or perspective.

Mixed economy. A balanced philosophy that seeks to synthesize the extreme positions of capitalism and communism. It accepts the socialist proposition that larger and more interdependent population groupings need more comprehensive and interactive central planning to harmonize human affairs for the good of everyone. It also embraces the capitalist notion that the productive capability and capacity of society are best stimulated when left in the hands of private entrepreneurs.

Polycentric corporations. These companies tend to organize themselves in a conglomerate mold with far-flung and diversified operations in many different parts of the world. The focus of effort is less upon the development of core businesses to achieve overall market share and earnings and more on allocating bottom line responsibility to regional affiliates that are left to their own devices in their particular markets.

QUESTIONS

2.1 Describe and explain how resource development and management theories and practices can differ among ethnocentric, polycentric, and geocentric organizations.

2.2 Describe and explain how the thrust and organization of a company's research and development effort can differ among ethnocentric, polycentric, and geocentric organizations.

2.3 Describe and explain how purchasing, sourcing, and production differ among ethnocentric, polycentric, and geocentric organizations.

2.4 Describe and explain how marketing and sales differ among ethnocentric, polycentric, and geocentric organizations.

2.5 Describe and explain how finance and accounting differ among ethnocentric, polycentric, and geocentric organizations.

2.6 Explain the distinctions in political organization, social objectives, and economic enterprise among capitalism, socialism, and the mixed economy.

CHAPTER 3

International Business Operations

INTRODUCTION

International business operations cover a range of activities from import–export transactions to foreign direct investments and foreign portfolio investments. Some of these operations are oriented toward the production and marketing of goods and services. Some are financially oriented and deal with the cross-border movement of funds. The various forms of cross-border activities in which large multinational corporations, along with smaller companies, engage are reviewed in summary form in this chapter.

These activities include merchandise importing and exporting (international trade), contract manufacturing, licensing and franchising, turnkey systems, management contracts, strategic alliances, and foreign direct investments in joint ventures and wholly owned subsidiaries. They also include foreign portfolio investments in stocks and bonds and a multitude of other financial transactions designed to maximize corporate after-tax profitability and return on invested assets.

A BREAKDOWN OF INTERNATIONAL BUSINESS OPERATIONS

Corporations engage in any number of these activities not only to maximize market opportunities and earnings, but also to capitalize on an array of variables such as transport and production costs, taxes, and a never-ending assortment of risk factors. Selecting the appropriate international activity mix often makes the difference between running a project at a loss or a profit.

Exporting

Most smaller firms begin to sell their products internationally through exporting. These firms may also typically import goods to complement their product lines for sale in the home market. The export sale trans-action becomes the end unto itself, the objective being to record a sale on company books for the same reason that motivates the domestic sales force.

Sales eventually become revenues to cover costs and generate profits. Companies may engage in importing for much the same reason, but here the process is more subtle. Importing is a procurement function in which the objective is not buying per se, but buying to meet local sales targets. Importing has become a function to achieve a separate objective, whereas exporting for many companies is both a function and a goal.

Most multinational corporations today no longer treat exporting as a revenue-producing function in its own right. The cross-border movement of merchandise is looked upon as one of several means to achieve broader and more complex ends. Companies are more interested in global market share targets, and exporting may or may not play a significant part in attaining them.

Rapid Market Access Through Exporting

The simplicity of exporting provides it with two distinct advantages. The first is that the cost of establishing and maintaining elaborate manufacturing operations in one or several countries is shifted to investors who are more comfortable doing business from a large fixed asset base. The second advantage is that exporting can help companies achieve experience curves and location economies. For example, by buying goods in one location and exporting them to another, it is possible to realize significant economies of scale as the result of global sales volume. It is also easier to switch to another industry when existing product lines achieve maturity.

Unfortunately, there are two major disadvantages to concentrating one's efforts on commodity trading. First, exporting from a firm's home operations can become inefficient if there are lower cost locations for manufacturing the product elsewhere. This is not an argument against exporting per se but rather against stubbornly producing a product and exporting it from a firm's home country without considering alternatives. For example, many U.S. firms have moved their operations to places where they can get low-cost yet highly skilled labor (like Mexico) and then export the products back to the United States and all around the world.

The second disadvantage to exporting is that high transport costs and national and regional trade restrictions can make it uneconomical. This is one of the reasons why countries like Japan produce some of their cars in the United States. Because these goods are produced on American soil, there are no transport costs and no import tariffs on the final product.

Export Trading Companies

Export trading companies (ETCs) are very large companies that are basically international traders and whose principal sources of income are derived from import–export activities. They tend to specialize in given industries and commodities and are highly knowledgeable in their markets as well as in the intricacies of international trade.

Some ETCs are risk takers, taking title to commodity inventories and then reselling them partially or in whole to high bidders in a worldwide marketplace. Some have exclusive arrangements with producers to handle select product lines. ETCs tend to concentrate their efforts on bulk commodities such as agricultural products and textile and petrochemical raw materials and intermediates.

Direct Exporting to End Users

Exporters have several options in choosing specific foreign entry strategies. One is an international version of direct marketing called *direct end-user exporting*. This approach involves developing an end-user customer base through mailing lists and local telephone directories.

Direct exporting offers the advantage of bypassing the local trade channels and permits more flexible price and payment arrangements between buyers and sellers. Relatively inexpensive and over-the-counter goods that are easily merchandised through magazine or newspaper coupon advertisements and require payment by check, money order, or credit card lend themselves to direct exporting techniques, as do high-technology products like printing presses in areas where distributorships and/or dealerships are not established.

The disadvantage of direct exporting lies in the absence of an after-sales service organization in the customer's region to extend manufacturers' warranties and service customer needs. This problem is not so apparent with consumables. It is more apparent with durable goods and high-technology processes (e.g., appliances, equipment, printing, and general imaging). The lack of a well-trained distributor–dealer organization in markets where such products are sold can slow a manufacturer's market inroads.

Exporting Through Foreign Import Distributors

The standard approach for exporting finished goods for small and large companies is to work with local import distributors or dealers. These trade organizations are often affiliates of the exporter (a licensee, joint venture partner, or wholly owned subsidiary) or they can be unrelated.

The difference between a distributor and a dealer is usually size. Distributors are direct importers that cover a relatively large region (e.g., a country or an area within a country, like a large city). They purchase directly from an exporter and then resell the goods to their own dealer organization. For example, BMW of North America is a wholly owned subsidiary of its German parent and performs what is basically a distributorship function. It imports vehicles from BMW Germany and/or orders vehicles from the BMW plant in South Carolina and then sells the automobiles to BMW dealers, which in turn sell them to consumers.

If foreign markets are small enough, as in the Caribbean and West Indies, a single distributor that is also a dealer may be sufficient to cover a given area. Some markets, like Russia, are so large and segmented that exporters may sell to dealers in some places and sell directly to distributorships in others.

There are two advantages to exporting to overseas distributors. The first is service; the second is financial. A well-developed distributor–dealer organization provides ongoing after-sales service to customers. This is important when the products involved are of a technical nature. The financial advantage lies in the fact that distributors and dealers make a direct purchase from a manufacturer from a published price list or sales agreement, setting up an accounts receivable for the seller and an accounts payable for themselves. Because the exporter–manufacturer no longer owns the goods, payment can be expected in accordance with the payment terms set forth in the price list or sales agreement.

The only disadvantage to selling to overseas distributors is if they are totally independent of control by the manufacturer–exporter. The fact that they buy a product from an exporter means that they have title to the item. This technically allows them to apply any markup or markdown and to sell in any territory, which may end up being outside their specific zone of operation. Court decisions in the United States and elsewhere have tended to favor the rights of independent distributors and dealers over those of manufacturers.

Exporting Through Foreign Import Agents

The distinction between an import agent and an import distributor or dealer lies in the implications derived from the word "agent." There is in most societies considered to be a fiduciary relationship between a principal and an agent who is presumed to act on behalf of the principal.

The general understanding of an import agent is that the agent does not purchase goods from a principal (in this case an exporter), but accepts goods on consignment. This means that no sale is made from export seller to import agent. A physical transfer of inventory without a title change merely takes place. Title to the goods remains with the exporter until the import agent sells them to a customer. That is when title flows directly from the exporter to the agent's customer.

Import agencies are normally established in free trade zones and other similar duty-free or in-bond warehousing areas where specialized or general materials management functions that have little directly to do with sales or marketing are needed. In these situations, a manufacturer wants to maintain total control over merchandise without making a branch or subsidiary office investment. Import agencies are also important where manufacturers' products require trademark, trade name, and territorial protection. Since a manufacturer owns the goods placed in an agent's facility until they are is sold, maximum marketing control over pricing policy, selling strategy, territory of operation, and after-sales service is maintained.

Contract Manufacturing

The best definition is by way of example. Cosmetics companies often offer specialty soaps and facial cleansers as extensions to their lines of perfume products. Many of these soap and detergent items are contracted out to one or several of the major soapers, such as Colgate-Palmolive, Procter & Gamble, or Unilever. Large aerospace companies like Boeing often contract out parts and components to smaller machine shops in the United States and abroad.

Many companies that contract some or all of their production abroad are small, have limited technology, and have few if any legally registerable or patentable intellectual assets in the form of patents, trade names, trademarks, or copyrights. Contract manufacturing arrangements with foreign producers for these type of companies can and do in fact provide viable alternatives to making costly long-term investments.

Contract manufacturing arrangements are also used by large companies as a means of limiting their wholly owned production units to the manufacture of what they consider to be their core product lines. Specifically, the large soapers produce detergents, soaps, toiletries, and cosmetics in their plants all over the world under their own respective names and have their own powerhouse marketing and sales organizations. But they also produce these same type of goods under contract for other independent companies, small or large, that do not have the same extensive production and technological resources. Independent bottling companies that perform contract-filling operations for Coca-Cola, Pepsi, and others also perform similar services for smaller and sometimes competitive beverage firms.

Companies enter into contract manufacturing (sometimes called contract-filling operations) when circumstances stop them from producing the product or products reasonably close to their markets, when market access is denied, or when their own costs are higher than having the goods made by someone else.

Turnkey Systems

A turnkey project is an arrangement whereby a firm that specializes in the design, construction, and start-up of a production facility contracts with a foreign client to perform such service in exchange for a fee. Once the firm has completed the project and trained the personnel to run it, the new facility is then turned over to the client for full operation. Turnkey projects are most common in the chemical, pharmaceutical, petroleum, and metal-refining industries.

The main advantage of turnkey projects is that they are a way of earning formidable returns on the asset of technological know-how without making a long-term investment. Another advantage is that in countries where political and economic environments are often questionable, a firm just constructs the facility, collects its money, and then leaves. Therefore, it is not subject to any possible loss if the government and/ or economy undergoes adverse changes.

The first disadvantage can potentially be caused by the second advantage above. Because the firm no longer has a vested interest in the facility it created, it is cut out of any future profits in the event the foreign country becomes a major market for the output of the process that has just been introduced. The second disadvantage is that a contractor firm that enters into a turnkey project with a foreign enterprise may inadvertently create a competitor. For example, many Western firms that sold oil-refining technology to firms in Saudi Arabia and Kuwait now find themselves competing head to head with these firms in other world oil markets.

Licensing

International licensing is an arrangement whereby a foreign licensee buys the rights to manufacture another firm's product in its country for a negotiated fee. This fee is usually a distributed through royalty payment based on units sold. The licensee puts up most of the capital necessary to get the overseas operation going.

The advantage of licensing is that a firm does not have to bear the development costs and risks associated with opening up a foreign market. It is a very attractive option for firms that lack the capital to develop operations overseas. Additionally, licensing is also attractive when a firm is unwilling to commit substantial financial resources to an unfamiliar or a politically volatile foreign market.

On the negative side, there are three serious drawbacks to this mode of entry. First, it does not give a firm the kind of control over manufacturing, marketing, and strategy that is required to realize experience curve and location economies. Licensing typically involves each licensee setting up its own manufacturing operations, which severely limits a firm's ability to realize experience curve and location economies by manufacturing its product in a centralized location.

The second disadvantage is that competing in a global market may require a firm to coordinate strategic moves across countries by using profits earned in one country to support competitive attacks in another; however, the very nature of licensing severely limits a firm's ability to do this. A third problem is the potential loss of control of technological know-how to foreign companies. For example, RCA Corporation once licensed its color television technology to a number of Japanese firms that quickly assimilated the technology and used it to enter the U.S. market.

Franchising

Franchising is similar to licensing, although it tends to involve much longer term commitments than licensing. Whereas licensing is pursued primarily by manufacturing firms, franchising is employed primarily by service firms, such as McDonald's and Hilton International. A franchising agreement involves a franchisor selling limited rights for the use of its brand name to a franchisee in return for a lump sum payment and a share of the franchise's profits. In contrast to most licensing agreements, the franchise agrees to abide by strict rules as to how it conducts business. For example, when McDonald's enters into a franchising agreement with a foreign firm, it expects that firm to run its restaurant in a manner identical to all the other McDonald's locations worldwide.

The advantages of franchising as an entry mode are very similar to those of licensing. Specifically, a firm is relieved of the costs and risks of opening up a foreign market on its own. Instead, the franchise typically assumes those costs and risks. Thus, using a franchising strategy, a service firm can build up a global presence quickly and at a low cost.

The disadvantages of franchising are not as apparent in comparison to licensing. Since franchising is used by service companies, there is no reason to consider the need for coordination of manufacturing to achieve experience curve and location curve economies. On the other hand, franchising may inhibit a firm's ability to take profits from one country to support competitive attacks in another.

Quality control and consistency are other factors to be considered. For example, when visiting the Paris Hilton, one would expect the same level of service as at the Hilton's Waldorf Astoria in New York. This is not always the case, however. One way in which companies have addressed quality control and consistency issues has been to establish management subsidiaries in each country or region targeted for expansion. These subsidiaries assume the responsibility of establishing and sometimes managing franchises throughout their designated territory with full compliance to prescribed standards. Consequently, the combination of close proximity and the smaller number of franchises to oversee helps provide quality assurance.

Strategic Alliances

These are intercorporate agreements between two or more companies designed to achieve various degrees of vertical and horizontal integration.

This vertical–horizontal integration is also possible with wholly owned subsidiaries where expansion takes place through merger, acquisition, and joint ventures.

The distinguishing feature of a strategic alliance lies in its informality. Exchanges of debt and equity are rarely involved, as in the case of joint venture arrangements. No formal mergers or acquisitions are involved. The strategic alliance is a temporary marriage of key human and other resources from the partnering firms to achieve certain synergies that could not be realized as quickly were the individual partners to go it alone. Once objectives are reached, it is normal for the alliance to end.

Foreign Direct Investments

Foreign direct investments (FDIs) are made by companies into foreign markets for the purpose of owning or co-owning, controlling, and managing a business enterprise with market share and earnings objectives. FDIs are made to achieve two objectives: vertical integration and horizontal integration.

The process of vertical integration establishes control over sources of production (e.g., supplies, technology, financing, labor, and other resources). It can also be used to create control over distribution, marketing, sales, and after-sales service. Strategic alliances between computer software companies like Microsoft and hardware companies like IBM are common in order to more productively link technology with information systems to be marketed to end users. They are also common in the aerospace system, where major contractors like Boeing continually cooperate with primary vendors like United Technologies (Pratt & Whitney) for engines and other components.

Horizontal integration is intended to achieve market control through understandings or cooperation agreements designed to allocate and maintain market share. Two or more companies selling in the same market can therefore agree to share the same sales force, the same marketing team, and pool their advertising and promotion funds in a single budgeted campaign. This is commonly done by beverage companies, restaurant chains, and the entertainment industry. Companies are ready for a strategic alliance when they come to believe that a measure of intercorporate cooperation may result in synergies that will more quickly achieve mutual or reciprocating objectives.

FDIs themselves fall into two major categories: joint ventures and wholly owned subsidiaries.

Joint Ventures

Establishing a joint venture with a foreign firm has long been a popular mode for entering new markets for two reasons. The first reason is that many capital- and technology-intensive investment projects require the resources of several different corporations in order to create the synergies needed to make them successful. The second reason is that many host nations encourage foreign investments to partner with local businesses in an effort to guarantee partial ownership and full participation.

Typically, joint venture enterprises are formed as corporations whose equity is divided among joint venture partners. They are, in a sense, formally structured strategic alliances. Corporate partners share decision-making processes as well as the distribution of earnings.

There are two advantages to joint ventures. First, a firm is able to benefit from a local partner's knowledge of the host country operating environment. For many U.S. firms investing abroad, their exposure has generally involved providing technology and know-how, and some capital, while the local partner has supplied the marketing expertise, knowledge, and business connections.

The second advantage is sharing the cost and risk, which are often high when entering a new market. There are also instances where political considerations make a joint venture the only feasible entry mode. For example, the only way American firms can set up operations in Japan is if they can acquire a Japanese partner.

There are two major disadvantages to the use of joint ventures. First, similar to licensing, a firm that enters into a joint venture risks losing control of its technology to a joint venture partner. A second disadvantage is that a joint venture does not give a firm the tight and complete control over operations that a subsidiary does. Hence, the completion of experience curves, location economies, and economies of scale may take longer. Nor does a joint venture give any specific partner the control that might be needed to engage in coordinated global attacks against rivals.

Wholly Owned Subsidiaries

A wholly owned subsidiary is a corporation whose equity is almost or entirely wholly owned by another corporation. The investing company becomes known as the "parent," and the subsidiary is colloquially called the "sub." A subsidiary company allows the parent more control over operations than other affiliate modes discussed above. However, absolute control is often tempered by requirements of local laws, which usually insist on an "arms-length" relationship between parent and sub in decision-making processes.

Establishing a wholly owned subsidiary in a foreign market can be done in two ways. A firm can either set up a completely new operation in a country or it can acquire an established firm and use that firm to expand operations.

There are two major advantages to using subsidiaries. First, when a firm's competitive advantage is based on technological competence, a wholly owned subsidiary will reduce the risk of losing control over that competence. Companies with technology-intensive goods and services would normally prefer the wholly owned subsidiary route. Unfortunately, they are too often either undercapitalized or focus on markets where host governments mandate joint ventures.

Second, a wholly owned subsidiary offers maximum global control over operations. This may be important if the parent has become geocentric in developing and implementing strategies governing all aspects of its business.

The major disadvantage of this type of entry mode is that it is the most costly approach for achieving a presence in foreign markets. Companies seeking to form subsidiary corporations must bear the full costs and risks of setting up and maintaining operations abroad.

Foreign Portfolio Investments

A foreign portfolio investment (FPI) is an investment in foreign-based securities (stocks and bonds). The objective is to generate income through interest, dividends, and capital gains. The larger portion of international investment flows in the world today are FPIs.

Their movement is more volatile than that of FDIs. In 1995, FDIs into other countries from the United States totaled $95.5 billion. U.S. FPIs abroad amounted to $98.9 billion. FDIs into the United States for 1995 were $99.3 billion and FPIs were almost $155 billion.

The mobility of FPIs accounts for their volatility. Investment and disinvestment decisions can be made and executed with surgical precision instantly. Indeed, the gradual "securitization" of international investments in the past decade is said to have contributed to the near economic collapse of countries such as Mexico in the mid-1990s.

CONCLUSION AND SUMMARY

This chapter has merely skimmed the surface in describing the various types of international business operations available to multinational corporations. The focus has been mainly on the overseas activities of manufacturing companies whose major thrust is product production, sourcing, and marketing. Banks, insurance companies, educational institutions, the theater arts, museums, the entertainment industry in general, and the travel and leisure industries have not been included because these industries have international strategies that vary significantly from the more orthodox approaches discussed in this chapter.

KEY TERMS AND CONCEPTS

Contract manufacturing. Having another company manufacture one's products in accordance with prescribed specifications on a contract basis.

Direct exporting to end users. Exporters have several options in choosing specific foreign entry strategies. One is an international version of direct marketing called *direct end-user exporting*. This approach involves developing an end-user customer base through mailing lists and local telephone directories.

Exporting. The act of shipping goods outside the customs area of a country. A shipment of goods from the United States to Brazil would be classified as an export from the United States to Brazil. A shipment of these same goods to Puerto Rico would be classified as a domestic transaction because the latter is part of the United States.

Exporting through foreign import agents. An import agent generally imports goods on consignment from an overseas principal and therefore takes no title to merchandise. Title to goods held by an agent in the seller's name (principal) flows directly from seller to buyer (the import agent's customer).

Exporting through foreign import distributors. The standard approach for exporting finished goods for small and large companies is to work with local import distributors or dealers. These trade organizations are often affiliates of the exporter (a licensee, joint venture partner, or wholly owned subsidiary) or they can be unrelated. In general, an import distributor buys goods from an exporter, takes title to the goods, and then resells them in the local market.

Export trading companies (ETCs). Very large firms that are basically international traders whose principal sources of income are derived from import–export sales activities. They tend to specialize in given industries and commodities and are highly knowledgeable in their markets as well as in the intricacies of international trade.

Foreign direct investments (FDIs). Investments made by companies into foreign markets for the purpose of owning or co-owning, controlling, and managing a business enterprise with market share and earnings objectives. FDIs are made to achieve two objectives: vertical integration and horizontal integration.

Foreign portfolio investments (FPIs). Investments into foreign-based securities (stocks and bonds). The objective is to generate income through interest, dividends, and capital gains. The larger portion of international investment flows in the world today are FPIs.

Franchising. Franchising is similar to licensing, although it tends to involve much longer term commitments than licensing. Whereas licensing is pursued primarily by manufacturing firms, franchising is employed primarily by service firms, such as McDonald's and Hilton International. A franchising agreement involves a franchisor selling limited rights for the use of its brand name to a franchisee in return for a lump sum payment and a share of the franchise's profits.

Importing. The act of bringing into the customs area of a country goods made in another nation. Goods made in Brazil and shipped to the United States would be classified as an import from Brazil to the United States. Import of these same goods from Puerto Rico to the mainland United States would be classified as a domestic transaction because the former is part of the United States.

Licensing. International licensing is an arrangement whereby a foreign licensee buys the rights to manufacture another firm's product in its country for a negotiated fee or royalty. This fee is usually a distributed royalty payment based on units sold. The licensee puts up most of the capital necessary to get the overseas operation going.

Strategic alliance. Intercorporate agreement between two or more companies designed to achieve various degrees of vertical and horizontal integration. This vertical–horizontal integration is also possible with wholly owned subsidiaries where expansion takes place through merger, acquisition, and joint ventures.

Turnkey system. A firm that specializes in the design, construction, and start-up of a production facility contracts with a foreign client to perform such service in exchange for a fee. Once the firm has completed the project and trained the personnel to run it, the new facility is then turned over to the client for full operation.

QUESTIONS

3.1 When would a company use an overseas (import) distributor and/ or dealer network? When would the use of import agents be appropriate? What are some of the pitfalls in using either import distributors or import agents? What are the alternatives when a company is committed to exporting and not to manufacturing abroad?

3.2 Explain how smaller companies can gain by working through export trading companies. Describe the advantages and disadvantages.

3.3 Your company is a small industrial solvent manufacturer with a strong regional niche market in the United States. The company also enjoys a good market in European Union (EU) countries through an import distributor network. Restrictions against solvent imports are rising and threaten to force you out of the market unless your products are produced within the EU area. What is the solution and why?

3.4 Explain exactly how a company would set up and manage a contract manufacturing arrangement in another country.

3.5 Describe and explain the similarities and differences between strategic alliances and joint venture agreements.

3.6 Describe the pros and cons of turnkey arrangements, wholly owned subsidiaries, and joint ventures.

CHAPTER 4

The Monetary System

INTRODUCTION

The monetary system that influences trade, investments, and even daily private and public sector operations can be traced back to the early nineteenth century. It evolved from the monetization of gold as a nation's holder of value in due course and coincided with the increasing use of paper currency in the late eighteenth century. The themes of this chapter are to show how the current monetary system developed into its current form, how it affects all aspects of a company's global activities, and what shape the monetary system may take in the future.

WHAT IS THE INTERNATIONAL MONETARY SYSTEM?

An Amalgamation of Many Loosely Coordinated Banks

There are over 200 independent nations today. Over 180 of these countries are members of three interrelated organizations: the United Nations, the World Bank, and the International Monetary Fund (IMF). These and other organizations are discussed in Part III of this book. Essentially, the IMF and other related international and supranational financial institutions interact with a loose association of national and regional banks to create the existing monetary environment that is euphemistically called "the monetary system."

Two Hundred Independent National Banking Systems with Separate Currencies

Almost every nation has its own banking system and individual currency to serve the interests of specific resident constituencies. These include individuals and groups that reflect the complex diversity of the entire society: individuals, businesses, government agencies, banks, brokerage firms, pension funds, civic groups, religious organizations, producers' cooperatives, and indeed anyone who engages in international trade, investments, or travel.

When any of these constituencies participates in an international activity, which can be as mundane as a family from the United States taking a trip to visit relatives in a foreign country, it trades the use of one currency for another. Billions of dollars in cross-border currency trading takes place daily. The level of foreign exchange transactions rises almost geometrically as the globalization of economic transactions accelerates.

Foreign Currencies Lead Their Own Lives

To further complicate matters, money and interest rates are increasingly treated today by banks, traders, and investors like speculative commodities. Hence, they are traded in pretty much the same way as pork bellies, in addition to being considered mediums of economic exchange. This means that foreign currency prices have a life and value of their own apart from the demand for the goods and services whose supply and demand variables they are supposed to reflect. It was an unpredictable degree of wild currency price fluctuation in Asian monetary markets in the late summer and early fall of 1997 that prompted Malaysian Prime Minister Makathir Mohamed to complain that foreign exchange trading "was immoral" and should be made "illegal" (*Wall Street Journal*, September 23, 1997, p. C-13).

The Monetary System to the Rescue

The international monetary system as it exists today is an informal association of public and private banks that function under a set of national and international understandings (protocols), rules, regulations, procedures, and laws that serve to maintain some sort of discipline and order in monetary markets. This is done by managing cross-border currency flows, foreign exchange prices, and interest rates through the coordinated activities of central banks (government-owned banks like the U.S. Federal Reserve System), the network of large private global banks, and the IMF.

HISTORICAL BACKGROUND

Two Hundred Years of Scrip With and Without Gold Backing

Before the Napoleonic wars, the general practice was for governments to exchange gold and silver coins or bullion in exchange for goods and services traded domestically and internationally. The so-called "coins of the realm" were the monies minted by a ruling government and issued sparingly to whoever provided goods and service to the reigning sovereign. This practice helped establish the rule that the power to create and/ or mint money was a monopoly reserved for the central government. This power is considered sacrosanct today by most nations as well as by the United States.

Wariness concerning the use of gold as a medium of exchange to be used directly in discharging financial obligations grew in the Napoleonic era between 1800 and 1815 as continuing war made the movement of monetary gold hazardous. Paper scrip (fiat money) backed by gold became a prudent alternative to the risky process of physically shipping the precious metal across unsecure areas. These government-issued credit notes, fully backed by gold held in government vaults, became legal tender and gradually gained popular acceptance, eventually replacing gold as the immediate holder of value in due course. For example, in 1821, the U.S. mint price was $20.67 per avoirdupois ounce. The British pound, set at 53,17 shillings and 10.5 pence per troy ounce of gold, then bought $4.87.

Backing Paper Money with Pure Gold

The current monetary system finds its roots in the gold standard, which gained popularity among the world's more powerful economies in the early 1800s when they saw a need to cultivate a climate of stable exchange rates for commonly traded currencies that were being printed on paper. It was the first modern attempt by nations to create a universally acceptable standard, namely gold, as backing for all major paper currencies in use at the time.

The gold standard turned into the gold exchange standard in 1934. That arrangement lasted until 1971, when the floating rate exchange rate system was introduced. The era of floating rates continues today.

The Gold Standard and Fixed Exchange Rate System

The gold standard was maintained by participating nations through a system of fixed currency exchange rates in which relative currency prices were based upon a nation's monetary unit as defined by a given weight and quantity of gold. A country's money supply was limited in part to the amount of monetary gold held by a national government's central bank. Gold standard countries generally agreed that all paper money backed by gold could be redeemed for the metal on demand at the tendered value shown on the paper certificates. Needless to say, in many cases a government's promise was not quite as good as gold!

The Central Banking System

International foreign exchange management was largely the domain of government-owned banks called central banks. These banks were off-shoots of the exchequers who had been handling the treasuries and finances of European monarchies since the Middle Ages. They replicated quite successfully in many instances the financing abilities of wealthy titled families (the Italian Medeci and the French Rothschilds) who had previously funded state budgets consumed primarily by military conflicts.

By the early nineteenth century, central governments found it cheaper and more expedient to become their own bankers. This also made it possible for them to put a muzzle on the emerging private banks, whose unrestrained activities occasionally brought about economic collapse when they failed. It was then that the concept of a central banking system came into its own.

A notable exception is the United States, where the Federal Reserve System was not formed until 1913. The creation of the Federal Reserve was more a reaction to the eclectic banking practices of J.P. Morgan and his clique of banker–financiers than an attempt to place private banks under government authority. In actuality, the J.P. Morgan banking and financial network helped reduce the economic severity of several crashes and recessions through its clever manipulation of the money supply. These tactics were eventually incorporated into the Federal Reserve's arsenal of monetary policy practices that have proven very effective in more recent years.

Privatization of Economic Enterprise

International commerce was only beginning to separate itself from state ownership or franchise in the nineteenth century. Private traders and investors were dependent upon the emerging central banks for licenses with which to send and receive monies in payment for specific transactions or to fund investments.

European central banks still concerned themselves with the foreign currency and monetary gold affairs of their respective governments, which then accounted for the great majority of international transactions. But they also expanded their jurisdiction to regulate the international financial flows stemming from private sector transactions.

Exchange Control Authority

The power of a central bank to control international financial flows is called its "exchange control" authority. This authority is still held by many central banks. It means that the central bank has the right to allocate its country's foreign exchange reserves (stocks of foreign currencies) to individuals and companies that wish to travel abroad, invest in other countries, and/or import goods and services from abroad. It also has the power to support its national currency or that of other nations by engaging in foreign exchange operations in international currency markets. The U.S. Federal Reserve, which acts as a central bank in many respects, has no exchange control authority.

How the Gold Standard Worked with Central Banking

A country's money supply was determined by the central bank's stock of monetary gold. Because nations discharged their international financial obligations with a transfer of monetary gold, a merchandise trade surplus would result in a net gold inflow. This would allow the trade surplus country to either print more money or up-value its currency. A trade deficit country would be in a reverse position. It would lose monetary gold and would have to reduce its money supply or devalue its currency.

Determining the Foreign Exchange Rate

Central banks controlled their nations' money supply in much the same manner they do today. Hence, if country X had 16 ounces of gold and "printed" 16 francs and country Y had 8 ounces of gold and "printed" 16 guilders, it meant that, relative to the price of gold, 1 franc was worth

2 guilders. The foreign exchange rate or currency price of francs to guilders would be 1 franc per 2 guilders or, in reverse, 1 guilder per 0.5 franc.

In other words, a country that insisted on issuing as much currency as another country but which had less monetary gold would possess the cheaper currency.

Currency Price Changes and Commodity Price Changes

Given a cross-border environment (which does not always exist in reality) of price equality for all goods and services, a canned beverage that cost a consumer 5 francs in country X would cost a consumer in country Y 10 guilders.

If country Y accumulated some significant trade surpluses or engaged in other international activities that would raise its monetary gold stock to 16 ounces, it would have three options. The first option would be to do nothing and maintain the existing foreign exchange rate with country X, thereby raising its money supply to 32 guilders.

The second option might be to leave its money supply alone at 16 guilders and raise (up-value) the guilder price against the franc. In effect, the franc would be devalued (floated down) against the guilder, or the guilder would be up-valued (floated up) against the franc.

The third option would be for country Y to increase its money supply to some intermediate level. Countries on the gold standard often adopted a "split-the-difference" monetary policy, making only slight adjustments in the money supply and in exchange rates in order to maintain long-term monetary stability.

Central Bank Intervention and Monetary Stability

Cooperation among central banks to help preserve international currency price stability started with the gold standard and has continued to the present day. Central banks have found it mutually beneficial over the years to develop a mutual support system that consists of purchasing weaker currencies with stronger ones to maintain foreign exchange stability. The feeling was, as it remains today, that inherently stable currency prices are the key to preserving harmony in international monetary markets.

This support system continues to exist today and is called central bank intervention, with order, stability, and predictability as its principal objectives. This made it possible for trade and investments to grow with the economies of their respective nations. The monetary system created a relatively secure atmosphere for the entire international trading and investment community. Cross-currency prices (foreign exchange rates) were fixed in the sense that they could not change without official sanction from the central banking system. No daily foreign exchange rate fluctuation was allowed; hence, currency speculation was kept to a minimum.

The Gold Exchange Standard and the Variable Fixed-Exchange Rate System, 1934–71

This era is best understood in terms of two distinct historical phases. The first phase was the Great Depression. The United States saw creating and implementing a modified gold standard as a partial antidote to the economic ills of the time. This new standard was expanded after 1945 by making the system of fixed exchange rates more flexible.

The Gold Exchange Standard

Most countries had discarded the gold standard by the early 1920s. World trade and investments were growing so rapidly that the general sentiment was that limiting economic growth and development to a state of nature was no longer practical. The problem is that growth began to stagnate in many parts of the world in the early 1920s. Growing protectionism further hindered international cooperation to the point that, as the depression deepened after 1929, production, trade, and investments came to a virtual standstill as prices fell precipitously on many goods and services. Dwindling demand helped destroy the trading value of many currencies that were no longer backed by gold, and there was a growing perception that national monies had become debased.

The gold exchange standard started in 1934 with a unilateral declaration by the United States that it would buy back any U.S. dollars held abroad by residents of other countries with gold at the officially posted price of $35 per troy ounce. This was an effort by the United States to shore up the dollar's value by backing it directly with gold, thus giving new life to the aging gold standard. The system was finally hammered into place when the IMF was created in 1944.

The gold exchange standard preserved the traditional fixed exchange rate system but made it more flexible. Exchange rates were now allowed several percentage points of fluctuation around the fixed rate before central bank intervention was called for.

The U.S. Dollar as Currency of Ultimate Redemption

This was the major change under the new system. The U.S. dollar became the currency of ultimate redemption and hence the world's key international reserve currency. The international understanding was that, as the currency of ultimate redemption, the U.S. dollar was as good as gold and could therefore be used as legal tender by the rest of the world.

Central Banks Coordinate Their Activities with the IMF

The central banks of countries that joined the IMF allowed their currency support processes to become coordinated by the IMF and thus subject to more oversight than in the past.

Finally, it was possible for foreign exchange rates to fluctuate freely within prescribed bands of a fixed exchange rate. The exchange rate was no longer an inflexible price unyieldingly maintained by a central bank until there was no choice but to mandate a change. The official foreign exchange rate became a target to be supported, allowing daily movement in cross-border currency prices. Those changes came to be viewed as a barometer of what was going on in the world of international commerce and as a guideline for central bank monetary policy.

When a national currency showed signs of short-term weakening, namely that its price was falling toward a preset "floor," central banks along with the IMF would intervene by buying up quantities of the weaker currency with stronger ones to bolster its price in international currency markets. If a national currency moved toward a similarly preset ceiling, the same process would occur in reverse. Central banks would sell off the currency at lower prices to bring the foreign exchange rate back down to the official level.

The Floating Rate System, 1971 to Present

The gold exchange standard ended in 1971 amid speculation that the United States might no longer be able to make good on its 1934 pledge. There was also a feeling, especially among monetarists in decisional power positions in the United States, that central banks had become sufficiently skilled in monetary policy that paper money, if properly managed, could carry its own intrinsic value in mirroring an economy's fundamental strength.

The End of Fixed Foreign Exchange Rates

The gold exchange standard, with its variable fixed-exchange rate system, ended in 1971, leaving all currencies to seek their own price level based on global supply and demand. This system, which continues through the present day, is called the floating rate system. Stability in international currency markets is still maintained by the IMF and its network of central banks. The system receives ad hoc support from the large private financial institutions and multinational corporations, all of which have strong vested interests in also maintaining global monetary stability.

How Floating Rates Work

The use of gold as backing for currency is minimized under a floating rate system. Indeed, monetary gold, or gold held as international reserve assets by nations in the system, has been essentially demonitized since the 1970s. Under a floating rate system, currency prices are determined by the supply and demand for specific currencies based upon relative inflation rates, current events, and changes in trade and investment patterns.

Hard Currencies and Soft Currencies

A country facing high domestic and international demand for its goods and services and whose government practices sound fiscal and monetary management will usually find itself with a currency that is universally acceptable, basically stable, and freely convertible. Such countries are often called "hard currency" states.

A country whose goods and services are not in high demand, whose economy tends to be highly inflationary, and whose political and economic policies lead to instability and unrest will generally find itself with a low-demand currency and may come to be known as a "soft currency" nation. This constitutes the great majority of countries.

Pegged Currencies

Many countries have currencies "pegged" to those of stronger economies. For example, the currencies of many Caribbean and West Indian nations are pegged to either the U.S. dollar or the U.K.'s pound sterling. The Bahamian dollar is pegged to the U.S. dollar at a one-to-one ratio. This means that the Bahamian dollar rises or falls along with the U.S. dollar against all other currencies against which the latter floats.

INTERNATIONAL LIQUIDITY, INTERNATIONAL RESERVE ASSETS, AND THE OFFICIAL SETTLEMENT OF INTERNATIONAL OBLIGATIONS

What Countries Do to Pay Their International Obligations

Nations, just like people, have bills to pay. This involves creating a debit on their financial assets in order to establish a credit against their so-called accounts payables (i.e., what they owe to other nations). They must thus hold a quantity of international liquidity, also known as international reserve assets, that can be used to discharge official international debts.

A Country's Checking Account

These international reserve assets can be compared to a personal or business checking account. When the account is depleted, one's liquidity is gone. For nations, liquidity consists of monetary gold, special drawing rights, reserve position with the IMF, and foreign exchange (foreign currency) reserves. When a country's international reserve assets are low, it then becomes necessary to borrow from foreign official sources such as other countries' central banks.

If a nation has net surpluses in its international transactions, it can increase its international liquidity and become a lender to other deficit countries.

Borrowing and Lending Funds

Nations also engage in what are known as "official" borrowing and lending operations. A country with depleted financial assets may then borrow the necessary reserves from other nations. This increases its international liquidity but at the same time raises its international indebtedness. Surplus countries, to the contrary, pare down their debt or become lenders to other states.

Monetary Gold

The use of monetary gold was widespread until the 1970s. Countries rarely use gold today to settle international payments. The prevailing attitude, supported by the United States, is that economic growth and development on an international scale should not be held hostage to a state of nature. The United States does not back its own currency with gold, either domestically or internationally, and the feeling is that other nations do not need to do so either. Gold has been largely demonetized, except for occasional gold auctions held by the IMF, and efforts to restore a gold or gold exchange standard have thus far been unsuccessful.

Special Drawing Rights

The supply of special drawing rights (SDRs) has remained unchanged since the early 1980s. There are about 10 billion SDRs (US$15 billion) in circulation. Originally conceived as a means of expanding the international liquidity of nations (they were to be used as a form of foreign currency reserve), no new SDRs have been issued because of disagreement about the allocation formula. A country's allocation of SDRs allows it to debit that special account with the IMF to discharge its accounts payables. In turn, countries owed money by other nations can also accept payment in SDRs, banking them with the IMF for future use. It should nevertheless be noted that the existing stocks of SDRs are in widespread use and are considered an active international reserve asset.

Deposits with the IMF

Nominally classified as reserve assets, these funds are unavailable for normal use. IMF deposits are initially made by countries joining the fund. This makes it possible for them to borrow from the IMF against the collateral created by their local currency deposit. Were a nation to draw down its IMF deposit, it would also be reducing the total amount of fund credit available to it.

Foreign Exchange

This is a country's "quick cash." In today's floating rate system, a country's most important international reserve asset is its foreign exchange position, namely, the quantity of foreign currencies it possesses. These are cash inventories against which a country can draw to discharge its international accounts payables, that is, to pay for its imports and other international obligations. That stock can be compared to a personal checking or short-term savings account used to pay current expenses. These foreign exchange reserves are held by private banks, central banks, and other financial institutions.

Foreign exchange reserves are not always located in the nation where they are claimed as assets. For example, U.S. banks often hold their foreign exchange in overseas banks to make it easier for foreign-based exporters that ship their goods to the United States to be paid on time. This enables them to quickly settle foreign claims by debiting local currency accounts in overseas banks. The same is true insofar as U.S. exporters are concerned. They too expect on-time payment. Therefore, foreign banks maintain dollar (their foreign exchange) deposits with U.S. banks that can be conveniently debited to pay for U.S. exports.

CONCLUSION AND SUMMARY

The current monetary system is in a constant state of flux as political borders are rearranged, new nations come into existence, and old states disappear. The miracle is that the system works. Perhaps it works because the entire world population has a vested interest in seeing some system—any system—work over the long term. One of the more popular recommendations to simplify the complexities of dealing with a proliferation of currencies is single-currency zones that cover specific geographic regions.

This is the idea behind the attempt by Western Europeans to introduce the "Euro" in the next few years to replace the 15 different currencies currently in use by the European Union's 15 member countries. The reluctance of the individual states to move wholeheartedly to complete creation of their European Monetary System and European Monetary Union is understandable. A single regional system could entail shifting authority for monetary policy away from the individual sovereign states to a less nationally accountable supranational central bank. Many countries are not yet ready to address this proposition.

KEY TERMS AND CONCEPTS

Fixed exchange rate. The foreign exchange rate of a country's currency is determined by its stock of official monetary gold. The rate cannot fluctuate without an official central bank act of monetary devaluation or upvaluation.

Floating exchange rate. The current system. International currency prices float freely based on the short-term demand for and supply of specific currencies.

Foreign exchange reserves. A country's reserves of foreign currencies. Commonly known as "quick cash," they can be used immediately to finance imports and other foreign payables.

Gold exchange standard. A modified gold standard stemming from a pledge by the United States in 1934 that it would buy back U.S. dollars held by foreign residents at US$35 per troy ounce of gold.

Gold standard. A monetary system whereby currency was directly backed by a nation's stock of gold officially held by a central government to finance international transactions and control the quantity of money in domestic circulation.

Hard currency country. A country facing high domestic and international demand for its goods and services and whose government practices sound fiscal and monetary management will usually find itself with a currency that is universally acceptable, basically stable, and freely convertible. Such countries are often called "hard currency" states.

International liquidity. A country's official gold reserves, reserve position with the International Monetary Fund, special drawing rights, and foreign exchange reserves. A country draws on this liquidity (usually its foreign exchange reserves) to discharge its short-term international obligations (accounts payables).

International monetary system. The system as it currently exists is an amalgamation or loose association of national central banks working through the International Monetary Fund to provide short- and long-term exchange rate stability.

Pegged currencies. Many countries have currencies "pegged" to those of stronger economies. For example, the currencies of many Caribbean and West Indian nations are pegged to either the U.S. dollar or the U.K's pound sterling.

Soft currency country. A country whose goods and services are not in high demand, whose economy tends to be highly inflationary, and whose political and economic policies lead to instability and unrest will generally find itself with a low-demand currency and may come to be known as a "soft currency" nation.

Variable fixed-exchange rate. A country's foreign exchange rate is fixed but can fluctuate within prescribed percentage points of the official rate.

QUESTIONS

4.1 Describe and explain how the monetary system much of the trading world knew in 1800 evolved into the prevailing system today.

4.2 Describe and explain, using specific examples, what a central bank is and what its exchange control authority means. What distinctions might be made between the U.S. Federal Reserve System, the International Monetary Fund, and the Bank of England?

4.3 You are the finance minister of country X, which is faced with a huge trade and services deficit. Incoming foreign investments are few and tourism is way down. Name and justify some options you might exercise. (Cooking the books and leaving the country is not one of them.)

4.4 Discuss the possibility and probability of the North American Free Trade Association developing a single currency to cover Canada, Mexico, and the United States. What steps might be taken to move in that direction?

4.5 Discuss the merits of returning to a gold standard. What steps might be taken to move in that direction?

4.6 You are the treasurer of a large U.S.-based multinational corporation. Discuss what type of monetary system would be best for your company.

CHAPTER 5

The Balance of Payments

INTRODUCTION

In this chapter, international trade, business, and investments are analyzed from the perspective of the flow of cross-border exchange of debits, credits, and payments among nations. These exchanges are recorded in a country's national accounts statistics, called "the balance of payments."

THE SIGNIFICANCE OF THE BALANCE OF PAYMENTS

A national balance-of-payments (BOP) statement in its entirety is probably less important to a business executive than its separate parts for making investment, trade, and financial decisions. Individual transactions recorded within an overall BOP statement can be used as predictors of what may happen to cross-border currency prices and interest rates in the short term.

DEFINING THE BALANCE OF PAYMENTS

A country's BOP can be defined as the systematic recording of all economic transactions between residents of one country and residents of another country over a specified period of time. An accounting definition can also be applied to the BOP: the structure of the BOP is based upon double-entry bookkeeping. Therefore, all transactions must net out to "zero."

For example, should country A export $2 million worth of merchandise to the rest of the world in 1997 and import $1 million in merchandise in the same time frame, it would record a merchandise trade deficit of $1 million. Assuming there were no other international transactions that year, its BOP would show a "deficit" of $1 million resulting from the debt created by the trade imbalance.

Country A could exercise one of two options (it could actually exercise both options) to handle its indebtedness. It could draw down its international reserves in the amount of $1 million, or it could sell $1 million worth of government bonds to foreign central banks. It could also settle the debt by executing both options (i.e., drawing down $500,000 of its own reserves and borrowing $500,000 from foreign central banks). The result would be a "zero" balance in its BOP.

This explains why there are no "deficits" or "surpluses" in a country's BOP; there are only balancing and/or compensatory items to offset any imbalances (disequilibrium) that occur in its economic transactions with other countries.

This leads to a third definition of the BOP as a measure of the net changes in a country's official international reserve assets plus net changes in claims by foreign official monetary authorities (central banks and the International Monetary Fund) needed to make the country's total debits equal total credits.

In the case of country A, a $500,000 drawdown or sale of its monetary assets (international reserves) would be recorded as a credit (+). The act of borrowing $500,000 from foreign central banks through the sale of government bonds would also be recorded as a credit (+), even though it would simultaneously increase foreign official claims against country A's monetary assets.

The "credit" entry is created because the immediate effect of the transaction would be tantamount to generating a cash inflow for country A. These two "credit" transactions, totaling $1 million, would offset the net negative $1 million trade imbalance recorded as a "debit" in country A's international accounts. Its BOP, on an official settlements basis, would be back in equilibrium, although the country would now have acquired a new foreign debt in the amount of $500,000 and drawn down its reserves by another $500,000.

COMPONENTS OF THE BALANCE OF PAYMENTS

A country's international economic transactions are broken down into components for systematic classification in a formalized reporting structure. The format used by the United States as reported annually by the U.S. Department of Commerce in its publication "Survey of Current Business" is reproduced in the Appendix at the end of this book.

Economic Transactions

Economists are interested in the notion of "equilibrium" wherein the impact of given activities should be offset by the effects of others in order to achieve and maintain harmony or a balance in international exchange. They therefore tend to think of the BOP in terms of autonomous and compensatory transactions. Autonomous transactions are those that occur for market reasons (merchandise imports and exports and foreign investments, shown on lines 2, 16, 43, and 56 of the Appendix) where players have no idea of the economic ramifications of their actions. In country A's merchandise trade transactions (see preceding section), its export of $2 million and import of $1 million would be called "autonomous." Indeed, all items from lines 1 through 32 of the Appendix are considered autonomous in that sense.

Its $1 million merchandise trade deficit creates an economic imbalance (places it in a position of economic disequilibrium). The correction of that imbalance takes place through a "compensatory" transaction that somehow makes up for the deficit. When country A exercises some or all of its options (see preceding section) in eliminating the transaction disequilibrium, its economy (at least in terms of that singular activity) will be back in balance. Hence, compensatory transactions are those that are intended to restore equilibrium to a country's BOP (see lines 34 and 49 of the Appendix). These compensatory activities may not cure deeper rooted socioeconomic problems that lead to the initial disequilibrium like country A's merchandise trade deficit, but they will at least help in "balancing the books."

The fact that they actually do not fully bring the BOP back into a bookkeeping equilibrium is due to errors and omissions. These creep into the BOP's computation for two reasons. First, it is still technically impossible to capture all economic transactions that transpire among nations. Second, central banks charged with the authority to participate in the compensatory process do not have up-to-the-moment real-time data and then create more confusion by often entering into foreign currency transactions for their own account. A "plug" is thus needed. That is provided by the "statistical discrepancy" row shown on line 63 of the Appendix which, as defined, is "the sum of the above items with sign reversed." The statistical discrepancy entry will supply the fill-in figure to yield a "zero" balance when the addition of the autonomous plus compensatory transactions does not.

Residency

Residency in a country is determined by physical domicile and not by citizenship, although citizenship is often used by the governments of many countries as prima facie evidence of residency. Residency refers to an individual's or a business's physical domicile, or where one "lives" for most of a calendar year. The term "most of the calendar year" is understood in many countries to mean more than 180 days or more than 270 days, depending on the type of tax treatment being sought. Hoffman LaRoche (U.S.) is therefore a corporate resident of the United States despite the fact that most of its voting stock is owned by its parent, Hoffman LaRoche of Switzerland. A shipment from the U.S. subsidiary to its Swiss parent would be treated as a merchandise export from the United States on line 2 of the Appendix.

The Balance of Payments Is a Combination Income Statement and Balance Sheet

The BOP, as suggested in the preceding section on economic transactions, can be compared to a corporate balance sheet that consists of assets and liabilities. The equalizing entry in any balance sheet is the "earned surplus," which on occasion may also consist of a "plug" figure to account for recording discrepancies and errors. Companies engage in market-driven operations (sales, the purchase of inventories, etc.) which can be called autonomous transactions. These activities must be financed either internally by writing a check against some existing bank account or by acquiring debt or selling equity. These latter acts can be considered compensatory in nature because they are intended to support current and future operations.

A nation functions internationally in much the same way. It engages in autonomous transactions such as the foreign sale and purchase of goods and services. If there is an imbalance in its autonomous sector, it then engages in compensatory activity to restore the balance. Any difference between these two sets of transactions is offset by a "plug" entry. The International Monetary Fund calls this "Net Errors and Omissions." The United States labels the entry "Statistical Discrepancy" (see line 63 of the Appendix).

The Current Account

Business economists and finance executives who use the BOP as a tool to determine a country's sources and uses of funds will be more interested in analyzing transactions from a cash flow or monetary perspective. Instead of fitting economic activity among nations into autonomous and compensatory headings, the designations current and capital accounts are used. Lines 1 through 32 of the Appendix are included as part of a country's current account, and its credits and debits are reconciled under "Memoranda" (line 70 of the Appendix). These transactions are under the current account heading because they are treated as sales and purchases in almost the same sense as they would be on a corporate income or cash flow statement. All current account activity is also considered autonomous. A surplus in current account transactions represents a net inflow of funds, while a deficit represents a net outflow of funds. Major subsets of the U.S. current account position are listed below.

- *Balance of merchandise trade.* The merchandise trade balance refers to the balance between exports and imports of physical goods such as automobiles, machinery, and farm products. A positive or favorable balance occurs when exports are greater than imports. Merchandise exports and imports are the largest single component of most countries' international transactions (lines 2 and 16 of the Appendix).
- *Services.* International trade involves exports and imports of both goods and services. Services include such items as foreign military expenditures, interest and dividends, travel and transportation, plus fees and royalties (lines 3 and 17 and lines 11 and 25 of the Appendix).

  A country's purchases of goods and services represent imports and are recorded as debit (–) entries. A country's sales of goods and services to foreigners represent exports and are recorded as credit (+) entries. The same rule is applied to remittances of fees, royalties, dividends, and other forms of income. Inflows are shown as credits and outflows are listed as debits.

- **Unilateral transfers.** Gifts, grants, pensions, and other private annuities are included in a country's unilateral transfer account. Private gifts and grants include personal gifts of all kinds, philanthropic activities, and shipments by relief organizations. For example, money sent abroad by immigrants to their families would represent a private transfer of money. Any monies leaving a country in this fashion would be considered a debit transaction, whereas money coming in would be considered a credit. If a resident of the United States moves to a foreign country upon retirement to establish residency and has his or her social security checks, pensions, and other annuity income forwarded, these funds are also recorded as unilateral transfers (line 29 of the Appendix).

The Capital Account

Activity in this account is divided between autonomous and compensatory transactions. Summarily, all foreign direct investments and all foreign portfolio investments are considered autonomous transactions are included in the BOP's current account.

- **Foreign direct investments.** These are investments into other countries, with the objective of owning partially or entirely an economic enterprise for the purpose of establishing market share and generating revenue and profits that can ultimately be transformed into stockholders' dividends. U.S. businesses invested $87.8 billion in other countries in 1996, while foreign resident businesses invested $76.9 billion in the United States (lines 44 and 57 of the Appendix).
- **Foreign portfolio investments.** These are investments into financial instruments such as stocks and bonds, where the objective is not to actively engage in business but instead to generate dividend and/or interest income and capital gains. Foreign portfolio investments by U.S. residents in 1996 were $98.9 billion (lines 45, 46, and 47 of the Appendix), while foreign portfolio investments by foreign residents into the United States that year were $348.2 billion (lines 58 through 61 of the Appendix).
- **Compensatory capital transactions.** Part of the capital account is used to record those central bank activities that are intended to

restore equilibrium to the BOP due to any imbalances caused by one or several autonomous transactions. These include changes in a country's official international reserve assets (international liquidity) and changes in foreign official claims on those monetary assets.

For example, autonomous transactions recorded by the United States in 1996 indicate that its current account position was a negative (–) $148.184 billion. Outbound U.S. foreign direct and foreign portfolio investments together were $358.4 billion, contrasted against inbound investments totaling $425.2 billion, creating a positive autonomous private capital account balance.

This positive autonomous capital account balance in the amount of $66.8 billion offset the current account deficit of $148.1 billion, leaving the United States with a net deficit in its BOP of $81.3 billion to be financed. This was done by drawing down U.S. official reserve assets by $6.668 billion (line 34 of the Appendix) and by borrowing $122.354 billion from foreign central banks. The sell-off of U.S. liquidity assets plus the official central bank (Federal Reserve) borrowings resulted in offsetting the deficit by $48.722 billion* ($130.022 billion less the deficit of $81.3 billion). The statistical discrepancy figure was thus duly recorded in the amount of (–) $48.927 billion to restore a "zero" balance.

The U.S. BOP position on an autonomous transactions basis was therefore a negative (–) $131.1 billion. The financing of this deficit was accomplished by allowing foreign official claims on U.S. monetary assets to rise in the amount of $109.757 billion. However, instead of the country also drawing down its own official reserve assets (monetary gold, special drawing rights, reserve position in the International Monetary Fund, and its stock of foreign currencies), it actually increased those reserves by a net $9.841 billion, offsetting the compensatory impact of the foreign-based financing.

- *The statistical discrepancy account.* The country's statistical discrepancy account entry should have normally read a positive (+) $21.707 billion to adjust for the difference between the autonomous BOP deficit and the inadequate financing. Instead, it had to be raised to a positive (+) $31.548 billion to reflect the increase in reserves.

---

* The difference between the two figures results from the author's rounding.

IMPORTANCE TO GOVERNMENTS AND THE BUSINESS COMMUNITY

The BOP helps business managers and government officials to isolate specific international economic pressure points that impact a country's global competitive position. An overall deficit or surplus of autonomous transactions in any given year is relatively unimportant except in determining the level of compensatory financing that might be required. A long-term position of disequilibrium is probably of greater concern, especially if the disequilibrium leads to a continuing depletion of reserve assets and rising foreign public sector debt levels.

The Issue of Long-Term Deficits

The United States has been sustaining long-term deficits in its autonomous transactions, concentrated in its merchandise trade balances, since 1971. External financing through loans from foreign central banks, if unliquidated, accumulates through an increase in official foreign debt levels. This is not a problem for countries whose income growth meets or exceeds increases in debt levels. The situation becomes more precarious for countries whose economic growth fails to keep pace with debt expansion.

Short-term impacts. If a country maintains a merchandise trade deficit and runs short of foreign exchange reserves, there will be pressure on its currency to float down (devalue) against others not pegged to it. Floating down the currency is a mechanical adjustment process managed by central banks and will not address any structural problem in the economy that gave rise to trade imbalances in the first place.

A currency's downward float may help increase exports if devaluation-related inflation does not erase the advantage of having a cheaper currency. However, it will also raise the price of imports. Equally important, it will make foreign investments more expensive for residents of the devaluating currency's nation. Investments from other countries will be attracted because foreign currencies can buy additional quantities of foreign exchange for the same price.

Anticipating possible or probable currency price changes is an essential facet of doing business internationally. Carrying out protective strategies to minimize foreign exchange risk is one of international business's daily chores. Hedging functions ranging from forward contracts to dabbling in the more speculative currency futures market serve as effective risk minimizers and help companies maintain predictability in their global operations.

Long-term impacts. These are seen in a gradual realignment of major currencies and in interest rates. For example, the yen price of U.S. dollars in 1970 was 360 Japanese yen per U.S. dollar. The trading range today is between 115 and 125 Japanese yen per U.S. dollar. In 1970, the special drawing right (SDR) was priced at one SDR per U.S. dollar. Today, the average exchange price is about US$1.35 per SDR. The U.S. dollar has gently floated down against the SDR and its market basket of major currencies since 1970, affecting every aspect of domestic and international commerce.

THE ADJUSTMENT PROCESS AND RESTORING BALANCE-OF-PAYMENTS EQUILIBRIUM

The adjustment process in bringing the BOP back to equilibrium or a "zero" balance is mechanical in nature. It does not address situations in a country's economy that may have triggered the disequilibrium in the first place. A country, through its central bank, can bring the BOP back to an accounting equilibrium by either floating down or floating up its currency if the source of the imbalance is a persistent current account deficit or surplus without there being any offsets in its autonomous capital transactions. In the event of a continuing deficit, floating down (devaluing) one's currency might have the effect of increasing exports and decreasing imports by making exports less expensive for foreign countries to buy and making imports more expensive for domestic customers to purchase.

Currency devaluation could also have the effect of attracting foreign source investments due to the lower price for the host country's currency. It might at the same time reduce the attractiveness of making investments overseas because of the higher cost of foreign currencies. The net result of changing one's currency price in international monetary markets can bring the country's BOP back to equilibrium, assuming conditions abroad remain unchanged during the process, which unfortunately is not always the case.

Another option available in the adjustment process is to draw down one's international reserves and/or to tap the SDR account (line 36 of the

Appendix). This would be the same as dipping into one's checking or savings account to liquidate an accounts payable. This option would minimize the need to change currency prices.

Borrowing or lending among central bank monetary authorities can also be used for adjustment purposes (line 49 of the Appendix). Borrowing from the central banks of other countries has traditionally been the way the United States has financed its BOP deficits on autonomous transactions over the years.

CONCLUSION AND SUMMARY

An examination of the international BOP accounts of many countries reveals varying levels of indebtedness resulting from annual deficits in their autonomous transactions. The United States is no exception. The United States is also typical of many countries whose deficits are attributable to merchandise trade deficits. Whether large trade deficits or surpluses are intrinsically bad or good for a country is a matter of opinion too often colored by political motive. A more appropriate approach to the entire issue of deficits might be to inquire into a country's debt affordability and manageability. How much debt can a nation afford and manage before there is a serious impact on its processes of economic growth and development?

KEY TERMS AND CONCEPTS

Adjustment process. A number of steps or options taken by governments to bring their BOP back to equilibrium or a "zero" balance (e.g., devaluing one's currency to make exports more competitively priced abroad).

Autonomous transactions. Transactions that occur for market reasons where players have no idea of or concern about the economic ramifications of their actions.

Balance of payments. The systematic recording of all economic transactions between residents of one country and residents of another country over a specified period of time. An accounting definition can also be applied to the BOP: the structure of the BOP is based upon double-entry bookkeeping. Therefore, all transactions must net out to "zero."

Compensatory transactions. Transactions intended to restore equilibrium to a country's balance of payments (see lines 34 and 49 of the Appendix).

Foreign direct investments. Investments into other countries, with the objective of owning partially or entirely an economic enterprise for the purpose of establishing market share and generating revenue and profits.

Foreign portfolio investments. Investments into financial instruments such as stocks and bonds, where the goal is not to actively engage in business but to seek dividend and/or interest income and capital gains.

Residency. Residency in a country is determined by an individual's or a corporation's physical domicile, or where one "lives" for most of a calendar year.

Statistical discrepancy. Normally a "plug" figure as on line 63 of the Appendix which, as defined, is "the sum of the above items with sign reversed." The statistical discrepancy entry will supply the fill-in figure to yield a "zero" balance when the addition of the autonomous plus compensatory transactions does not equal out to "zero" on their own.

QUESTIONS

5.1 You are the finance minister of a country with a BOP position that indicates a huge net surplus of foreign portfolio investments. What policy recommendations would you make and why?

5.2 The United States has sustained a continuing merchandise trade deficit since 1971. Discuss how this deficit impacts the nation's economic welfare. Explain how it impacts your personal economic welfare.

5.3 Discuss the BOP adjustment process to help bring it to a bookkeeping equilibrium.

5.4 Discuss the measures a country can consider to restore equilibrium to its BOP over the long term.

5.5 Discuss with examples how monetary policy can be used to maintain BOP equilibrium.

5.6 Discuss with examples how fiscal policy can be used to maintain BOP equilibrium.

CHAPTER 6

Foreign Exchange and Foreign Exchange Management

INTRODUCTION

The understanding and management of foreign exchange have become a major preoccupation for multinational corporations. Essentially, foreign exchange gains can mean extra profits for companies. Foreign exchange losses can turn a profitable enterprise into a losing proposition.

Changes in cross-border currency prices occur continually throughout the world. Some fluctuations are a result of rapid changes in the supply and demand for specific currencies, such as U.S. dollars and Japanese yen. Some currency price differentials are a function of time zone variations. Sudden shifts in currency prices are often a consequence of uncertainty, fear, and speculation.

Over the long term, foreign exchange rates change as fundamental economic relationships among countries change. The concept and operation of the foreign exchange market and how companies manage their foreign currency assets to minimize the risk of sustaining foreign exchange losses are the focus of this chapter.

FOREIGN EXCHANGE AND CURRENCY DEFINED

Foreign exchange is defined as another country's currency or money. Thus, the U.S. dollar would be foreign exchange to a resident of Germany, and the deutsche mark would be foreign exchange to a resident of the United States. As an example, the deutsche mark rate from the point of view of a U.S. importer would be 1.50DM/U.S. dollar or 1.00DM/$0.75.

Foreign exchange as a term is synonymous with the expression foreign currency or foreign money. The words "money" and "currency" may seem to be synonymous, but they are not quite the same.

Money, in order to be an acceptable medium of international exchange, must have currency. This means it must have three characteristics: it must be universally acceptable, it must be freely convertible, and it must be inherently stable over the long term as a holder of value in due course. In other words, money must have currency or validity in order to be in demand as a medium of exchange.*

Hard and Soft Currencies

Bankers often make a distinction between "hard" and "soft" currencies. A hard currency is one which has the three features that define a holder of value in due course. It is a currency whose use is in global demand, such as the Japanese yen. Soft currencies are in more limited demand. They also tend not to be very stable.

Pegged Currencies

Some currencies which may tend to be "soft" are often "pegged" to hard currencies to maintain their stability. A "pegged" currency, like the Bahamian dollar or the peso of the Dominican Republic, is linked to the movement of a major "hard" currency, so that when the lead currency floats up or down, the "pegged" money will also float in the same direction in the same proportion. The problem is that "pegged" currencies often have little value in monetary markets outside of their link with the lead currency.

Foreign Exchange Rates

A foreign exchange rate is the price of one currency stated in terms of another. Traders occasionally use the expression "cross-border currency

---

* Foreign currency prices, cross rates, spot rates, and selected forward contracts and currency futures are published in *The Wall Street Journal*. Currency prices for all countries are published weekly in *The Wall Street Journal*. Currency prices are also available in real-time quotes through the Internet.

prices." Both mean the same. Two other terms often used are "spot rate" and "forward rate."

The Spot Rate

The spot rate for a currency is its foreign exchange price quoted for immediate delivery. When one calls a bank's currency trading desk for a deutsche mark quote, the response will most likely be the spot price (e.g., 1.50DM/U.S. dollar). This means that if no decision is made to trade currencies (dollars for deutsche marks) at that time and the caller hangs up and then tries an hour later, the foreign exchange rate may have changed to 1.48DM/U.S. dollar. There would have been no commitment by currency traders to execute an order at the old price.

Although it is defined as immediate, in practice, settlement actually occurs two business days following the agreed-upon exchange date. Thirty percent of all foreign exchange transactions are executed at the spot rate.

The Forward Rate

The forward exchange rate is a foreign exchange rate quoted for future delivery, which can be up to 180 days. Most forward rates rarely go beyond 120 days. Using the deutsche mark example above, if the spot rate is quoted at 1.50DM/U.S. dollar, then the 60-day forward rate might hypothetically be quoted at 1.60DM/U.S. dollar.

Forward transactions come in two varieties: outright and swaps. Forward outrights are typically traded for the major volume currencies for maturities of 30, 90, 120, 180, and 360 days. They represent 5% of all foreign exchange transactions.

Forward swaps are the most common type of forward transaction, comprising 60% of all foreign exchange transactions. In a swap transaction, two companies exchange currency immediately for an agreed-upon length of time at an agreed exchange rate. At the end of the time period, each company returns the currency to the former owner at the original exchange rate with an adjustment for interest rate differences.

Forward contracts serve a variety of purposes, but their primary purpose is to allow firms to lock in a rate of exchange on foreign currency funds that may be needed in the future. This enables companies to avoid potential foreign exchange losses on trades at times when prices on desired currencies rise or fall.

The foreign exchange prices on trades taking place at spot and forward rates are published daily in the business press of most countries and are also available through the Internet and other specialized computerized services.

The other 5% of forward transactions occur in currency futures markets. These trades take place in specific locations like the Philadelphia Stock Exchange.

The Spread

Currency buying and selling commissions and transactions that take place across different time zones create an ever-changing spread between buying and selling prices and also impact the basic foreign exchange rate, depending on where in the world the trade is to occur. This knowledge becomes handy for those who feel that better currency prices may be had in places other than where they reside. With today's information technology, it becomes as easy to be a global currency trader as it is to buy and sell stocks and bonds with a computer.

Foreign Exchange Markets and How They Work

Foreign exchange markets, despite the presence of central banks and the International Monetary Fund (IMF), which does a reasonably good job of preventing chaos and panic during times of crisis, come closest to Adam Smith's concept of the "invisible hand" in an unregulated environment for two reasons:

- *Floating exchange rates.* The world has been functioning on a floating exchange rate system since 1971, with only reactive intervention by central banks and the IMF to maintain order.
- *Technology renders government action obsolete.* The mechanical ease and speed with which cross-border financial transfers can be undertaken make the presence of any national or international regulatory or monitoring agency virtually obsolete. Hence, most currency transactions today emerge more from the need to meet specific open market objectives than a need to meet international public policy goals.

The Exchange Rationale

In the simplest case scenario, before two companies, each in a different country, can do business with one another, they or their intermediaries must be able to exchange currencies. After all, a firm domiciled in the United States that sells goods to Argentina would prefer being paid in dollars to being paid in pesos. Importers that bring in products from other countries must also first obtain the currency in which the product is sold.

The United States, whose banking system has over $200 billion in foreign exchange reserves, consisting mainly of hard currencies, has few exchange control restrictions. Therefore, importers can readily buy foreign currencies through their banks upon demand. However, it may be worthwhile for an importer purchasing on an open account basis to look into buying foreign exchange on a forward contract.

Both exporters and importers, as well as foreign investors, can also enter into forward foreign exchange contracts or even play the currency futures markets without restriction.

Forward Contract

A forward contract is an arrangement between two parties to trade specified amounts of two currencies at some designated future due date at an agreed price. More than a formal hedge against unforeseen changes in currency prices, it guarantees certainty in the foreign exchange rate at the contract's delivery date.

A U.S. importer of textile machinery from Germany may have been quoted a CIF (cost, insurance, and freight) price of DM150,000, which would now cost the importer at spot US$100,000. However, the importer knows that the equipment will not be shipped for over 2 months and that the payment terms will be 30 days sight draft. If the importer believes that, for a number of economic and political reasons, the deutsche mark will float up against the dollar in the next few months, it might be worth hedging against that probability.

A quick call to the importer's bank or a look at the business press might reveal a 90-day forward rate of 1.40DM/U.S. dollar. Should the spot actually move to the forward rate to become the future spot rate, then the importer's $100,000 would only buy DM140,000, leaving a shortfall of DM10,000, which would cost another $7,143. Doing nothing, and assuming that the rate moved as expected, would raise the importer's CIF cost from $100,000 to $107,143.

While finding someone to enter into a forward contract at the current spot rate is unrealistic, it would be possible to locate a partner at perhaps 1.45DM/U.S. dollar. This might be a company looking to lock into a set amount of dollars for use in the near future and thus avoid being subject to market vagaries. Thus, the importer entering into a forward contract for DM150,000 at 1.45DM/U.S. dollar for delivery in 90 days would pay $103,449, which would guarantee or fix the CIF import cost at that amount.

Doing nothing may cost the importer more if the deutsche mark rises as predicted, or the importer could gain if the currency stays unchanged or even falls against the dollar. That is the gamble with a forward contract. However, as stated at the outset, it does freeze the foreign exchange rate for a particular transaction, creating certainty about costs and making it possible for all parties to plan their financial needs. Forward contracts are multinational corporations' hedge of choice and are estimated to cover over 70% of all cross-border currency transactions.

Currency Futures

These markets operate based on a concept similar to forward contracts. The latter are bilateral agreements that can cover any quantity of currency for execution at any agreed time. The former are commodity agreements for large, specific quantities of foreign currencies where buyers and sellers are not immediately known to one another. Currency futures are traded in formal arenas, just like pork bellies. The oldest and still active currency trading exchange in the United States is the Philadelphia Stock Exchange, which has been in continuous operation since 1792.

International Liquidity and Reserve Assets

A country's foreign exchange reserves (i.e., foreign currencies held by domestic banks, central banks, and other financial institutions) form part of its international liquidity position. The components of international liquidity position are also called international reserve assets. These reserve assets consist of the following:

- *Foreign exchange reserves.* The current U.S. position is over $270 billion. This stock of foreign currencies is "quick" cash that importers access through their banks in order to pay for goods purchased from other countries.
- *Currency reserves with the IMF.* These are dollars and other currencies on deposit with the IMF. These reserves are drawn down mainly in times of financial crisis, when a country is forced to bring its balance of payments back into equilibrium.
- *Monetary gold reserves.* These reserves still exist, but little or no gold has been traded among nations since the early 1980s.

- *Special drawing rights (SDRs).* These special credits, created by the IMF in 1969, were intended to expand the international liquidity of IMF member countries. However, members to date have disagreed on the allocation methodology. The result is that although SDRs are officially called "active" reserve assets, no SDRs have been issued since 1981.

While the composition of IMF reserves, gold reserves, and SDRs may change from time to time, they have little immediate impact on international trade. A change in a country's quantity of foreign exchange reserves (especially reserves of hard currencies) will affect imports and exports right away.

If the U.S. stock of hard currency reserves declines, their prices will quickly rise, which means that the dollar will start floating (devaluing) down rapidly. This will make imports more expensive and, of course, will make forward contracts more popular. Exporters, however, may seize a short-term advantage because foreign importers will be able to buy dollars at a cheaper price.

If the U.S. inventory of hard currency reserves rises, their prices may actually drop, which means that the dollar will start floating up (upvaluing). This will make imports less expensive. Exporters will end up at a disadvantage because the dollar will now be more expensive in other importing countries.

Scenarios do not always play out as indicated above because of a number of other variables that affect short-term foreign exchange prices, not the least of which are current political and economic events. However, for international traders of any size, heightened sensitivity to foreign exchange fluctuations is essential for business survival and growth.

THE PURCHASING POWER PARITY THEORY (HOW TO "GUESSTIMATE" FUTURE CURRENCY PRICES)

In order to find the rate at which one currency can be exchanged for another in the near future, the purchasing power of the two economies in question must be analyzed. For example, if the price of a moderate bottle of wine in the United States is $10.00, the precise exchange rate would be that which exchanges $10.00 for the number of French francs it would take to purchase a moderate bottle of wine in France. The underlying assumptions are that the economic profile of a buyer of specific goods would be globally uniform and that, after factoring away logistics, taxes, and other exogenous factors, the only variable left would be inflation, and that would be assumed to have a nationally simultaneous impact on costs, prices, wages, and salaries.

Therefore, without inflation, if the price of a moderate bottle of wine in France is 30 French francs (FFr), then the exchange rate that equalizes the purchasing parity would be

$$FFr\ 300/US\$1.00$$

In this example, each U.S. dollar is equal to three French francs regardless of in which country the wine drinker is located. This is the essence of the purchasing power parity theory. It can be used to help predict short-term forward rates (up to 180 days). The purchasing power parity exchange rate is simply the rate that equalizes the price of an identical product or service in two different currencies.

The formula for the purchasing power parity theory is:

$$Fr = Sr \times (PIfr1 - PIfr2/PIus1 - PIus2)$$

where Fr = forward rate of francs to dollars, Sr = spot rate of francs to dollars, PIfr1 = beginning year price index of France, PIfr2 = end year price index of France, PIus1 = beginning year price index of the United States, and PIus2 = end year price index of the United States.

Assuming that the spot rate is two francs per dollar and that France's price index moved from 100 to 110 in one year while that of the United States remained at 100 for the same period, the forward rate of francs to dollars should move from Fr 3.00/US$1.00 to the future spot rate of Fr 3.30/US$1.00. In other words, the value of the French franc will have devalued (depreciated) 10% or floated down against the U.S. dollar because France's inflation rate as reflected through its price index is 10% higher than that of the United States.

THE FOREIGN EXCHANGE MARKET

The foreign exchange market is an international market that exchanges financial instruments denominated in different currencies. The financial instruments involved range from cash, drafts, checks, and wire and telephone transfers to contracts to buy and sell currency in the future.

The most common instrument of foreign exchange is the telephone transfer among banks. It usually involves transactions in excess of $1 million. This part of the foreign exchange market is known as the inter-bank market. Brokers sometimes assist in the transfer of funds confidentially. The central banks of governments may participate in the foreign exchange market in order to implement governmental policies regarding the value of their currencies.

The market for foreign currencies is a worldwide market that is informal in structure. This means that there is no central pit, place, or floor. The "market" is actually the thousands of telecommunications links between financial institutions around the globe, and it is open 24 hours a day. Although the foreign exchange market has no central location, trading volume is concentrated in the United States, the United Kingdom, and Japan.

The structure of the foreign currency market leads to some interesting problems. Since there is no single exchange location or floor, there is no one exchange rate.

EXCHANGE RATE QUOTATIONS AND TERMINOLOGY

Foreign exchange rates can be found in newspapers such as *The Wall Street Journal* and *The New York Times*.

The exchange rate between the U.S dollar (USD) and the French franc (FFr) can be expressed in either U.S. or European terminology.

U.S. terms. U.S. terms gives the price of a franc in relation to the U.S. dollar or its U.S. dollar equivalent. For example, USD/FFr or $/FFr = $0.1707 means that 1 French franc is equal to or would cost 0.17071 U.S. dollar or slightly more than 17 U.S. cents.

European terms. European terms gives the price of a U.S. dollar in relation to its French franc equivalent. For example, FFr/USD or FFr/$ = 5.8580 FFr means that 1 U.S. dollar is equal to or would cost 5.8580 French francs.

In the interbank market, almost all quotations are for sale or purchase of U.S. dollars against a foreign currency using the FFr/USD form. These two exchange rates are actually reciprocals of each other. Once one of the rates is known, the other can be easily calculated. A reciprocal is any number divided into one; thus, if the USD/FFr rate is 0.17071, the FFr/USD can be calculated as follows:

$$\frac{1}{0.17071} = 5.8580$$

Cross rates. Although it is common to quote foreign currencies against the U.S. dollar, it is not necessary. Any currency's value can be stated in terms of any other currency. When the exchange rate for a currency is stated without using the U.S. dollar as a reference, it is referred to as a cross rate. For example, suppose the German mark and the Japanese yen are both quoted in terms of the U.S. dollar: DM 17175/USD and yen 104.70/USD. If the yen/DM cross rates are needed, it is simply a matter of division:

$$\text{Yen } 104.70/\text{USD} = \text{Yen } 60.96/\text{DM}$$
$$\text{DM } 1.7175/\text{USD}$$

This means that if would take 60.95 Japanese yen to purchase 1 German mark.

CONCLUSION AND SUMMARY

Understanding and managing foreign currencies and foreign currency markets is the key to effective financial control over international markets. The general thrust of corporations, individuals, and even governments is to avoid soft currency exposure by maximizing hard currency holdings and to avoid foreign exchange fluctuation risk through forward contracts and futures. This allows the financial planning process to go forward multinationally in a world of many competing currencies.

KEY TERMS AND CONCEPTS

Currency futures. These markets operate based on a concept similar to forward contracts. The latter are bilateral agreements that can cover any quantity of currency for execution at any agreed time. Currency futures are traded in formal arenas, just like pork bellies. The oldest and still active currency trading exchange in the United States is the Philadelphia Stock Exchange, which has been in continuous operation since 1792.

Currency reserves with the International Monetary Fund (IMF). Dollars and other currencies on deposit with the IMF. These reserves are drawn down mainly in times of financial crisis, when a country is forced to bring its balance of payments back into equilibrium.

Foreign exchange. Another country's currency or money. U.S. dollars would be foreign exchange to a resident of Germany, and deutsche marks would be foreign exchange to a resident of the United States.

Foreign exchange rate. The price of one currency stated in terms of another. Traders occasionally use the expression "cross-border currency prices." Both mean the same. Two other terms often used are "spot rate" and "forward rate."

Foreign exchange reserves. The current U.S. position is over $270 billion. This stock of foreign currencies is "quick" cash that importers access through their banks in order to pay for goods purchased from other countries.

Forward contract. An arrangement between two parties to trade specified amounts of two currencies at some designated future due date at an agreed price. More than a formal hedge against unforeseen changes in currency prices, it guarantees certainty in the foreign exchange rate at the contract's delivery date.

Forward swap. The most common type of forward transaction, forward swaps comprise 60% of all foreign exchange transactions. In a swap transaction, two companies immediately exchange currency for an agreed-upon length of time at an agreed exchange rate. At the end of the time period, each company returns the currency to the former owner at the original exchange rate with an adjustment for interest rate differences.

Hard and soft currencies. Bankers often make a distinction between "hard" and "soft" currencies. A hard currency is one which has the three features that define a holder of value in due course. It is a currency whose use is in global demand, such as the Japanese yen. Soft currencies are in more limited demand and tend not to be very stable.

International liquidity and reserve assets. A country's foreign exchange reserves (i.e., foreign currencies held by domestic banks, central banks, and other financial institutions) form part of its international liquidity position. The components of international liquidity position are also called "international reserve assets." These reserve assets consist of foreign exchange reserves, currency reserves with the International Monetary Fund, monetary gold reserves, and special drawing rights.

Monetary gold reserves. These reserves still exist, but little or no gold has been traded among nations since the early 1980s.

Money. This is currency. Money, in order to be a "holder of value in due course" and an acceptable medium of international exchange, must have "currency." This means it must have three characteristics: it must be universally acceptable, it must be freely convertible, and it must be inherently stable over the long term as a holder of value in due course.

Pegged currencies. Some currencies which may tend to be "soft" are often "pegged" to hard currencies to maintain their stability. A "pegged" currency, like the Bahamian dollar or the peso of the Dominican Republic, is linked to the movement of a major "hard" currency, so that when the lead currency floats up or down, the "pegged" money will also float in the same direction in the same proportion.

Purchasing power parity theory. The formula for the purchasing power parity theory is

$$Fr = Sr \times (PIfr1 - PIfr2/PIus1 - PIus2)$$

where Fr = forward rate of francs to dollars, Sr = spot rate of francs to dollars, PIfr1 = beginning year price index of France, PIfr2 = end year price index of France, PIus1 = beginning year price index of the United States, and PIus2 = end year price index of the United States.

Special drawing rights (SDRs). These special credits, created by the International Monetary Fund in 1969, were intended to expand the international liquidity of fund member countries. However, members to date have disagreed on the allocation methodology. The result is that although SDRs are officially called "active" reserve assets, no SDRs have been issued since 1981.

Spot rate. The spot rate for a currency is its foreign exchange price quoted for immediate delivery.

Spread. Currency buying and selling commissions and transactions that take place across different time zones create an ever-changing spread between buying and selling prices and also impact the basic foreign exchange rate, depending on where in the world the trade is to occur. This is known as the "spread."

QUESTIONS

6.1 The current spot rate for German deutsche marks into U.S. dollars is 2.00DM/U.S. dollar. This year's inflation rate for the United States is expected to run its price index up from 105 (January 1, 1997) to 110 by December 31, 1997. Germany's inflation rate is expected to run its price index up from 110 to 121. Suppose the treasurer of a U.S.-based company is interested in entering into a forward contract to purchase 2 million deutsche marks for delivery in 90 days. The treasurer is assuming that both countries' inflation rates will be evenly distributed throughout the year, with no sudden seasonal or unforeseen surges. Calculate the future or forward rate based upon this information.

6.2 Discuss the circumstances under which the purchasing power parity theory might and might not work well. Give specific examples.

6.3 Describe and explain the similarities and differences between spot rates, forward and future rates, and the future spot rate.

6.4 Describe and explain the differences between how forward markets and currency futures function.

6.5 Describe and explain how fixed exchange rates vary from pegged exchange rates.

6.6 Describe and explain the role of central banking and foreign exchange in international trade transactions.

PART II

International Trade and Business Operations

CHAPTER 7

International Trade Practices: The Parties

INTRODUCTION

In this chapter, the parties involved in the practice of international trade and how they interface to create and complete an import–export transaction are reviewed. This chapter also scans the operating environment of international trade, introduces the major parties in an import–export transaction, and explains their roles. The major parties are the exporter, the importer, the freight forwarder, the customs broker, the bank, the common carrier, and the insurer. There are others, depending on the type of transaction, but these are the primary movers.

U.S. INTERNATIONAL TRADE IN GOODS AND SERVICES

According to the July 1996 issue of *Survey of Current Business,* the United States exported $575.9 billion worth of goods and imported $749.3 billion. This is the largest single set of international transactions recorded in its balance-of-payments accounts (see the Appendix).

The export and import of services are growing rapidly for the United States, but they remain far smaller than merchandise trade. In 1995, $210.6 billion in services was exported in exchange for $142.2 billion in services imported. Services trade should continue to expand in the future, but so will merchandise trade. The globalization of corporate activities accelerates the cross-border interaction market forces, leading to a greater exchange of all goods and services in order to achieve optimum economies of scale, minimize costs, and maximize revenues. This exchange takes place through international trade.

The Operating Environment

Over 300 distinct political entities are engaged in trade throughout the world. Each has its own rules and regulations to control the flow of goods, services, and the payments that are generated by these flows. While it is difficult for one company located in a particular area to be familiar with trading customs the world over, there are practices that are fairly common to all nations.

Vive la différence. The import–export environment differs from that of domestic enterprises because all transactions are cross-border in nature and are thus impacted by international laws and by the national laws and politics of at least two countries that govern the conduct of sellers, buyers, and all other related parties.

Confusion and conflict. Aside from a confusing assortment of sometimes conflicting laws and regulations, there are logistical constraints on the physical movement of goods. Energy utilization and adaptation specifications vary among countries. There are differences in banking procedures, currency prices, and just about everything else that affects international trade.

Reliance on specialized services. Consequently, traders rely on services that specialize in given areas of international trade. These include, in addition to those named above, cargo surveyors, marine insurers, inspection and quality assurance firms, and government agencies, to name a few. They all make sure that goods are properly handled and documented and that all parties fully understand their rights and obligations.

THE PARTIES TO AN IMPORT–EXPORT TRANSACTION

The Exporter

The exporter is considered to be the seller and shipper of record. Were one to export a compressor to a customer in Indonesia, the exporting company's name would appear as the shipper of record. This implies that the exporting company is making the sale and has title to the unit until some agreement between the two parties indicates that title is to be transferred from seller to buyer. The name of the foreign buyer would be shown as the ultimate consignee, the party intended to receive the goods and title to the compressor and from whom payment was expected.

Most product manufacturers are also exporters. Multinational corporations tend to export their output directly to a global network of affiliates. These overseas companies may be dealers, distributors, or agents; they can also be producers that buy for their own consumption and not for resale.

When is an export an export? Whether the foreign customer is an independent company, a wholly owned subsidiary, or something in between is irrelevant to the import–export buyer/seller relationship. For international trade transaction recording purposes, it is only important that the exporter be a resident of one country and the importer be a resident of another. An export sale is completed once title has passed from exporter to importer, an invoice has been issued, an accounts receivable established, and the transaction recorded in the international accounts ledgers of the countries involved.

When is an export not an export? Consignment shipments are export shipments with no title change from exporter to importer. There is only a physical transfer of inventory from one country to another. A final invoice is not cut, and no accounts receivable is created. Recording errors frequently occur among nations because of mistakes made by the trading community in appropriately labeling shipping documentation as either a sale or a consignment.

Export trading company. An export trading company (ETC) is a mercantile firm that buys from local supply sources and resells overseas. These traders can be helpful to small manufacturing companies that are not in a position to develop their own foreign markets. A U.S. company that sells merchandise to an ETC is making a domestic sale. The ETC is the exporter and shipper of record.

The Importer

The importer is the buyer or ultimate consignee. As stated above, its name appears on all relevant documents which serve as evidence that an export sale has taken place.

No strangers here. Exporters and importers are usually well known to one another. This is especially true in the case of multinational companies, where a U.S. exporter's foreign customer can be its own subsidiary or a joint venture partner. Even small businesses are familiar to one another multinationally through a web of credit checks and financial references that today are available on a global basis.

"Arms-length" rule of law. Under the "arms-length" rule of law in the United States and in most countries, buyers and sellers are considered "unrelated" persons or residents for transaction purposes. Hence, a U.S. exporter like Allied-Signal that ships goods to its wholly owned subsidiary in Indonesia, Allied-Signal Indonesia, will be shown as the seller and shipper of record, and Allied-Signal Indonesia will be the buyer and ultimate consignee.

Importers have different shapes. Parties importing directly from an exporter are not always those that plan to use or consume the items purchased. They may be distributors or dealers that resell to consumers or end users. Exporters thus have some choices in their overseas marketing strategies. They can target end users, they can sell their goods to import distributors, or they can try to sell through import agents, who function as local sales representatives. When selling through import agents, title will probably not flow from exporter to agent; it will flow to the agent's customer when a sale in the foreign market is finally consummated by the agent.

The Freight Forwarder

The freight forwarder is to the exporter what a travel agent is to a traveler. The freight forwarder's function is to arrange for the transportation of goods from the exporter's warehouse to the importer's port of entry and/or warehouse destination. It is also the responsibility of the freight forwarder to prepare all export and shipping documentation on behalf of the exporter and to present the documents to an international bank for collection.

Many forwarders tend to be small and concentrate on airfreight, overland, or ocean freight shipments. Some are multinational in scope, with offices in many countries, and will handle any form or combination of shipment.

The Customs Broker

The customs broker's function is to help clear imported merchandise through local customs on behalf of the buyer. This includes the payment of all import taxes and charges and arranging for the transport of the goods to the buyer's facility.

The customs broker represents the importer in much the same way as the freight forwarder represents the exporter. Large customs brokers and freight forwarders tend to be part of the same multinational transport and customs services companies.

International Banks

International banks are designed to facilitate trade by helping exporters and importers expedite the flow of documents and payments. It is important that both the seller's and the buyer's banks have correspondent relationships. This means that each bank may represent the other in specified transactions.

The correspondent relationship. In effect, the exporter's bank should have power of attorney to act on behalf of the importer's financial institution. If there is no correspondent relationship, extra expenses and delays can be expected.

For example, if an importer in Indonesia banks at Standard Bank and an exporter banks at Citibank in the United States and both insist on using their respective banks, then Citibank and Standard Bank will act as correspondent banks for one another for this transaction, assuming they already enjoy such a relationship.

In fact, most multinational banks like Citibank and Standard Bank maintain correspondent banking affiliations with most major banks throughout the world. It would nevertheless be more convenient, faster, and more cost effective for the buyer and seller to agree to use only one of the two banks, as Citibank and Standard Bank both have banking subsidiaries in both countries.

If a correspondent relationship between the two banks is not possible, either bank will usually locate a third-party bank with which both original banks have a correspondent arrangement. Again, this situation should be avoided because it increases processing costs and can create delays.

The Common Carrier

The common carrier is the transportation firm that hauls the freight. Goods move via truck, airfreight, ocean freight, or through any combination of these modes. Most shipments are now containerized or bulk/

tanker shipped. The traditional break-bulk (less than container load) methods of shipment that prevailed in earlier generations exist mainly in lesser developed areas where new materials management technologies have not yet been introduced.

Individual pieces of equipment, unless they are too heavy or oversize, are generally shipped airfreight despite what may appear to be a higher initial cost. Greater speed and safety make airfreight a very attractive alternative to ocean freight, which often involves time-consuming piggyback transport modes.

Containerized ocean freight shipments are commonly used today when airfreight is not an option. Slower than airfreight, they offer the advantage of warehouse-to-warehouse transport under a single freight bill. In addition, many containerization companies have their own in-house customs brokers and freight forwarders, which eliminates the need to deal separately with such parties.

Insurance

In-transit insurance is rarely legally required, but it makes good business sense to have goods insured against loss and/or damage while moving from one country to another. Further, many letters of credit specify that marine insurance must be obtained and that a certificate of insurance must be furnished along with other required documents before payment can be made.

The general practice is to insure a shipment from the seller's warehouse to the buyer's warehouse. Either the exporter or the importer should cover the goods with adequate insurance. This critical issue is generally resolved during the negotiation stage of a sale.

Comprehensive and overall insurance coverage by the exporter will lessen liability resulting from all sorts of unforeseen events, such as a general average situation. This condition occurs when a vessel is damaged or lost at sea. Exporters, as charter parties, can become collectively liable for repairs to or the replacement cost of the vessel unless it can be shown that the goods were sold free on board (FOB factory), freight along the outbound ship or vessel (FAS dock), or free on board vessel (FOB vessel) "freight insurance collect," with title changing before the vessel left the port of embarkation.

Freight forwarders, customs brokers, carriers, and banks, in the interest of promoting trade and as a service to their clients, are usually in an excellent position and more than willing to recommend reliable insurers.

CONCLUSION AND SUMMARY

International trade is an arena in which small and large companies can compete effectively. Modern information and communications technology make it possible to enter the import–export business with a home office and a computer. All one needs is access to a marketable product line.

Trade is an indispensable part of a national economy. Society would rapidly come to a standstill without trade. It is estimated that a full 20% of the labor force in the United States is directly or indirectly employed in the international trade sector.

KEY TERMS AND CONCEPTS

Common carrier. The common carrier is the transportation firm that hauls the freight. Goods move via truck, airfreight, ocean freight, or through any combination of these modes. Most shipments are now containerized or bulk/tanker shipped. The traditional break-bulk (less than container load) methods of shipment that prevailed in earlier generations exist mainly in lesser developed areas where new materials management technologies have not yet been introduced.

Customs broker. The customs broker's function is to help clear imported merchandise through local customs on behalf of the buyer. This includes the payment of all import taxes and charges and arranging for the transport of the goods to the buyer's facility.

Exporter. The exporter is considered to be the seller and shipper of record. Were one to export a compressor to a customer in Indonesia, for example, the exporting company's name would appear as the shipper of record.

Freight forwarder. The freight forwarder is to the exporter what a travel agent is to a traveler. The freight forwarder's function is to arrange for the transportation of goods from the exporter's warehouse to the importer's port of entry and/or warehouse destination.

Importer. The importer is the buyer or ultimate consignee. Its name appears on all relevant documents which serve as evidence that an export sale has taken place. The importer would be responsible for making payment on the goods shipped.

Insurance. In-transit insurance is rarely legally required, but it makes good business sense to have goods insured against loss and/or damage while moving from one country to another. Further, many letters of credit specify that marine insurance must be obtained and that a certificate of insurance must be furnished along with other required documents before payment can be made.

International banks. International banks are designed to facilitate trade by helping exporters and importers expedite the flow of documents and payments. It is important that both the seller's and the buyer's banks have correspondent relationships. This means that each bank may represent the other in specified transactions.

Merchandise trade. According to the July 1996 issue of *Survey of Current Business,* the United States exported $575.9 billion worth of goods and imported $749.3 billion. This is the largest single set of international transactions recorded in its balance-of-payments accounts. This fact also holds true for most other countries. Indeed, the more investments increase internationally, the more cross-border trade increases.

Trade in services. The export and import of services are growing rapidly for the United States, but they remain far smaller than merchandise trade. In 1995, $210.6 billion in services was exported in exchange for $142.2 billion in services imported. Services trade should continue to expand in the future, but so will merchandise trade. The globalization of corporate activities accelerates the cross-border interaction market forces, leading to a greater exchange of all goods and services in order to achieve optimum economies of scale, minimize costs, and maximize revenues. This exchange takes place through international trade.

QUESTIONS

7.1 Why is exporting more actively supported by the U.S. government than importing?

7.2 Why are imports in large quantity that lead to a merchandise trade deficit sometimes regarded as being against a nation's economic and national interests?

7.3 When exporting, should a company be concerned with insuring in-transit shipments?

7.4 What payment terms should be negotiated with foreign buyers?

7.5 What are the alternatives to exporting if the importing climate in some countries becomes overwhelmingly restrictive?

CHAPTER 8

The Legal Environment of International Business

INTRODUCTION

In this chapter, the legal environment of international business practices is examined. Many questions concerning the rights and obligations of those participating in cross-border transactions must be addressed before committing time, energy, resources, and money to overseas ventures. Important issues to consider are legal relationships created between buyers and sellers through one-time-only transactions and ongoing distributorship and agency agreements, differences in the laws of individual nations that affect commercial agreements, manufacturers' rights and obligations that emerge from product warranty and product liability claims, claims relating to the protection of intellectual assets (i.e., patents, trademarks, trade names, and copyrights), national employment protection laws, and the protection of industrial property from seizure (expropriation).

LEGAL RELATIONSHIPS AMONG PARTIES TO A BUSINESS TRANSACTION

The Concept of Residency and the Legal Persona of the Foreign Affiliate

The laws of most countries seem to identify the residency of individuals, businesses, and other organizations in terms of their physical domicile for the better part of one year, usually defined as being at a location within a national jurisdiction for longer than six months. There are exceptions and variations to this general rule in many nations, and each jurisdiction should be studied carefully by international taxation specialists and other experts before committing a company to a course of action.

Wholly Owned Subsidiary

A wholly owned subsidiary located in the United States and owned by a foreign parent is a U.S. "resident" for taxation and international transaction recording purposes. Thus, the pharmaceutical firm Hoffman LaRoche, located in the state of New Jersey, would be considered a resident of the state of New Jersey and the United States under state and federal law and under the laws of other nations that have tax treaties with the United States.

It just so happens that this corporation is wholly owned by its parent, Hoffman LaRoche of Basel, Switzerland, which means that its outstanding common shares (voting stock) are all owned by a foreign entity. Both companies (the corporate parent and its subsidiary) are treated under the laws of their respective countries and by most international tribunals and mediation and arbitration groups as residents of the respective countries where they are principally domiciled.

The Arm's-Length Concept

This implies that two companies, connected by financial equity and related by culture, will be treated in many instances as if they were independent of each other. This would be true if the parent corporation was Company ABC of the United States and its foreign subsidiary was Company XYZ of Indonesia.

Therefore, international commercial relations between the two affiliates are almost always subject to an "arms-length" rule, namely, that the actions they have undertaken together would also have normally been undertaken with an unrelated company in a similar context. If not, actions between the two firms may be suspected of some form of illegal collusion by either or both national governments.

The logical extension of this rule suggests that buy–sell transactions and all other agreements among affiliates can be scrutinized by authorities and subjected to legal tests of arm's-length independence.

The Operational and De Jure Independence of the Parties to a Transaction

In a practical sense, a U.S. multinational corporation, whether it is dealing with a foreign subsidiary, an overseas joint venture partner, or a totally and truly unrelated company, should consider all these firms as independent entities within their countries of residence if only to avoid the political onus of foreign domination of local economic affairs.

Local courts in host countries are frequently under pressure to rule against foreign corporate parents and affiliates whenever it can be shown that local business decisions were influenced by overseas owners and managers. The issue of whether a company in Indonesia is an agent or distributor of its American parent will be decided not so much by the financial connection between the two companies as by the intent of the parties in the transaction in question.

The same thinking applies to warranty, liability, patent, and other intellectual asset infringement situations and even extends to questions of taxation and nationalization. The earlier corporate attitude that a U.S. company and its executives and other employees will not suffer judgments passed against them in foreign courts is invalid today. A resident of Indonesia can now just as easily sue a resident of Florida or Indonesia. Indeed, the Florida resident may be surprised to learn that foreign judgments can be enforced today as easily in the United States as abroad.

International Distributorship Arrangements

An international distributorship arrangement is a generic descriptor for a buy–sell contract in which the exporter is selling to a foreign company that plans on reselling the purchased items in the local market. These import distributors may be large wholesalers or smaller dealers, working individually or as part of an affiliated network. Orders placed by these import distributors may involve single non-repeat business or a continuing relationship with repeat business over time. Orders negotiated on the premise of non-repeat business in general expose exporters to less liability than those that form part of a longer term commercial relationship in which various degrees of exclusivity are rightly or wrongly envisioned.

One-Time-Only Orders

Initial import–export transactions between sellers and buyers are often accomplished on a one-time-only basis. These transactions are like trial orders, where no enduring relationship is planned or where a probationary relationship between the exporter and the foreign distributor is in order. This gives both parties an opportunity to evaluate their respective organizations in terms of product quality, service, attitude, and anything else they believe is necessary to establish a continuing relationship.

Longer Term Distributorship Agreements

Once a relationship has been established, buyers and sellers can start considering a distributorship arrangement. This may expose the exporter to certain risks that are more easily contained in one-time-only transactions. The seller will probably have to provide warranty services if needed in any buy–sell situation. These warranty services and obligations become more urgent as the buy–sell relationship endures and the local market grows.

The seller may also be exposed to product liability and to third-party liability situations. One way in which sellers try to reduce these forms of exposure is to build disclaimers into their buy–sell agreements. A prior disclaimer statement before the sale will not eliminate a seller's exposure, but it will at least help reduce risk parameters. However, the success of these disclaimer clauses, which are almost standard in most contracts, during litigation in foreign courts has been mixed at best.

Even assuming that the terms of a disclaimer clause are acceptable to the foreign buyer, who may be in a position to perform unassisted warranty work and in fact carries product liability insurance, litigation often results when the perceived damage is sufficiently large. Local courts will often disallow contractual disclaimers as a violation of their national laws.

Import Agents

Import agents are preferred by companies that consider maximum foreign market control to be important. An agent (importer) functions in a fiduciary relationship with a principal (the exporter). This means that the importer may act based on the exporter's express and/or implied instructions. Goods imported on consignment through an agent means that although the physical inventory has moved from the exporter's warehouse to that of the import agent, title to the goods remains with the exporter until the agent makes a sale. Title then passes directly from the exporter to the agent's customer. An export receivable is created at that point.

Advantages. The advantage of an import agency relationship lies in the fact that because ownership of the goods remains with the exporter until sold by the agent, the exporter can define the local market selling price, the sales strategy, the sales territory, the payment terms, and anything else considered to be of importance to the long-term market success of the product or product line. Marketing control is thus maximized and more easily maintained with an import agency agreement than with a formal or informal distributorship arrangement.

There are instances when import agency arrangements are necessary. Goods brought into free trade zones are often consigned to agents prior to their final disposition. Participants at trade shows often consign goods to agents if unsure of making a final sale. Some items are so large and bulky or so great in weight, volume (e.g., tractors, earth movers, and petrochemicals), or value (jewelry and works of art) that they are better off being stored or bunkered fairly close to their final point of sale while remaining in the physical custody of the exporter's agent in the given market.

Disadvantages. The disadvantages of an agency arrangement to an exporter are both financial and legal. Legally, exporters are vulnerable to possible third-party liability lawsuits in which unrelated parties alleging injury seek monetary damages.

Financially, exporters are saddled with higher costs and non-payment risks. Goods warehoused overseas and owned by U.S. companies must be insured, protected, and maintained as they would be back in the home market. This invariably carries a high logistical cost. The exporter, in all probability, will have at least prepaid all transport and insurance charges from the United States to the foreign destination. Unsold inventory may have to be financed through loans or returned. Finally, the longer goods remain unsold and/or unpaid for in a foreign market, the greater the risk of financial loss.

Local Labor Law Conflicts

Another area of concern is the principal's possible responsibility for local employees hired by the agent to handle the new workload. Employment laws in many South American countries provide lifetime job guarantees once a probationary period is completed and mandate generous severance packages when long-term employees are fired with or without cause. The exporter can be accused of inducing the import agent to hire more people in anticipation of new business and can be held responsible for compensatory damages.

Import Distributors

An import distributor, by definition, is an independent company that buys and then resells goods for its own account. It assumes title to the exporter's goods on or before delivery of those goods to its warehouse. As a general rule, title to the goods will pass to the buyer by the time the goods clear customs.

Advantages. The advantages of an import distributorship are both financial and legal. Once title passes from seller to buyer, a receivable (a claim on the buyer's assets) is established, and the clock starts ticking toward the collection due date based on agreed-upon payment terms. This title change removes the exporter from any liability regarding the importer's actions and behavior in the local market.

Another advantage is that distributorship arrangements can be on an ad hoc basis without involving a term contract. Agency agreements normally require a well-crafted document that spells out the understanding between the parties. Distributorships that are not couched in a binding contract can usually be terminated at will by either party, which is often seen as an advantage by both parties.

Finally, a distributor, using its own finances, will be under greater pressure to sell the exporter's products than an agent that receives the goods on a consignment basis and has made no financial commitment.

Disadvantages. These relate mainly to the exporter's lack of marketing and management control in view of the fact that the goods are now owned by the distributor. Therefore, it is almost impossible for export sellers to control distributor resale prices, even if clauses guaranteeing that right are built into the distributorship agreement.

Where price is part of the overall product image, this can be a problem. This disadvantage can be partially overcome if the exporter's product enjoys a high level of brand awareness among consumers or end users through effective advertising and promotion in the local market. While Coke, Pepsi, and GE may enjoy that curbside appeal, lesser names may not enjoy the same reputation.

A Binding Contract or Just a Loose Arrangement?

Just how good are formal distributorship contracts? The answer is that they are only as good as the intent of the parties to seek a mutually rewarding relationship. Few firms enter into a transaction with the goal of "buying" a lawsuit. A written contract may be unnecessary from that point of view.

However, if the exporter is suddenly doing business in a growing number of overseas markets at once, formal contracts may be needed to preserve a written record of the understandings the parties have reached and under which they are operating. A distributorship contract will not prevent a lawsuit, but it may at least help clarify the issues.

CONCLUSION AND SUMMARY

It is common practice among market-oriented exporters and importers to agree informally to resale prices. This practice is predicated on the proposition that both exporter and distributor share the same vested interest in maximizing sales and profits.

It is also a fairly common practice not to have binding term and/or territory-defining agreements. Many lasting relationships between exporters and overseas distributors are based only on their successful track records. Distributorship and agency agreements that imply a need for formality between the parties may not be appropriate for all import–export situations, especially for small start-up companies. Informal arrangements may be the better way to go.

KEY TERMS AND CONCEPTS

Arm's-length concept. This implies that two companies, connected by financial equity and related by culture, will be treated in many instances as if they were independent of each other. This would be true if the parent corporation was Company ABC of the United States and its foreign subsidiary was Company XYZ of Indonesia.

Import agent. Preferred by companies that consider maximum foreign market control to be important. An agent (importer) functions in a fiduciary relationship with a principal (the exporter). This means that the importer may act based on the exporter's express and/or implied instructions. Goods imported on consignment through an agent means that although the physical inventory has moved from the exporter's warehouse to that of the import agent, title to the goods remains with the exporter until the agent makes a sale. Title then passes directly from the exporter to the agent's customer. An export receivable is created at that point.

Import distributor. An import distributor, by definition, is an independent company that buys and then resells goods for its own account. It assumes title to the exporter's goods on or before delivery of those goods to its warehouse. As a general rule, title to the goods will pass to the buyer by the time the goods clear customs.

Residency. The laws of most countries seem to identify the residency of individuals, businesses, and other organizations in terms of their physical domicile for the better part of one year, usually defined as being at a location within a national jurisdiction for longer than six months. There are exceptions and variations to this general rule in many nations, and each jurisdiction should be studied carefully by international taxation specialists and other experts before committing a company to a course of action.

QUESTIONS

8.1 Describe and explain the characteristics, advantages, and disadvantages of an import distributorship.

8.2 Describe and explain the characteristics, advantages, and disadvantages of an import agency.

8.3 Discuss some of the problems that the concept of residency can create for a U.S.-based company and its overseas affiliates.

8.4 Discuss some of the problems that the "arms-length relationship" concept can create for a U.S.-based company and its overseas affiliates.

CHAPTER 9

Product Warranty and
Product Liability Issues

INTRODUCTION

It is generally recognized throughout the world today that a producer of goods has an obligation to offer satisfaction on defective products through a product warranty. It is also the manufacturer's general obligation to make sure that the handling and use of those products cause no harm. This obligation is global and is not limited to a product's country of manufacture. The various aspects of a company's rights and obligations in terms of product warranty and liability are discussed in this chapter.

PRODUCT WARRANTIES

These are promises by a manufacturer that its products will perform as stated in published literature. They can be explicit or implicit. Warranties are explicit when a manufacturer includes a written statement describing what guarantees it offers in the event of product performance failure and for how long a period of time those guarantees are good.

Warranty Disclaimers

Warranty disclaimers (e.g., "goods sold as is," etc.) should be in writing. If written warranties are not offered and if there are no written disclaimers, then courts in many countries usually hold producers liable under the principle of implied warranty. This means that a full warranty is in force for a "reasonable" time.

Disclaimers have limited value. Disclaimers are generally issued by exporters and/or their manufacturers that sell in areas where a dealer network with after-sales service facilities does not yet exist. They are a popular approach to a difficult problem and are viewed dimly by local courts. These disclaimers are usually discounted by local courts, which may apply their own time-honored rules of implied warranty.

Every sale is a potential claim. It would be preferable for a manufacturer to make sure, prior to closing a sale with a foreign buyer, that warranty service can be supplied. Any export sale has a chance of becoming a warranty claim, and it is incumbent upon the U.S. seller to make sure that the foreign customer is as protected as a domestic consumer.

Be a broker if warranty service is impossible. It is possible for a mercantile exporter (export trading company) to avoid warranty situations altogether by expressly stating to all parties concerned that it is functioning strictly in a brokerage capacity and not as part of the distribution chain.

Warranty breaches. This creates problems for exporters that do not issue written warranty statements, especially if they are resellers. The issue of what constitutes a "reasonable" time is always open to question, thus exposing the maker of the product to litigation. It also opens the exporter to the same lawsuit, as the latter would be considered to be part of the producer's global distribution chain.

In some areas, breach-of-warranty judgments are arbitrary, discriminatory, capricious, and rendered in absentia. They can lead to stiff fines and even to prison sentences. In some cases, the exporter, which is often more visible than the original manufacturer, will be held as the scapegoat.

Full warranty data should always be communicated. Complications can arise when the manufacturer publishes a warranty but the warranty documents and their contents are not forwarded and/or communicated effectively to the foreign buyer and end user. This failure to make an express warranty known to foreign customers forces local courts to treat the case as if there were an implied warranty and perhaps even deceit and fraud on the exporter's part.

Advantages of express warranties. A well-detailed written warranty statement by a seller defines the time frame within which the warranty and warranty service are valid. It also defines the obligations of both the seller and buyer, making it more difficult for foreign buyers and users to lodge warranty claims long after products have been in use.

Importance of a warranty-competent overseas distributor or dealer network. Manufacturers' warranty statements should be conveyed to all parties in the distribution chain, from the export resellers to the foreign import distributors to the local dealers to the end users.

If no distributor or dealer network exists in a foreign country (often a problem in developing areas), a decision not to sell may have to be considered unless the manufacturer or the exporter is in a position to provide on-site after-sales warranty services.

The need for a good foreign distributor/dealer network. The effective execution of product warranty and more general after-sales service is the key to overseas market survival and growth. This fact highlights the need to build an experienced distributor network and a competent dealer organization in foreign markets. The U.S. manufacturer, the U.S. exporter, and the foreign customer will rely upon that network and organization to provide a long-term mutually rewarding relationship.

PRODUCT LIABILITY

This thorny issue comes up when someone has been injured or property has been damaged by the direct or indirect use of a product. Sometimes a product liability situation can arise out of a warranty problem. Many times, it happens because of the incorrect use of a product; sometimes it occurs because a product falls on someone or something or breaks up or explodes and destroys property and injures people.

The Extent of Product Liability

Product liability exposure accompanies a product anywhere the product goes. It is rarely successfully disclaimed. If an item is going to Mongolia, its producer and anyone else connected with its sale, shipment, and servicing will be legally exposed if it is found to have caused damage to people and/or to property in Mongolia or on the way there.

Protection from product liability exposure. It is important for a manufacturer to make sure that the installation, operating, and usage instructions are fully understood by all parties concerned. A working familiarity with the local language may be needed to that end. It is also essential that a product destined for sale in overseas markets be covered by adequate product liability insurance.

Smaller exporters that serve as resellers may not normally be held accountable in product liability situations as long as they have not altered the merchandise being shipped. However, they should satisfy themselves that their vendors have adequate liability insurance to provide worldwide coverage and that they too may find shelter under that umbrella.

Small business exporters that are also manufacturers should consult with legal counsel, who will probably recommend the purchase of a product liability insurance policy before anything is shipped overseas. ***Be a broker if no product liability insurance is available.*** Again, exporters that explicitly take a brokerage position, and can show that this is their customary way of conducting business, should issue product liability disclaimers on every transaction to all parties concerned, specifying their role in the transaction clearly and in writing.

CONCLUSION AND SUMMARY

It is important for business executives contemplating marketing their goods and services in other countries to become familiar, through competent legal counsel, with the prevailing local legal environment. It is also important to realize that it might be better not to sell in those areas where it is difficult or impossible to offer warranty service and where product liability insurance is either unavailable or very expensive.

KEY TERMS AND CONCEPTS

Product liability. A manufacturer's liability when someone has been injured or property has been damaged by the direct or indirect use of a product. Sometimes a product liability situation can arise out of a warranty problem. Many times, it happens because of the incorrect use of a product; sometimes it occurs because a product falls on someone or something or breaks up or explodes and destroys property and injures people.

Product warranty. Promise by a manufacturer that its product will perform as stated in published literature. Warranties can be explicit or implicit. They are explicit when a manufacturer includes a written statement describing what guarantees it offers in the event of product performance failure and for how long a period of time those guarantees are good.

QUESTIONS

9.1 Explain the differences between a warranty and a liability claim.

9.2 Explain the differences between an express warranty and an implied warranty.

9.3 Discuss the different ways in which an exporter can minimize warranty and liability exposure.

CHAPTER 10

Protection of Intellectual Assets

INTRODUCTION

This chapter explores the nature of intellectual assets and their importance to companies doing business internationally. The protection of these assets is growing in importance as goods and services are being produced, marketed, and traded on a global scale.

INTELLECTUAL ASSETS AND GOODWILL

Intellectual Assets

Intellectual assets consist of patents, trade names, trademarks, and copyrights, the sum of which identify a company's goods and services as belonging to it. They are duly granted and registered documents which announce to all parties that assets consisting of specified inventions, innovations, works of art, original writings, music, business names, product names, corporate logos, and package designs and labels are proprietary to their creators and may not be replicated without specific permission.

Intellectual Assets Are Intangible

Someone who breaks into a company's offices and steals a computer or telecommunications equipment robs their owner of a tangible and measurable asset, and the owner is often painfully aware of the loss. However, the theft of intellectual assets, though it may go undetected for a long time, is far more injurious and costly to legitimate businesses. Intellectual assets are, for many companies, their most valuable property.

Exclusivity and Infringement

As indicated above, patents, trademarks, trade names, and copyrights that identify goods and services as belonging to a specific producer mean that no one else in a given jurisdiction may replicate those intellectual assets without the express permission of their owner. While infringements occur routinely in the United States, they are often more flagrant in many other countries.

Trade Name

This can be the name under which a business functions. The simple act of initially registering a trade or business name at the city, county, or state level for tax purposes protects the use of that name from infringement by others without the consent of the business owner. However, this protection is only statewide at best. Should the business ever contemplate becoming a player in the national marketplace, the registration of its trade name in Washington, D.C. would be appropriate. Once that is done, trade name protection in other countries can be achieved through a similar process.

Trademarks

These are the company and product logos and names that symbolically describe a company's goods and services, making them recognizable to end users and consumers and distinguishable from those of the competition. A trademark can be a word, symbol, drawing, or design or some sort of combination of all these expressions which identify a product, product line, service, or artistic creation as being proprietary to an individual or firm.

Trade names, once registered, can be considered in the same category as trademarks. Hence, the Coca-Cola Company is both a trade name and trademark due to its unique shape and spelling. So too are the words Coke and Diet Coke. The Coca-Cola Company and all its products would not be where they are today were it not for the zeal and jealousy with which corporate executives and their legal staffs guard these assets globally.

An unregistered trademark may be protected by common law in the United States, but only in those few states that still subscribe to common law. Common law usage is also declining in the United Kingdom as the nation starts to harmonize its commercial practices with those of its European Union (EU) partners.

In the United States, trademarks may be registered with the Federal Patent and Trademark Office. Once issued, a trademark is valid for ten years, after which it can be renewed. However, trademark owners must file their intent to continue the use of their registered trademarks within the first five years of trademark life.

In the past, U.S. companies that wished to legally protect their trademarks from infringement by residents in other countries would have to proceed on a nation-by-nation basis to register them. Unless a bilateral treaty existed between the United States and the country in question, the American firm would actually have to petition for a trademark as if it were a first-time application.

This situation has improved over the years. The United States has treaties with over 100 countries, allowing U.S residents to simply register their trademarks in the country without contest if they are already in use in the United States. The process is even more streamlined in the EU, where since 1975 it has been only necessary to file with the EU government in Brussels, Belgium, in order to have coverage throughout the Western European region. However, it should be noted that treaty violations, especially in developing areas, are frequent.

Copyrights

These are the word, shape, and symbol combinations that appear on labels and packaging. They can be protected from infringement nationally and internationally by registering them in all markets where a company plans to operate. As in the case of trademarks, there has been progress over the years in simplifying the process of arranging for copyright protection abroad. A number of bilateral treaties between the United States and other individual countries have largely done away with the tedious, time-consuming, and expensive country-hopping process.

Patents

These are inventions and unique innovations that a company possesses which distinguish its products from all others. The patent itself is a temporary government grant that allows the patent holder to deny everyone else the right to make, use, and/or sell the registered invention. A patent is valid for a non-renewable period of 19 years, although it may be extended for an additional number of years under some circumstances.

Market-oriented companies like Coca-Cola, Nestle, and Disney do not rely as much on patent protection as do technology-oriented firms such as Westinghouse, IBM, and Hewlett-Packard. Crossover businesses such as Microsoft depend on patent, trademark, trade name, and copyright protection.

There are three types of patents: utility (product) patents, design patents (good for a maximum of 14 years), and plant (process) patents. A utility patent protects the invention. To qualify, it must be shown that the item will serve a "useful" purpose and is significantly (patently) different from anything else currently on the market.

Patents are thus also available for innovations that expand the use or application of the original device. Hence, a four-legged seating device with a backrest, the whole thing being called a "chair" and never having been in evidence before, could be eligible for a utility patent. Additional patents could be granted if arms or rockers were subsequently added. The way or process by which the chair is made, if it is sufficiently unique, might be eligible for a plant patent.

Plant patents are more important to protect than utility patents, mainly because very often the process governs the invention. When the Polaroid camera was developed, it was covered by more than 300 distinct process patents that took Eastman Kodak over 25 years to decipher. When Kodak finally caught up and introduced its own instant camera in time for the U.S. bicentennial in 1976, it was clobbered by a paralyzing lawsuit that resulted in a settlement of over $900 million to Edwin Land's company years later.

Design patents protect the uniqueness of a design, like that of a chair or vehicle which may have ornamental and aesthetic purposes. Interesting desk lamps and computer icons are occasionally given design patents.

The Importance of Protecting Technology, Know-How, and Name

The United States is a net exporter of technology. This technology is sold in the form of intellectual properties (patents sold for a fee or rented as part of a licensing agreement).

Royalties and fees received by U.S. companies in 1995 were four times greater than those paid out to foreign corporations. However, this does not negate the fact that many intellectual properties of U.S. origin are stolen without compensation by residents of other countries. Even where licensing agreements have been negotiated, U.S. companies often find their foreign licensees less than honest in reporting production and sales figures. It has also been revealed that licensing arrangements have on occasion been sought by overseas residents primarily to acquire technology and know-how without having any plan to compensate U.S. inventors.

Very often, governments encourage or at least do not discourage this form of activity. The rights of U.S. citizens in trying to protect their patents, trademarks, and copyrights from infringement in countries like China and Brazil are usually ignored. The result has been a proliferation in recent years of product piracy and counterfeiting, inflicting serious market losses on U.S. companies.

·Goodwill

Business executives normally think of assets in terms of cash, inventories, accounts receivable, buildings, desks, motor vehicles, and a host of other tangible items that have a purchase cost, a book value, and a discernible market value. Business executives are also familiar with the notion of goodwill as an asset, but small companies often tend to treat goodwill in a casual manner, as if it is there but not worth much.

Goodwill can exist without intellectual assets. A company that has survived for a number of years will have goodwill even if it holds no registered patents, trademarks, trade names, or copyrights. This goodwill is the accumulated appeal that a company enjoys with the trade, its customers, and even with its competition.

Goodwill is a company's image. Corporate goodwill is encapsulated in a corporate image and personality. Goodwill items are all those attributes that give small and large companies recognition and appeal—things to which companies can claim pride but no legal ownership. These may include charitable acts and sponsorships, participation in public works and education, and a reputation for fairness, prompt service, and product excellence, among many others. A company with a high level of goodwill may find it easier to establish market share and finance expansion. A company with limited goodwill may find market access blocked and may experience difficulty obtaining necessary government licenses and general acceptance of its goods and services.

Goodwill as a marketable asset. Goodwill is especially marketable when one wants to sell the business and when the enterprise is small and local. However, goodwill alone becomes less marketable as a business grows large and multinational. The problem is that no individual or firm can legally claim exclusivity to goodwill. A company's goodwill must therefore be complemented by specific and legally protectable intellectual assets if the business is to remain intact.

The International Legal Environment

The General Agreement on Tariffs and Trade, superseded today by the World Trade Organization, the Paris Convention for the Protection of Industrial Property, the Berne Convention for the Protection of Literary and Artistic Works, and a number of other international organizations, has been addressing piracy and counterfeiting issues for many years.

The United States also has in place many treaties with other nations that are supposed to protect the rights of U.S. patent, trademark, and copyright holders. The only real progress has been with the EU, where U.S. intellectual property is protected about as well as it is in the United States.

A poor record of protection. Patents, trademarks, and copyrights are currently poorly protected in Brazil, China, India, Korea, Indonesia, Malaysia, Mexico, the Philippines, Taiwan, Singapore, Saudi Arabia, and the United Arab Emirates. Product piracy and counterfeiting are ongoing problems in all these areas and in many others as well.

CONCLUSION AND SUMMARY

There seems to be an obvious need for a more sincere global monitoring of intellectual property rights. Companies with important technologies, valuable know-how, and well-known product and process names routinely investigate, at great expense, legal environments overseas before making a sale or an investment in which they can end up losing their intellectual assets to a local copycat competitor. The problem is that this happens all too often, and lawsuits brought overseas are expensive and their results do not always fall on the side of the presumably injured U.S. company.

A question that should be pondered by an exporter before making that first tempting sale is: Does the foreign buyer really want to purchase and use the article, or is it seeking a prototype for its own local production?

KEY TERMS AND CONCEPTS

Copyright. The word, shape, and symbol combinations that appear on labels and packaging. They can be protected from infringement nationally and internationally by having them registered in all markets where a company plans to operate.

Goodwill. The accumulated appeal that a company enjoys with the trade, its customers, and even with its competition.

Intellectual assets. The patents, trade names, trademarks, and copyrights, the sum of which identify a company's goods and services as belonging to it.

Patent. Inventions and unique innovations that a company possesses which distinguish its products from all others. The patent itself is a temporary government grant that allows the patent holder to deny everyone else the right to make, use, and/or sell the registered invention.

Trademark. Company and product logos and names that symbolically describe a company's goods and services, making them recognizable to end users and consumers and distinguishable from those of the competition.

Trade name. This can be the name under which a business functions. The simple act of initially registering a trade or business name at the city, county, or state level for tax purposes protects the use of that name from infringement by others without the consent of the business owner.

QUESTIONS

10.1 Discuss the differences among the different types of patents for which an inventor can apply.

10.2 Describe and explain, giving specific examples, the differences between trademarks and copyrights.

10.3 Discuss some arguments in favor of considering inventions and works of art and literature as proprietary in nature.

10.4 Discuss some arguments in favor of considering inventions and works of art and literature as belonging to society at large.

10.5 Some argue that forcing poor countries to pay for technology that has already made a profit for its owner is industrial piracy or blackmail. Discuss this argument.

10.6 Discuss the efforts made to develop a global standard with regard to the management of intellectual properties.

CHAPTER 11

International Trade Logistics

INTRODUCTION

The transportation environment is often ignored by business executives in planning international business strategies for their companies. It is frequently looked upon as a minor detail to be handled by freight forwarders, banks, and customs agents and brokers. However, in-transit shipping, insurance, documentation, and banking costs for moving goods from one country to another can mean the difference between making a profit and incurring a loss.

The specialized terminology used in international trade to define the rights and obligations of all parties to a transaction is examined in this chapter. In-transit insurance, without which the physical distribution of goods internationally would be riskier than it is, is considered in detail.

SHIPPING AND SELLING TERMS

The language used in defining and determining the time and place for goods to change ownership from seller to buyer is reviewed in this section. It is important to pinpoint this ownership change, or change of title, for insurance purposes. It is also important in determining when a sale has been completed for invoicing purposes.

Terminology

A shipment cannot be invoiced without clear knowledge that title has passed. Unless an invoice can be issued, a receivable on the exporter's books, creating a claim on the importer's accounts payables, cannot be created.

Shipping/Selling Terms Define Shippers' Rights and Obligations

Equally important as pinpointing the change of title are shipping and selling terms (FOB [free on board] factory, CIF [cost, insurance, and freight] port of entry, etc.), which identify the respective rights and obligations of exporters and importers while goods are in transit (on the way from the seller's facility to the importer's receiving point).

Seller and Buyer Preferences

Sellers would like to unload title to their goods as soon as they leave the loading dock, or at least once physical custody of the goods is given up. Hence, they would prefer FOB factory selling terms because in most instances that is where they lose physical control over the merchandise.

Importers would naturally prefer to delay taking title until they actually receive the goods, an excellent display of human nature. Somewhere between the FOB factory selling point and the foreign buyer's receiving warehouse, both seller and buyer will agree on a point in place for goods to change ownership. This point in place will be determined by the shipping/selling terms in the seller's invoice and other relevant documentation. The payment terms, as spelled out in the drafts drawn by the exporter, identify the time and place of payment but will have little to do with merchandise title changes.

Shipping and Selling Terms Defined

The shipping and selling terms in this section are known in the trade as INCOTERMS, or international rules for the interpretation of trade terms. They are excerpted from the International Chamber of Commerce, which periodically updates the data as trade practices evolve.

Ex works (ex factory, ex mill, ex plantation, ex warehouse, etc.). "Ex works" means that the seller's only responsibility is to make the goods available at its premises (i.e., works or factory). In particular, the seller is not responsible for loading the goods on the vehicle provided by the buyer, unless otherwise agreed. The buyer bears the full cost and risk involved in bringing the goods from the seller's premises to the stated destination. This represents the seller's minimum obligation.

FOR/FOT (named departure point, sometimes called FOB factory). FOR (free on rail) and FOT (free on truck) are synonymous, because the word "truck" relates to the railway cars. They should only be used when goods are to be carried by rail. The seller's responsibility ends when the goods are loaded upon the outbound truck. FOB always means "free on board."

FAS (named port of shipment). FAS means "free alongside ship." Under this term, the seller's obligations are fulfilled when the goods have been placed alongside the ship on the quay (wharf) or in lighters. This means that the buyer has to bear all costs and risks of loss of or damage to the goods from that moment. It should be noted that, unlike FOB, this term requires the buyer to clear the goods for export.

FOB (named port of shipment). FOB means "free on board." The goods are placed on board a ship by the seller at a port of shipment named in the sales contract. The risk of loss of or damage to the goods is transferred from the seller to the buyer when the goods pass the ship's rail.

C&F (named port of shipment). C&F means "cost and freight." The seller must pay the costs and freight necessary to bring the goods to the named destination, but the risk of loss of or damage to the goods, as well as any cost increases, is transferred from the seller to the buyer when the goods pass the ship's rail in the port of shipment.

CIF (named port of destination). CIF means "cost, insurance, and freight." This term is the same as C&F but with the addition that the seller has to procure marine insurance against the risk of loss of or damage to the goods during the carriage. The seller contracts with the insurer and pays the insurance premium. The buyer should note that under this term, unlike "freight/carriage and insurance paid to," the seller is only required to cover insurance on minimum conditions.

Ex ship (named port of destination). "Ex ship" means that the seller will make the goods available to the buyer on board the ship at the destination named in the sales contract. The seller has to bear the full cost and risk involved in bringing the goods there.

Ex quay (duty paid...named port). "Ex quay" means that the seller makes the goods available to the buyer on the quay at the destination named in the sales contract. The seller has to bear the full cost and risk involved in bringing the goods there.

There are two "ex quay" contracts in use: ex quay "duty paid" and ex quay "duty (import taxes) on buyer's account" in which the liability to clear the goods for import is to be met by the buyer instead of the seller.

It is recommended that parties always use the full descriptions of these terms (ex quay "duty paid" or ex quay "duty on buyer's account") to avoid uncertainty as to who is to be responsible for the liability to clear the goods for import.

If the parties decide that the seller should clear the goods for import but that some of the costs payable upon the import of the goods should be excluded, such as value-added taxes (VATs), the intent should be made clear by adding words to this effect (e.g., "exclusive of VAT," etc.).

Freight/carriage paid to... (named point of destination). Like C&F, "freight/carriage paid to..." means that the seller pays the freight for the carriage of the goods to the named destination. However, the risk of loss of or damage to the goods, as well as any cost increases, is transferred from the seller to the buyer when the goods have been delivered into the custody of the first carrier and not at the ship's rail.

This term can be used for all modes of transport, including multimodal operations and container or "roll on–roll off" traffic by trailers and ferries. When the seller has to furnish a bill of lading, waybill, or carrier's receipt, the seller duly fulfills this obligation by presenting such a document issued by the person with whom the seller has contracted for carriage to the named destination.

Freight/carriage and insurance paid to... (named point of destination). This term is the same as "freight/carriage paid to..." but with the addition that the seller has to procure transport insurance against the risk of loss of or damage to the goods during the carriage. The seller contracts with the insurer and pays the insurance premium

Delivered at frontier (named place of delivery at frontier). "Delivered at frontier" means that the seller's obligations are fulfilled when the goods have arrived at the frontier but before arrival at the customs border of the country named in the sales contract.

This term is primarily intended to be used when goods are to be carried by rail or road, but it may be used irrespective of the mode of transport.

To avoid misunderstandings, it is recommended that parties contracting according to this trade term qualify the word "frontier" by indicating the two countries separated by that frontier and also the named place of delivery (e.g., "delivered at Franco-Italian frontier [Modane]").

Delivered duty paid... (named place of destination in the country of importation). While the term "ex work" signifies the seller's minimum obligation, the term "delivered duty paid," when followed by words naming the buyer's premises, denotes the other extreme, the seller's maximum obligation. The term "delivered duty paid" may be used irrespective of the mode of transport.

If the parties determine that the seller should clear the goods for import but that some of the costs payable upon the import of the goods should be excluded, such as VATs and/or other similar taxes, this should be made clear by adding words to this effect (e.g., "exclusive of VAT and/or taxes").

FOB airport (named airport of departure). The rules set forth hereunder for delivery on FOB terms for carriage of goods by air have been carefully drafted to reflect the usages usually observed in trade. It should be noted that the expression "FOB" (which means free on board) is not, in relation to air transportation, to be taken literally but rather as announcing that the next word (i.e., the airport named) constitutes the point where the seller's responsibility is to terminate.

FOB carrier (named point). This term has been designed to meet the requirements of modern transport, in particular such multimodal transport as container or "roll on–roll off" traffic by trailers and ferries.

It is based on the same basic principle as FOB except that the seller's obligation is fulfilled when the goods are delivered into the custody of the carrier at the named point. If no precise point can be mentioned at the time of the contract of sale, the parties should refer to the place or range where the carrier should take charge of the goods. The risk of loss of or damage to the goods is transferred from seller to buyer at that time and not at the ship's rail.

Agreement by Exporters and Importers to Follow Prescribed Rules

Foreign trade definitions have been issued by organizations from many countries with an almost infinite number of interpretations. It is important that sellers and buyers agree that their contracts are subject to a set of terms to which both parties, including their judicial systems, agree.

The above definitions, used alone on a formal offer of sale or on an invoice, do not in themselves imply a change of title from exporter to importer. The exact place where international traders intend for title to goods to pass from one party to another should be expressly stated in all shipping and banking documents.

International traders frequently rely on the INCOTERMS put out by the International Chamber of Commerce. While adherence to any single reference source is not mandatory, it is a good idea to consult with independent authorities on the subject.

Some terms that sound alike are not the same. In addition to the foreign trade terms listed above, other terms are used at times, such as free harbor, CIF&C (cost, insurance, freight, and commission), CIFC&I (cost, insurance, freight, commission, and interest), and CIF landed (cost, insurance, freight landed), among others. None of these terms should be used unless there is a definite understanding as to their exact meaning. It is unwise to attempt to interpret other terms in light of the terms given herein.

Abbreviations are unwise shortcuts. It is unwise to use in quotations or in contracts abbreviations which might be subject to misunderstanding. When giving quotations, the familiar terms "hundredweight" or "ton" should be avoided. A hundredweight can be 100 pounds (of the short ton) or 112 pounds (of the long ton), A ton can be a short ton (2,000 pounds), a metric ton (2,204.6 pounds), or a long ton (2,240 pounds). The type of hundredweight or ton should be clearly stated in quotations and in sales confirmations. These common-sense rules also apply to terms that refer to quantity, weight, volume, length, or surface area.

Explicivity of detail is important. If inspection, or certificate of inspection, is required, it should be agreed, in advance, whether the cost thereof is for the account of seller or buyer. Unless otherwise agreed upon, all expenses are for the account of seller up to the point at which the buyer must handle the subsequent movement of goods.

Rules on "customary" practices. A number of elements in a contract may not fall within the scope of the foreign trade definitions reviewed above but are part of the customary relationship between parties or within specific industries. These practices should also be set forth in writing and defined before the start of transactions.

INSURANCE

The thrust of this section is to discuss the importance of insurance in international trade. Political and credit risk insurance is not at issue here.

The concern is with hazard, casualty, and liability insurance which protects both buyers and sellers in the event that something goes awry with a shipment.

The general impression among many business executives is that if their invoices read "FOB factory" or "freight and insurance collect," they have no responsibility for the goods beyond their warehouse loading point. This view is misleading.

The Seller's Exposure

If the exporter, and not the importer, has booked passage for the goods directly or through a freight forwarder, then the exporter has a "charter party" relationship with the carrier. This means that the exporter, even if a claim can be made that the goods belong to the importer, may suffer some losses should something happen to the goods on board and even should something happen to the vessel while the merchandise is on board.

Either the exporter or the importer must cover the goods with insurance. Practically all letters of credit specify that marine insurance must be obtained and that a certificate of insurance must be furnished along with other required documents before the money can become available to the shipper. Many countries require the seller to cover shipments with warehouse-to-warehouse insurance. This is especially the case when a foreign government is the buyer or ultimate consumer. Brazil makes an exception, allowing FOB quotations on most transactions with insurance to be carried by the importer.

Insurance Coverage

Insurance coverage is generally offered on the basis of 110% of the CIF value as indicated on the exporter's invoices if the exporter is carrying the insurance charges. The exporter prepays the insurance mainly on CIF shipments.

Many exporters purchase a covering policy, called an "open cargo policy," on all shipments. This provides coverage even when importers expressly state that they are insuring the goods. This might seem like redundant coverage, but it helps to remember that there is no absolute guarantee to exporters, whatever statements are made to the contrary by their foreign buyers, that a viable insurance policy covering a shipment in question in fact exists.

Protection from General Average Situations

A comprehensive open cargo policy covers all modes of transport and is not limited to ocean freight. However, this type of policy will protect shippers from liability that arises from a "general average" claim. This is a situation limited to ocean freight carriers in which the vessel suffers damage or is destroyed. More specifically, "general average" denotes a loss, damage, or expense that is incurred while a vessel is in operation (transit) for the general benefit of its charterers (those who have themselves or their cargo on board).

A "particular average" is a partial loss or damage accidentally sustained by either cargo or vessel. In the case of a "particular average" claim, the loss and damage to the cargo or the ship falls on its owner. The effect of a "general average" assessment is that the shipping company can expect contributions from cargo owners (exporters) to make good on the vessel.

Thus, the shippers of record (exporters) become automatically liable for the replacement costs of the damaged parts and/or the vessel itself, unless it can be shown that the exporter shipped its goods FOB factory, FAS, or FOB vessel, freight and insurance collect, with title changing before the vessel left on its voyage.

Obligations of Common Carriers

The best approach in order to avoid any exposure is to have comprehensive insurance coverage. Carriers do not normally provide any automatic insurance coverage to shippers beyond a standard "Carriage of Goods by Sea Act" contract of affreightment, which provides little protection. Carriers with consolidation and/or containerized services often offer a group policy to exporters upon request.

This benefits small or occasional exporters that may be unable to afford an open cargo policy. An alternative to the group policies is policies offered by some large multinational freight forwarders and customs brokers. These tend to be more inclusive and, of course, more expensive, but they are still cheaper than an individual policy.

Liability by Ocean Carriers

The liability of ocean carriers in international commerce generally revolves around the Carriage of Goods by Sea Act of 1936, other laws passed since then, and whatever valid clauses may be contained in the carrier's contract of affreightment.

A carrier's liability is limited under these circumstances to just an obligation to move freight from one point to another and to be held accountable for acts of gross negligence should that primary objective not be achieved.

Group Insurance Coverage

This type of policy taken by carriers covers goods only while they are in the care, custody, and control of the carrier and/or its agents or its independent contract pickup and delivery carriers, except in very special instances subject to advance negotiation. There are two principal types of coverage available for general merchandise (not including war and strikes, riots, and civil commotions insurance): marine risks (a generic term that also applies to non-marine carriage) and all risks.

Marine risks. This is to insure the shipper against most of the causes of loss for which the carrier cannot be held liable. Called "perils of the sea," these causes include:

- Fire and explosion
- Collision, stranding, and sinking
- Jettisons, assailing thieves, and battery
- Latent defects of the vessel
- Faults or errors in navigation and/or management of the vessel
- General average and salvage charges

Marine risk insurance also protects goods while on shore against the following:

- Fire, lightning, sprinkler leakage, and explosion
- Hail, flood, earthquake, and windstorm
- Landslide, volcanic eruption, and avalanche
- Subsidence of docks and structures

Goods are generally insured for their CIF value plus 10%. That value must be declared by the shipper. The coverage is against physical loss only and excludes any kind of "loss of market" claim or claims caused by delay, regardless of what caused the delay. The coverage also excludes losses due to war, strikes, riots, and civil commotions, although such insurance can be obtained for an additional premium.

Buying the complete insurance package. In order to get the complete package, a shipper need only request in writing (on the bill of lading or in a letter) "Insure against 'Marine Risks' for $_____ (+ War, S.R. & C.C.)" plus "To cover against all risks of physical loss from any external cause whatsoever..."

Riots and Civil Commotions Coverage

In addition to "loss of market" or other consequential loss and damage due to delays (no matter what caused the delay), war and strikes, riots, and civil commotions are usually excluded, according to the terms of the American Institute of Marine Underwriters Warranties. These exclusions are also found in all U.S. and British cargo insurance policies.

Shippers can request coverage, for an extra premium, by asking for "Insure against 'All Risks' for $_____ C.C. + War, S.R. & C.C.)."

Not All Goods Qualify for Full Coverage

The following merchandise is not accepted for "all risks" insurance, and special contracts must be requested. It is recommended that the exporter negotiate directly with the insurer.

- Aircraft, boats, automobiles, and other self-propelled craft and vehicles
- Animals, birds, cattle, livestock, and other living creatures
- Candy, confectionery
- Chilled, frozen, or otherwise refrigerated cargo (subject to special conditions)
- China, glass, enamelware, porcelain, and similar fragile articles or fixtures
- Dangerous chemicals
- Fresh fruits, vegetables, and other perishable foods (unless in refrigerated containers subject to special conditions)
- Gold, platinum, silver, and other precious metals and bullion
- Grains, flour, and meal in bags or bulk
- Iron and steel angles, bars, girders, pipes, sheets, wire, tinplate, and similar ferrous products
- Jewelry, watches, furs, and precious stones (cut and uncut)
- Liquid products in glass containers—unboxed
- Money, notes, securities, stock certificates, and other valuable papers

- Nuclear fissionable, fusionable, and otherwise radioactive materials
- Paintings, statues, and other works of art
- Refrigerators, stoves, washing machines, and other major appliances
- Sugar
- Used and/or reconditioned machinery, household and personal effects, and used goods and/or merchandise of any kind

Other Specialized Insurance

This coverage includes refrigerated goods to protect against the perils listed in "marine risks" above, as well as partial losses payable only in the event of sinking, stranding, fire, or collision. Coverage is also available for deterioration losses caused by a vessel's mechanical breakdown or malfunction of its refrigeration machinery, provided the breakdown lasts for 24 hours or more. Goods which are not in mechanically refrigerated containers may not be insured against deterioration, however it may have been caused. The shipper requests "Twenty-four-hour Reefer Clauses (+ War, S.R. & C.C.)."

Insurance Policy Costs

Open cargo policies are relatively expensive. They are underwritten and sold on the basis of annual premiums, which can be broken down into quarterly and even monthly payments. The amount of the premium is determined by the nature of the items to be shipped, the mode of transportation, and the geographical area of destination.

It goes without saying that explosive materials shipped to a war zone will be subject to a very high insurance premium. On average, an annualized open cargo insurance policy may cost the exporter from 2 to 5% of invoice value. It is worth planning ahead to build these costs into a company's export selling price structure. Whatever the costs, it is not worth making a shipment without knowing conclusively that the goods are adequately insured.

CONCLUSION AND SUMMARY

According to U.S. balance-of-payments data, over $57 billion was spent in 1995 on transporting merchandise in and out of the country. This did not include freight forwarding, customs brokerage, bank charges, inland freight and insurance, wharfage and handling, special packaging and airfreight preparation, in-transit insurance, legal fees, and myriad other costs connected with the physical movement of goods traded internationally. It is estimated that almost $100 billion is spent annually to logistically support U.S. exports and imports.

KEY TERMS AND CONCEPTS

Marine insurance. A generic name for casualty and loss insurance coverage for freight moving internationally, whatever the means of conveyance. Most policies offer warehouse-to-warehouse insurance coverage at 110% of the freight's cost and freight invoice value.

Shipping and selling terms. The language used in defining and determining the time and place for goods to change ownership from seller to buyer. It is important to pinpoint this ownership change, or change of title, for insurance purposes. It is also important in determining when a sale has been consummated for invoicing purposes. The shipping and selling terms also help establish exporters' and importers' respective obligations while the goods are in transit and beyond their physical control.

QUESTIONS

11.1 Discuss the shipping/selling terms a company would use to relinquish title as soon as possible and still pay the freight and insurance charges to a foreign customer's point of receipt.

11.2 Discuss the shipping/selling terms a company would use to retain title to a foreign customer's point of receipt but not pay freight and insurance charges beyond its FOB point.

11.3 Discuss how exporters shipping hazardous materials may avoid becoming involved in a "general average" situation.

CHAPTER 12

Financing Trade:
The Banking System

INTRODUCTION

The international banking system and documentation that must be prepared by international traders as shipments proceed to their destination are described in this chapter. The paperwork, which includes the seller's commercial invoices, is commonly called "documentation." Its accurate and timely preparation and distribution (the collection process) will enable importers to receive their goods and make it easier for exporters to receive on-time payment.

SHIPPING DOCUMENTATION

A typical set of export shipping documents might include:

- Commercial invoices
- Shipper's Export Declaration
- Sight or time draft
- Bill of lading or other transport document
- Certificate of origin
- Insurance policies or certificates

Documentation

These are legal documents describing the nature and value of a particular shipment. They also identify the exporter and importer, along with the carrier, insurer, banks, and all other parties participating in the transaction. Without the proper documentation, obviously shipments cannot be completed and payment cannot be rendered.

Commercial Invoices

These are the standard invoices a seller would normally issue upon making a shipment to a domestic customer. They will probably be more detailed in the sense that a more elaborate description of the goods shipped, along with a more complete explanation of the shipping/selling and payment terms, may have to be included to satisfy local customs authorities abroad and to meet letter-of-credit conditions, other financial requirements, as well as U.S. Customs regulations.

In some cases, the invoicing will have to be in both English and the local language and may also have to bear a qualifying stamp from the country's consulate in the exporter's region. Invoices are normally prepared by the seller.

Shipper's Export Declaration

This is a U.S. government form that describes the merchandise exported in accordance with official commodity definitions and commodity numbers. The form also indicates the quantity and value of what the seller exported. It is on the basis of the information supplied on this form that the U.S. government is able to compile and record the country's international trade statistics. The Export Declaration does not usually follow the rest of the documentation abroad; it is lodged with U.S. Customs. The form is generally prepared by the freight forwarder.

The Draft

The draft, generically known as a bill of exchange, is the critical document without which payment by importer to exporter cannot be made, whatever the payment terms may be. It is a written order by the drawer (exporter) directing the drawee (importer) to make payment at sight or at a determinable future date. Depending on the tenor of the draft associated with a documentary collection, the collecting bank requests either payment or acceptance of the draft before releasing the documents. Without the documents, the importer may not be able to claim the merchandise.

The Bill of Lading or Other Transport Document

This is a receipt given by a common carrier (a transportation company that uses trucks, planes, boats, or any other form of conveyance) to a seller for goods physically consigned for shipment. The old axiom that a bill of lading is a negotiable instrument is subject to much qualification today.

A bill of lading is essentially a contract between the exporter and the common carrier or between the importer and the common carrier, depending upon who has title to the goods while they are in transit, along with other factors.

It is therefore important to carefully review contractual provisions in the bill of lading and then consult with legal counsel concerning rights and obligations. Such counsel is helpful for container shipments that involve a combination of truck–air or truck–ocean shipments with door-to-door service provided by the carrier.

The only document that is considered negotiable is a "clean, on board" ocean bill of lading. This means that only one seller's goods are covered by the document, that those goods have not been consolidated with any others on the vessel, that they have been placed on board apart from other shipments, that they have been entered separately on the ship's manifest (inventory list), and that their entry on the vessel has been witnessed and signed by the skipper or a responsible agent (freight forwarder).

If a bill of lading is negotiable, the transportation company will not release goods to the foreign buyer without first having the document surrendered back to the carrier. This lends credence to the collection process, which otherwise may be meaningless to the exporter.

Without a negotiable bill of lading, an overseas customer does not really have to accept any drafts presented by the local collecting bank because there is no need to retrieve the bill of lading in order to claim the merchandise lying at the pier, air cargo terminal, or container holding area.

"Thru-bills" issued "warehouse to warehouse" by containerization companies are not normally negotiable. Neither are airline bills of lading. Thus, exporters making shipments under which bills of lading are non-negotiable might explore the option of consigning the goods to either the carrier or the collecting bank. This would ensure that the merchandise would not be released before the draft and the payment terms contained therein have been accepted by the buyer. The problem is that not all banks and carriers are interested in being physical consignees of goods for collection purposes, especially to suit small business owners. Some airlines offer a COD (collect on delivery) service, but only to a few designated areas.

Certificate of Origin

This is not a special form and is not required by all countries. U.S. law requires that commercial invoices and/or exporters' declarations contain a statement as to the origin of the goods. A few countries, however, do have formal paperwork that must be completed to attest to the origin of the goods and fair market prices.

Certificate of Insurance

This is written proof that goods being shipped internationally are insured against theft, loss, or damage. Many orders covered by letter-of-credit payment terms require the exporter to cover the shipment with insurance while the goods are in transit. The requirement is waived in most other cases. Some countries require the importer to buy insurance locally in order to conserve scarce foreign exchange reserves.

The International Payments Collection Process

Exporters normally want to maintain control over goods until the importer either pays for the merchandise or provides a satisfactory promise of payment in the future. The exporter's bank-initiated collection (outward foreign collection) may help meet that goal, depending on its structure. The amount of protection afforded the exporter, however, depends on the conditions of the collection.

An international collection is the process by which a bank, known as the remitting bank, acting upon the instructions of an exporter, presents document(s) associated with a sales transaction to the importer. This is done with the assistance of a second bank, known as the collecting bank.

The exporter's bank (the remitting bank), acting upon the exporter's instructions, will present documents associated with a sales transaction to the importer through the overseas correspondent bank (the collecting bank). The collecting bank presents the documents to the importer and, following stated instructions, obtains from the importer either a payment (sight draft) immediately upon "sight" of the documents or a trade acceptance (time draft), which means that the importer will be obligated to pay at some future specified date. An "acceptance" means the importer undertakes an obligation to make payment upon the maturity of a time draft drawn on the account of the importer and accepted by the importer.

The Parties to the Collection Process

Drawer. The drawer (exporter) writes the draft, which becomes part of the shipment's documentation. The drawer is also called the principal.

Freight forwarder. The freight forwarder, as a broker–agent, will most likely be the party preparing all the documentation on behalf of a small business exporter and presenting same to the bank for collection.

Remitting bank. The remitting bank is the bank chosen by the exporter to forward the documents to the importer's country for collection through a collecting bank. This may be the exporter's regular business bank or a bank that specializes in international transactions and has a network of correspondent banks abroad.

The remitting bank prepares an instruction letter. This letter sets forth when and under what conditions the collecting bank should release the documents to the importer, based on agreements reached earlier by the exporter and importer.

Collecting bank. The collecting bank will usually be the importer's bank unless the parties agree to another financial institution. The collecting bank presents the draft and documents to the importer for either immediate payment or payment in the future.

Drawee. The drawee (importer) is the party to whom the documents are presented, in accordance with an instruction letter (sometimes referred to as the transmittal letter). This letter defines when and under what conditions the collecting bank should release the documents to the importer, based on the terms previously agreed to by the exporter and importer.

Types of International Collections

Collections fall under two general categories: "clean" and "documentary." Most export collections are of the latter type because they provide less risk and difficulty for sellers, although they are costlier in terms of documentation fees.

Clean Collection

This is a collection that involves only "financial" documents, including a draft (also referred to as a bill of exchange), promissory note, or check. The most common financial document is a draft.

Under a clean collection, the commercial (or shipping) documents relating to the draft may have been consigned and forwarded by the exporter directly to the importer without processing by banks. When the bill of lading or transport document is consigned directly to the importer, the importer is in a position to claim the goods upon arrival without paying or promising to pay for them.

Such transport documents are said to be "straight consigned." The endorsement of the shipper and/or the remitting bank and/or the collecting bank is not necessary. The role of the exporter's bank is merely to forward the draft to the bank in the importer's country (collecting bank) for payment or acceptance.

Clean collections are used among larger international corporate affiliates where speed is of the essence and the manner of payment is not an issue. They are not recommended for small business exporters unless there is a clear understanding of the risks of non-payment.

Documentary Collection

In this form of collection, "commercial" (or shipping) documents are transmitted. A financial document (draft) may be included as well. Under a documentary collection, the exporter's bank (remitting bank) forwards the documents and its instruction letter, which contains the collection instructions requested by the exporter, to the bank in the importer's country (the collecting bank). This letter defines when and under what conditions the documents should be released to the importer. The importer receives the documents only after complying with the specified conditions.

Compared to a clean collection, a documentary collection can be safer for the exporter if completion of the passage of title to the merchandise can be protected on behalf of the seller until the buyer has complied with the terms of the draft.

Title is protected when all original copies of the bill of lading or transport document are forwarded to the collecting bank and are consigned to the order of the shipper blank endorsed or to the order of the collecting bank. If consigned to the collecting bank, after the importer satisfies the collection conditions, the collecting bank endorses the bill of lading to the importer.

Common Problems Faced by Exporters

Situations that may arise during the course of a collection transaction may result in an increased financial burden as well as additional problems for the exporter. The remitting bank should be requested to act as an adviser to help the exporter anticipate and prevent problems. However, there is no onus on the remitting bank to be helpful because it essentially acts as an agent of the importer and the collecting bank.

Examples of common problems include:

1. The goods, if not claimed, may incur demurrage, warehousing, insurance, and other related charges billable to the exporter until such time as the importer wishes to pay for the collection or the exporter makes other arrangements to sell the goods. The goods may have to be reshipped at the exporter's expense.
2. Insurance coverage by the seller or buyer may be inadequate. If the merchandise is either damaged or lost, the importer would probably refuse to honor the collection. To avoid this problem, exporters should investigate "contingency" or "difference in conditions" insurance policies and consider protecting their financial interests on all foreign shipments.
3. The exporter may have to wait an indeterminate length of time to receive payment/acceptance. This is dependent on various factors, such as the method by which payment is made (terminal-based communication, SWIFT,* cable, or mail) and the availability of foreign exchange in the country of the buyer.
4. The importer may not have a valid import license, which could result in refusal to accept the goods or in a delay in payment or acceptance of the draft. The exporter should always verify that the importer has a valid license (if required) before shipping on a collection basis.

DRAFTS

A draft is a bill of exchange that is similar in many respects to a business or personal check. It gives the banking system the necessary instructions concerning who pays whom, how much, where, and when. A draft is a written order by the drawer directing the drawee to make payment upon sight of the instrument or at a determinable future date. Depending on

---

* Society for Worldwide Interbank Financial Telecommunication.

the tenor of the draft associated with a documentary collection, the collecting bank requests either payment or acceptance of the draft before releasing the documents.

Documentary Drafts

These fall into two categories: sight drafts and time drafts. Both types are used extensively in international trade. Sight drafts generally result in faster payment and less risk to exporters. Time drafts give importers more time to pay and therefore present more risk to exporters.

Sight Draft

If the draft is drawn at sight, the documents are released to the buyer (drawee) upon payment of the draft. This term of settlement is referred to as D/P (documents against payment) or CAD (cash against documents).

Time Draft (or Usance Draft)

If the draft is a time draft (drawn to be payable 30, 60, 90, etc. days after sight or date), the documents are released to the buyer upon acceptance of the draft. This term of settlement is referred to as D/A (documents against acceptance). Payment is to be made, at maturity of the draft, by the acceptor of the draft. The accepted draft is called a trade acceptance.

Terms of settlement based on a time draft imply trust on the part of the exporter. By agreeing to draw a time draft, the exporter is granting credit terms to the importer. After the draft is accepted by the importer, the exporter has only the importer's promise to pay at the maturity date. The collecting bank is not responsible for the payment at maturity of the draft.

Advantages and Disadvantages

As a method of obtaining payment, the risks involved in a collection fall between open account (which favors the importer) and cash in advance (which favors the exporter).

Advantages to the exporter. One advantage is reduced risk of premature release of goods. Under a documentary collection, the exporter may guard against the release of goods until the importer has paid or accepted a draft.

Although a collection provides less security to the exporter than cash in advance or a letter of credit, if the exporter judges that the commercial and political risks of a particular transaction do not require fuller protection, or that immediate payment is not necessary, a collection may be an excellent settlement method. A collection is less costly and burdensome to arrange than a letter of credit. Therefore, the exporter may be able to sell at a lower price, enhancing its ability to compete for business. The same can be said for the exporter's agreement to accept payment on a time draft basis. The underlying credit extension from exporter to importer, while increasing the exporter's risk, improves its competitive position.

Disadvantages to the exporter. One disadvantage is delays in or slow payment. If, for example, the importer is required to obtain an import license but has not yet done so, the exporter must wait until the license is approved and issued to obtain payment. Also, due to the slow way in which some countries process collections, payment may be delayed.

Another disadvantage is additional costs due to non-payment or non-acceptance by the importer. Should the importer refuse to pay or accept the draft, the bank is not responsible and has no legal basis for enforcing the collection. The result may be additional demurrage, storage, insurance, and other costs to the exporter.

Advantages to the importer. Buying on a collection basis means the importer avoids the detailed requirements of opening a letter of credit. This means a lower cost of importing. The importer also avoids the costs of an import letter of credit and may benefit from a lower purchase price as well, as the exporter may be able to pass along certain savings. This deferred payment collection method favors the importer in the timing of payment. Generally, payment or acceptances may be deferred until the goods arrive or often after their arrival.

Disadvantages to the importer. There can be damage to the importer's reputation if non-payment or non-acceptance is claimed. If the importer is unable to pay or accept the draft for some reason or chooses not to, the exporter may provide specific instructions to "protest" on its behalf. In many countries, protest is a formal, legal complaint registered to provide a basis for possible legal action later.

There is, therefore, greater reliance upon the use of negotiable and financial instruments as collection tools, unless the exporter is shipping abroad on an open account basis. An almost universally accepted language and code of procedures has evolved over time to make sure that all parties to an international transaction fully understand the essence and substance of their intentions and actions.

Despite the fact that many exporters persist in making open account shipments, either on a freight collect or freight prepaid basis, this is not a recommended practice. It is true that both buyer and seller may be in frequent contact with one another, but the fact remains that they are doing business across national borders. This can create difficulties, especially when the importer is in a soft currency country which imposes restrictions on the convertibility of local currency into dollars for transmittance back to the exporter.

On an open account shipment, the exporter might have to accept payment in the importer's currency or nothing at all. Operating through a bank, the exporter will at least know that its collection documents will be duly processed by the importing country's central bank and that payment will be made as dollars become available in the importing country's banking system. Thus, the great advantage of utilizing a formal system of export documentation and routing it through a bank lies in a fairly high assurance of payment.

Once the importer accepts the documents from its own correspondent bank, even if the payment terms are for an extended time period, the international banking channels through which the transaction has taken place automatically seek to make a collection on behalf of the exporter. This means that if the importer has funds deposited with its bank, its account may be debited to satisfy the amount outstanding owed to the exporter. If the funds on deposit are insufficient, the bank will press the importer for the collection on behalf of the exporter.

CONCLUSION AND SUMMARY

Banks dealing in international transactions may have a somewhat exposed position, particularly if they are advancing funds to either the importer or the exporter. By the same token, the positions of other intermediaries to an import–export transaction are almost equally exposed. Hence, banks, insurers, common carriers, forwarding agents, customs brokers, and even customs officials look to the documentation as prima facie evidence of performance in good faith by both buyer and seller.

The significance of this reliance upon the documentation means that there should be no discrepancies between statements and figures shown on the exporter's invoices and those on the bills of lading, bank drafts, and all other negotiable and/or financial instruments. Unless all the documents agree with one another, the exporter may not get paid and/or the importer may not receive its goods.

KEY TERMS AND CONCEPTS

Bill of lading (or other transport document). A receipt given by a common carrier (a transportation company that uses trucks, planes, boats, or any other form of conveyance) to a seller for goods physically consigned for shipment. The old axiom that a bill of lading is a negotiable instrument is subject to much qualification today.

Certificate of insurance. Written proof that goods being shipped internationally are insured against theft, loss, or damage. Many orders covered by letter-of-credit payment terms require the exporter to cover the shipment with insurance while the goods are in transit. The requirement is waived in most other cases. Some countries require the importer to buy insurance locally in order to conserve scarce foreign exchange reserves.

Certificate of origin. This is not a special form, and it is not required by all countries. U.S. law requires that commercial invoices and/or exporters' declarations contain a statement as to the origin of the goods. A few countries, however, do have formal paperwork that must be completed to attest to the origin of the goods and fair market prices.

Clean collection. Collection involving only "financial" documents, including a draft (also referred to as a bill of exchange), promissory note, or check. The most common financial document is a draft.

Commercial invoices. The standard invoices a seller would normally issue upon making a shipment to a domestic customer. Their context may vary from country to country, depending on U.S. export control regulations and local legal requirements.

Documentary collection. A form of collection that transmits "commercial" (or shipping) documents. A financial document (draft) may be included as well.

Documentation. Legal documents that describe the nature and value of a particular shipment. They also identify the exporter and importer, along with the carrier, insurer, banks, and all other parties participating in a transaction. Without the proper documentation, obviously shipments cannot be completed and payment cannot be rendered.

Draft. Known generically as a bill of exchange, it is the critical document without which payment by importer to exporter cannot be made, whatever the payment terms may be. It is a written order by the drawer (exporter) directing the drawee (importer) to make payment at sight or at a determinable future date.

Shipper's Export Declaration. A U.S. government form that describes the merchandise exported in accordance with official commodity definitions and commodity numbers. The form also indicates the quantity and value of what the seller exported.

Shipping documentation. A typical set of export shipping documents might include commercial invoices, shipper's Export Declaration, a sight or time draft, a bill of lading or other transport document, certificate of origin, and insurance policies or certificates.

QUESTIONS

12.1 Describe the nature and purpose of an import license.

12.2 Discuss the pros and cons of clean collections and documentary collections.

12.3 International banks often claim that their primary responsibility is to importers. Discuss this statement.

CHAPTER 13

Financing Trade: Payments and Collections

INTRODUCTION

This chapter focuses on the more popular payment terms used by companies in the export business. It also looks more closely at the role played by the international banking system in providing an operating environment that makes it easier for exporters to receive on-time payment for their shipments.

There are risks with all payment terms except prepaid. There are even risks with letter-of-credit transactions, as will be seen in the next chapter. However, an interesting point to consider is that bad debts from international trade worldwide are much less than those from domestic sales, despite the fact that most export sales involve the extension of trade credit through extended payment terms.

PAYMENT TERMS

Payment terms do not normally determine when and where title to goods changes hands. Payment terms establish who owes whom, how much, when payment is to be made and received, through which intermediaries (banks) payment is to be made, what currency is acceptable, and where (which country, city, and bank) the payment is to be made. Where and when a title change takes place is largely determined by the selling terms, sometimes called shipping terms.

Establishing Payment Terms

The definition of payment terms for specific overseas customers is more complex than establishing terms for domestic buyers. In addition to determining a foreign buyer's credit worthiness and financial viability, it becomes essential to evaluate the foreign country's financial, economic, and political environment, along with its relationship with the exporter's home country, where payment may be sent.

Investigating a foreign buyer's credit. In a domestic sale, a customer credit check through banks, Dun & Bradstreet, vendors, and creditors is enough to determine payment terms (i.e., open account or COD). It makes good sense to engage in the same precautionary credit checks with overseas customers. The domestic credit services that operate locally also operate overseas.

The foreign customer's country environment. In addition to clarifying the foreign customer's credit standing, an awareness of conditions within the importer's country is necessary before deciding on payment terms. Such questions as political stability, steadiness of the monetary system, ability of the country's banking and other monetary institutions to pay the country's bills on time, and import restrictions must be addressed and answered. This is where the international banking system comes into play.

The International Banking System

Most countries, including the United States, have their own individual monetary system and their own currency managed by a central bank similar in many ways to the U.S. Federal Reserve. The local currency is not legal tender in the United States, which means that it must first be converted into dollars before an American exporter selling goods into the area can be paid in dollars.

Currency convertibility problems. Difficulty experienced by the international banking community in converting a foreign currency into dollars or any other foreign exchange may be an indication that the overseas country's monetary system may be short of foreign exchange reserves. While such shortfalls are not unusual in international trade and tend to be temporary, they do create payment bottlenecks. The exporter's bank will know if such situations exist overseas and will convey that information to the exporter before any payment terms are established.

Banks are payment facilitators. The international banking system will help facilitate the payment function by handling all the documentation necessary to move funds from the importer's bank to the exporter's bank and have those funds converted into dollars in the process.

Selecting Appropriate Payment Terms

All payment terms carry risk unless payment is rendered well before shipment. Low risk to an exporter means high risk to an importer and vice versa. Cash-in-advance payment to the exporter means that the importer stands the chance of not receiving merchandise ordered and paid for. Based solely on this possibility, the importer might never send an order and there will be no sale.

The other extreme may be equally painful for the exporter. If the exporter grants open account payment terms, there is a high risk of not getting paid at all. It is thus entirely reasonable for an exporter to inquire: If cash in advance is 100% guaranteed, why bother with any other payment terms? There are three possible answers: an exporter may never get an order because of such inflexibility, most buyers resist paying for goods not yet received, and advance payments may be in violation of some foreign governments' currency control laws.

Buyers and sellers need a quid pro quo that will encourage all parties to assume an acceptable level of risk. Payment terms finally selected will often reflect a compromise between cash up front and open account.

Caveats About the Exporter's Favorite International Bank

A company selling overseas may believe that it has a "special" relationship with its bank, especially if it has been using the bank's services for several years. The company may believe that the bank will protect its interest as an exporter in dealing with an overseas bank and customer.

In fact, the exporter's bank is an agent of the overseas buyer's bank because of its correspondent relationship. It is only when the exporter becomes an importer that its local bank will act as a good-faith agent for the U.S. company.

The exporter's bank acts as a facilitator. The exporter's bank does not pay or routinely advance any funds to the exporter on the basis of an import–export transaction, unless it has specific instructions from the importer's bank. Even then, no payments will be made by the exporter's bank if it has reason to suspect it will not be reimbursed by the foreign bank in a timely manner.

Exporter's credit with the remitting bank. An exporter may be able to borrow money from a U.S. bank, but that loan will have to stand on the merits of the exporter's credit rating and will have little to do with the export transaction per se.

External credit and political risk insurance. Exceptions exist if the exporter has purchased political and credit risk insurance covering non-payment of export receivables through the Export-Import Bank of the United States. Some exporters have such coverage and are then able to discount or even to sell their receivables outright without recourse to themselves.

What the Exporter's Bank Does

The exporter's bank is officially the remitting bank. It is a conduit for the flow of paperwork (the routing of drafts and other documentation) and for the flow of funds resulting from the transaction. It plays a more active role only when letter-of-credit transactions are involved, but then only as a representative for the overseas bank.

The Collection Process

When an exporter makes a shipment where payment terms are other than "prepaid," a process called a "collection" is set in motion. The submission of export documentation (invoices, drafts, bills of lading, etc.) by the exporter or freight forwarder to the bank is "presentation for collection." The exporter's bank passes those documents on to the importer's bank, making its own "presentation for collection." The exporter's bank thus provides a processing service which will help the exporter secure either payment (sight draft) or a payment promise (time draft).

Data Verification

The two correspondent banks (the exporter's and the importer's) are responsible for verifying that certain conditions specified in the documentation as previously agreed upon by the selling and buying parties are met before the release of those documents. According to Chemical Bank, the banks (and certainly not the exporters) are not responsible for:

- *Verifying the quantity or quality of the merchandise being shipped against the documents.* Banks deal in documents alone, ensuring only that documents specified in the transmittal letter are provided to them by the exporter for presentation to the importer. Banks have no further obligation to examine the documents.

- *Guaranteeing payment in the event of non-payment or non-acceptance of the draft.* Banks are required to release documents only if specified conditions are met by the importer, usually including payment or acceptance of a draft.

Payment Terms

Without a draft, generically known as a bill of exchange, payment by importer to exporter cannot be made, whatever the payment terms may be. The draft contains all the instructions to the exporter's bank and the importer's bank as to who pays whom, how much, where, and when.

Essentially, a draft is similar to a seller writing a check on behalf of a buyer who has run out of checks. In lieu of the exporter executing a draft, the importer would write a check in the local currency and send it to the exporter in the United States.

This would result in a convoluted process in which the exporter would have to submit the draft to the U.S. corespondent bank for collection. The U.S. correspondent bank would route the draft back overseas for conversion into dollars before being able to make a deposit to the exporter's account. This can create difficulties in the importer's country, because if no dollar (foreign exchange) has been set aside for the transaction, the check in the local currency cannot legally be redeemed in dollars.

An exporter would not as a matter of routine policy make a shipment and have a draft issued unless guaranteed that the foreign exchange (dollars) has been made available for the transaction.

Sight Draft

If a draft is drawn at sight, the documents are released to the buyer (drawee) upon payment of the draft. This term of payment is often called D/P (documents against payment) or CAD (cash against documents). It means that the collecting bank will not release the shipping documents to the importer until payment has been rendered.

Time Draft

Under these terms (a draft drawn to be payable 30, 60, 90, etc. days after sight or date), the documents are released to the buyer upon acceptance (signing) of the draft. This term of settlement is referred to as D/A (documents against acceptance). Payment is to be made, at maturity of the draft, by the acceptor of the draft. The accepted draft is called a "trade acceptance."

Terms of settlement based on a time draft imply trust on the part of the exporter. By agreeing to a time draft, the exporter is giving the importer trade credit and has only a signed promise of payment at maturity. The collecting bank is not responsible for the importer's possible non-payment.

Time drafts as payment terms should probably be avoided by small business exporters unless they hold a paid-up credit and political risk insurance policy from the Export-Import Bank of the United States. Sight draft transactions can also be difficult to collect on unless both exporter and importer are well known to one another and can arrange for an alternative payment method if a problem occurs. The saving grace is that, in most instances, exporters want to sell, importers truly want to buy and to pay, and the international banking system sincerely wants to facilitate business.

Types of Collection

Clean Collection

This is a collection that involves only "financial" documents, including a draft (also referred to as a bill of exchange), promissory note, or check. The most common financial document is a draft. (See Chapter 12 for a more detailed explanation.)

Documentary Collection

In a documentary collection, "commercial" (or shipping) documents are transmitted. A financial document (draft) may be included as well. Under a documentary collection, the exporter's bank (remitting bank) forwards the documents and its instruction letter, which contains collection instructions requested by the exporter, to the bank in the importer's country (the collecting bank). (See Chapter 12 for a more detailed explanation.)

Common Problems Faced by Exporters

Situations that may arise during the course of a collection transaction may result in an increased financial burden as well as additional problems for the exporter. The remitting bank should be requested to act as an adviser to help the exporter anticipate and prevent problems. Examples of common problems include:

1. The goods, if not claimed by the importer, may incur demurrage, warehousing, insurance, and other related charges billable to the exporter until such time as the importer wishes to pay for the collection or the exporter makes other arrangements to sell the goods. The goods may have to be reshipped at the exporter's expense.

2. Insurance coverage by the seller or buyer may be inadequate. If the merchandise is either damaged or lost, the importer would probably refuse to honor the collection. To avoid this problem, exporters should investigate "contingency" or "difference in conditions" insurance policies and consider protecting their financial interests on all foreign shipments.

3. The exporter might have to wait an indeterminate length of time to receive payment/acceptance. This is dependent on various factors, such as the method by which payment is made (terminal-based communication, SWIFT,* cable, or mail) and on availability of foreign exchange in the country of the buyer.

4. The importer may not have a valid import license, which could result in refusal to accept the goods or delay in payment or acceptance of the draft. The exporter should always verify that the importer has a valid license (if required) before shipping on a collection basis.

CONCLUSION AND SUMMARY

International collections are usually governed in their treatment by the International Chamber of Commerce (ICC) Uniform Rules for Collections. The general provisions and definitions of this ICC publication are binding on all parties to a collection unless otherwise expressly agreed or unless contrary to the provisions of a national, state, or local law and/or regulation from which no departure may be made. Trading partners are encouraged, when operating under collection terms, to state in their sales agreement that the Uniform Rules for Collections published by the ICC apply. Domestic collections in the United States may be governed by the

---

* Society for Worldwide Interbank Financial Telecommunication.

Uniform Commercial Code. Exporters and importers should be knowledgeable about these rules.

KEY TERMS AND CONCEPTS

Collection process. When an exporter makes a shipment where payment terms are other than prepaid, a process called a "collection" is set in motion.

Draft. A bill of exchange. Without this critical document, payment by importer to exporter cannot be made, whatever the payment terms may be. The draft contains all the instructions to the exporter's bank and the importer's bank as to who pays whom, how much, where, and when.

International banking system. Most countries, including the United States, have their own individual monetary system and their own currency managed by a central bank, similar in many ways to the U.S. Federal Reserve. The local currency is not legal tender in the United States, which means that it must first be converted into dollars before an American exporter selling goods into the area can be paid in dollars.

Payment terms. Payment terms do not normally determine when and where title to goods changes hands. Payment terms establish who owes whom, how much, when payment is to be made and received, through which intermediaries (banks) payment is to be made, what currency is acceptable, and where (which country, city, and bank) the payment is to be made. Where and when a title change takes place are largely determined by the selling terms, sometimes called shipping terms.

Sight draft. If a draft is drawn at sight, the documents are released to the buyer (drawee) upon payment of the draft. This term of payment is often called D/P (documents against payment) or CAD (cash against documents). It means that the collecting bank will not release the shipping documents to the importer until payment has been rendered.

Time draft. Under these terms (a draft drawn to be payable 30, 60, 90, etc. days after sight or date), the documents are released to the buyer upon acceptance (signing) of the draft. This term of settlement is referred to as D/A (documents against acceptance). Payment is to be made, at maturity of the draft, by the acceptor of the draft. The accepted draft is called a "trade acceptance."

QUESTIONS

13.1 Discuss the circumstances under which exporters would sell to overseas customers on a time draft basis rather than offering sight draft payment terms.

13.2 Explain, with examples, the differences in purpose between selling/shipping terms and payment terms.

13.3 Discuss how factors other than the overseas customer's credit may impact the exporter's payment terms.

13.4 Describe and explain, with examples, the international banking system's obligation to importers and exporters.

13.5 Discuss the nature and purpose of a central bank's import licensing procedures.

CHAPTER 14

International Letters of Credit

INTRODUCTION

This chapter is about minimizing payment risk through the use of letters of credit. It will also be shown that these documents can be used to finance international trade.

LETTERS OF CREDIT IN GENERAL

The Letter of Credit

A letter of credit (L/C) is an issuing or opening bank's promise to pay a certain amount of money to a beneficiary subject to specific performance by that beneficiary within a given period of time. The issuing bank is the importer's bank, called the remitting bank in Chapter 13. Its correspondent bank will usually be the exporter's bank, called the collecting bank.

The process. When an L/C is opened by an importer's bank, it is routed to the beneficiary (exporter) via the correspondent bank, which appends to it a "letter of advice" setting forth the role it is prepared to play should the exporter opt to act under the terms of the L/C.

Whose promise to pay? In an L/C-backed transaction, the promise to pay as drawn on a draft by the exporter is transferred from the buyer–importer to the issuing bank, which opens the L/C based upon the importer's instructions.

Types of Letters of Credit

Standard Letter of Credit

Standard revocable L/Cs are most often used as personal L/Cs by individuals traveling around the world who need large amounts of cash on certain occasions. For example, a mountain climber from Kansas seeking to conquer Mt. Everest in Nepal may need $1 million in local currency to hire the sherpa crews and to buy food and gear in Katmandu, Nepal's capital and the starting point of the expedition.

The climber could go to Citibank in New York, assuming it had a correspondent affiliate in Katmandu, buy a $1 million L/C, cash it before its expiration date at Citibank in Nepal, and get the local currency equivalent. The L/C might require the climber to show a valid passport or driver's license to Citibank in Nepal, which would not be a problem because the L/C's beneficiary in this case is also the party that asked the opening bank in New York to issue the document in the first place.

Of course, today this form of personal L/C has been rendered partially obsolete by the introduction of wire transfers. Nevertheless, a revocable L/C is revocable by the issuing bank or by the party making the request of the bank at any time before documents are presented for collection. As far as an exporter is concerned, an order cancellation faxed to either the issuing or correspondent bank voids the transaction as long as the shipping documents have not yet reached the exporter's bank.

An importer that instructs the issuing bank to open a revocable L/C is in the position of being able to cancel an order up to the very last minute (i.e., a few days past the time of shipment) as long as the documentation showing evidence of shipment has not yet landed inside the door of the correspondent bank in the United States. This creates for the exporter the unpleasant prospect of having to pay round-trip freight for the goods or trying to have them sold at a customs auction in the importer's country.

Irrevocable Letter of Credit

Most L/Cs that involve single orders with no contracted repeat business are of this variety. The L/C is irrevocable by the issuing bank. This means that neither the buyer nor the opening bank can cancel the commitments made under the documents as long as the seller (exporter) performs as specified in the L/C.

An irrevocable L/C is sent by the opening bank to its correspondent bank (hopefully the exporter's bank, to save time and money), which then forwards the document with a letter of advice to the beneficiary (exporter). The letter of advice indicates that the covering text is "merely advice and conveys no engagement by the bank." This or similar wording is standard in such letters.

This is a good time to recall that, as stated several times earlier, the exporter's bank (the collecting bank) functions as a representative of its overseas corespondent bank and the importer buying the merchandise. It does not represent the exporter, even in an L/C transaction. Here again, it is possible that the importer's bank, or the entire banking system with which it is affiliated, may suddenly run aground. This would leave correspondent banks in the United States, with whom the foreign bank had opened dollar accounts to cover such L/C transactions, with insufficient funds to cover exporters' and other claims. True, an import license might have been issued by the importer's central bank, but the foreign exchange (dollars in this case) might have simply evaporated.

Other reasons for a U.S. correspondent bank not to honor a foreign bank's irrevocable L/C are political risk and fraud. On the political risk side, disputes among nations may bring retaliation by the U.S. government in the form of "freezing" foreign-owned bank accounts in the United States. Often, this also puts a lock on the U.S. dollar accounts of foreign banks. Until the dispute is put to rest, innocent exporters cannot ship and be paid, and innocent importers may not receive their merchandise even though they may have already paid for it in their local currency.

On the fraud side, an increasing number of fictitious L/Cs have been issued by overseas individuals and groups masquerading as banks. Consequently, a U.S. bank may receive an L/C and be suspicious of its origin.

Experienced exporters will always call their stateside bank upon receiving an irrevocable L/C from an overseas opening bank and ask if the U.S. bank will honor the document on presentation, assuming all the documentation is in order. In the majority of cases, the exporter's bank will agree over the telephone.

L/Cs from large international banks in Western Europe, Japan, Hong Kong, Singapore, and many other established markets and hard currency areas present few problems other than the usual headaches of careful order processing. Problems with L/Cs center around some developing areas with unsound central banking systems and unstable currencies.

Irrevocable Confirmed Letter of Credit

This type of L/C represents the least risk for an exporter, but it commits the foreign buyer to see the transaction through to its end. Up to this point, the promise to pay has been on the part of the issuing bank based upon the instructions of the importer. Now, the promise to pay shifts from overseas to the U.S. correspondent bank that confirms the document.

In other words, when the exporter's bank (again, assuming it is the correspondent bank) receives an irrevocable L/C from abroad, it sends it on to the exporter with the same covering "letter of advice," but in this case notes that it will "honor the L/C and all documents submitted with it." The exporter now has a solid guarantee of payment by its bank as long as performance meets the requirements of the L/C.

Charges are imposed by both opening and correspondent banks when L/Cs are created and processed. Confirmation of an irrevocable L/C by a correspondent bank imposes another add-on charge of up to two and three percentage points on top of the face value of the invoice on which the L/C is based. From a cost perspective, confirmation should therefore be avoided whenever possible.

In addition to being used by importers and exporters in cases where an air of uncertainty prevails, L/Cs are also used as third-party contracts (with the issuing and confirming banks as the third party) to complement the original buy/sell agreement between importer and exporter. Transactions that are very complex and take months or even years to consummate are often executed under L/C arrangements.

In general, L/Cs help increase trade by providing a bank's guarantee of "quick cash" to the exporter when shipment is made as called for. An L/C also guarantees to the importer that payments will not be made unless the exporter has performed as stated in the L/C.

Domestic L/Cs operate in the same manner as international L/Cs except that both buyer and seller are located in the United States and confirmation of an L/C is rare.

THE IMPORT LETTER-OF-CREDIT APPLICATION PROCESS

The purpose of this section is to acquaint importers with the nature of and the steps in applying for and obtaining an import L/C. In a sense, the term "import L/C" is somewhat of a misnomer because just about all L/Cs, except for personal L/Cs, are applied for by importers.

Definition and Nature of the Import Letter of Credit

The same definition given in the previous chapter applies here. In part, an import L/C is a bank's promise to pay a certain amount of money to a beneficiary (the exporter), subject to specific performance by that beneficiary (ship and show proof of shipment). It appears at first blush that the importer has committed funds to the transaction from the moment the opening bank issues the L/C, and that is true to an extent.

Importer needs no front money. In fact, the importer generally puts up no front money at all and merely signs a promissory note with the opening bank, so that the buyer's account will not be debited before the exporter is paid on the L/C. However, in reality in an L/C transaction, the goods will be paid for before the importer receives them.

Red tape. The general observation that the L/C application process can be tedious, annoying, and expensive is also correct. On the positive side, the importer's promise to pay is taken over by the bank, which will take all measures to make sure that payments are made to the seller without first knowing that the goods ordered by the buyer have indeed been shipped.

The Letter-of-Credit Application Process

The L/C application process is fairly standard no matter which bank is the issuing or opening bank (the remitting bank). An up-to-date set of financial statements usually accompanies new applications. This condition may be waived for repeat business.

Letter-of-credit terms vary considerably. The conditions are adjusted to fit the requirements of each individual transaction. However, all irrevocable L/Cs have certain characteristics in common. The seller of the goods is authorized to draw on the issuing bank, with the latter's understanding that the draft will be paid (if a sight L/C) or accepted for payment by the bank at a later date (if a time L/C), provided all documents presented are as stipulated in the L/C. In other words, the bank places the security of its name behind the buyer. Where irrevocable L/Cs are concerned, this security cannot be removed except by mutual consent of both the seller and the buyer.

By means of an L/C, merchants can set in motion the machinery that will make possible the shipment of goods from exporting countries (e.g., machinery from Germany, cotton from Egypt, wool from New Zealand, and many other types of goods which may be available in other parts of the world).

The Letter of Credit and the Draft

Most import and domestic L/Cs call for drafts to be drawn on the exporter's bank at sight. This means that when the bank receives the documents accompanying the draft, they must be checked to determine that they conform to the requirements of the L/C.

Banks pay only against documents. This accounts for the fact that banks will not pay sellers unless all their pertinent shipping papers are in good order. If an examination shows that the documents agree with the L/C provisions, the bank will then render payment and forward the documents so that foreign buyers can clear the goods through their own customs without delay. Banks will invariably hold back payment if the shipping documentation is not in order.

Prior financing arrangements. In the event arrangements for refinancing have been made (prior to opening documentary sight L/Cs), the shipping documents will be released to the importer upon its signing a financing agreement. The foreign buyer thus gives the banking system permission to pay the seller even though the documents may be flawed. The L/C is no longer the operative instrument in this case. The operative instrument is the draft, with the buyer receiving a loan from the bank to pay the exporter.

Time letters of credit. These credits have refinancing built into them. Instead of the importer's bank making immediate payment when documents are presented by the exporter through its bank, it will "accept" the draft calling for payment at a later date (possibly 30, 60, or 90 days but not over 180 days). The draft then becomes known as a "banker's acceptance," and the holder presents it for payment at maturity. The importer's account is debited at that time.

Banker's acceptance. Bankers' acceptances bear no interest because they are purchased by investors at face value, less the "discount" for the number of days the acceptance has to run to maturity. The "discount" is ordinarily for the shipper's account. The original L/C application should indicate those instances where importers agree to absorb the discount.

EXPORT LETTERS OF CREDIT

Export L/Cs are issued by U.S. banks on behalf of foreign correspondents for the accounts of their customers (to whom these are import L/Cs, as previously described). The U.S. banks directly advise the U.S. exporter beneficiary, unless otherwise directed by the overseas banking affiliate.

Inasmuch as export L/Cs originate outside the United States, there is usually little that can be done in terms of which U.S. bank should advise or confirm. However, many shippers ask their customers to have their banks open L/Cs at a specific U.S. bank with which the exporter already has a relationship.

CONCLUSION AND SUMMARY

Letters of credit, in and of themselves, do not constitute acceptable collateral security for obtaining bank credit. Under certain circumstances, however, they do make requests for bank credit more attractive. Therefore, if financing is needed in order to obtain merchandise from the supplier and the L/C is not transferable (formerly called "assignable"), banks may be able to work out a back-to-back or bridged L/C for an exporting customer.

If it is not possible to extend such credit, the supplier may be willing to accept an assignment of proceeds, a courtesy often extended to responsible shippers.

An L/C is not "money in the bank." It may contain stipulations that make it difficult or impossible to control the transaction for which it was issued, due to circumstances such as inability to obtain space prior to the shipping date, strikes, consul's office not open or consularization otherwise refused, embargo by the government, etc. An L/C becomes "money in the bank" only when a bank finally pays the exporter the document's face value.

Beneficiaries should check L/Cs carefully immediately upon receipt, to see that they conform with the sales contract or the customer's purchase order. If there is any discrepancy, the buyer and the banks involved should be advised immediately, without waiting until the shipment is ready or has already been made.

Exporters sometimes find that drafts and documents presented for payment are turned down because of discrepancies found when checked against the requirements in the L/C. Under certain circumstances, the paying bank may be willing to accept the beneficiary's guarantee to indemnify the bank should the foreign buyer (through the opening bank abroad) refuse to accept the documents because of such discrepancies.

Many exporters freely offer such guarantees, but others will not, inasmuch as final settlement then rests with the buyer, and it is possible that the buyer (particularly in a declining market) may decide it is to its advantage not to accept the documents as presented. To avoid this situation, which would offset the benefits of having an L/C, some exporters request the paying bank to cable the opening bank abroad for authority to pay against the documents as submitted.

KEY TERMS AND CONCEPTS

Irrevocable confirmed letter of credit. This type of L/C represents the least risk for an exporter, but it commits the foreign buyer to see the transaction through to its end. The promise to pay shifts from the issuing bank to the U.S. correspondent bank that confirms the document.

Irrevocable letter of credit. Most L/Cs that involve single orders with no contracted repeat business are of this variety. The L/C is irrevocable by the issuing bank. This means that neither the buyer nor the opening bank can cancel the commitments made under the documents as long as the seller (exporter) performs as specified in the L/C.

Letter of credit. An issuing or opening bank's promise to pay a certain amount of money to a beneficiary, subject to specific performance by that beneficiary within a given period of time. The issuing bank is the importer's bank, also known as the remitting bank. Its correspondent bank is usually the exporter's bank, also called the collecting bank.

QUESTIONS

14.1 An exporter wants to ship a million-dollar piece of equipment to a customer in Turkey and would like to give the customer 120-day payment terms. The exporter would also like to be paid in U.S. dollars as rapidly as possible. Using a specific example, explain how a letter-of-credit arrangement might benefit both exporter and importer.

14.2 Not all letters of credit are the same. Explain, using specific examples, the differences among the various forms of letters of credit available today.

14.3 Explain the ways in which letters of credit can be used to finance an exporter's transaction.

14.4 "A letter of credit is not money in the bank." Explain this statement.

CHAPTER 15

Foreign Manufacturing and Assembly

INTRODUCTION

This chapter discusses the use of turnkey systems, management contracts, and contract manufacturing agreements as means of introducing high-technology systems and/or goods produced in other countries expediently and without long-term foreign direct investments.

TURNKEY AGREEMENTS

Turnkey agreements are most commonly used in emerging markets during the design, procurement, assembly, and construction phases of a capital project. Companies that have the critical skills needed to coordinate the building of large capital projects (e.g., steel mills, petrochemical refining and processing facilities, resort and housing developments, commercial air terminals, etc.) become known as turnkey contractors.

How They Work

The process starts when a turnkey contractor responds to a bid invitation from a party in an emerging nation that lacks the resources and skills to successfully execute given industrial projects on its own. Bid awards are not necessarily made on the basis of price competitiveness. The criteria for winning a turnkey contract are usually couched in a company's demonstrated ability to effectively execute the project and sometimes to also provide financing for the project if funding has not already been allocated.

Advantages and Disadvantages

Advantages. There are three main advantages to turnkey projects. One advantage to contractors is that they are a way of earning returns on technological assets and know-how that might otherwise remain idle.

Another advantage is that the turnkey contractor merely constructs the facility, collects its money (usually on a percentage-of-completion basis), and then leaves. It is not subject to possible losses if the government and/or economy undergoes adverse changes.

A third advantage, this time to the recipients of turnkey projects situated in politically sensitive areas where investments from industrial countries are routinely suspect, is that the foreign contractor maintains a temporary presence and is then gone.

Disadvantages. The first disadvantage can be derived from the second advantage above. Because the firm no longer has a vested interest in the facility it created, it is cut out of any future profits in the event the foreign country becomes a major market for the output of the process that has been exported.

The second disadvantage is that a firm that enters into a turnkey project with a foreign enterprise may inadvertently create a competitor. For example, many Western firms that sold oil-refining technology to firms in Saudi Arabia and Kuwait now find themselves competing head to head with these firms in other world oil markets.

MANAGEMENT CONTRACTS

Management contracts are often instituted toward the last phase of a turnkey agreement. The new facility has been turned over to the new owner–operators, who find themselves temporarily without the experience required to manage the project. A professional management company may then be called in to operate, manage, and maintain the facility and to train the local work force, until it becomes self-sustaining.

CONTRACT MANUFACTURING

Many companies that contract some or all of their production abroad are small, have limited technology, and have few if any registerable or patentable intellectual assets such as trade names, copyrights, and inventions. For these types of companies, contract manufacturing arrangements with foreign producers can and do in fact provide viable alternatives to making costly long-term investments.

However, contract manufacturing arrangements are also used by large companies as a means of limiting their wholly owned production units to the manufacture of what they consider to be their core product lines.

Contract Manufacturing Defined

The best definition is by way of example. Cosmetics companies often offer specialty soaps and facial cleansers as extensions to their lines of perfume products. Many of these items are contracted out to one or several of the major soapers, such as Colgate-Palmolive, Procter & Gamble, and Unilever. Large aerospace companies like Boeing often contract out parts and components to smaller machine shops in the United States and abroad.

Specifically, the large soapers produce detergents, soaps, toiletries, and cosmetics in their plants all over the world under their respective names and have their own powerhouse marketing and sales organizations. However, they also produce these same type of goods under contract for other independent companies, small or large, that do not have the same extensive production and technological resources. Independent bottling companies that perform contract-filling operations for Coca-Cola, Pepsi, and other beverage companies also perform similar services.

Many well-known cosmetics companies routinely use Procter & Gamble's facilities for the production of expensive soap products sold under the cosmetics firm's logo and label. The same holds true in the beverage industry, the machine and appliance business—in just about every industry.

Companies enter into contract manufacturing (sometimes called contract-filling operations) when circumstances stop them from producing their products reasonably close to their markets, when market access is denied, or when their own costs are higher than having the goods made by someone else.

How Contract Manufacturing Agreements Work

The typical arrangement calls for a contract manufacturer to produce a fixed amount of inventory from given specifications at a negotiated total cost. A 50% prepayment of the total cost is often required; the balance is payable upon completion of the production run. Contract manufacturers can agree to warehouse and sometimes distribute the finished run upon receipt of shipping instructions from the contracting firm. These agreements are generally paid separately by the contracting firm.

Contract Manufacturing as an Advantage to Exporters

Small companies that enjoy niche markets overseas with non-branded products and for whom patent protection is not important may find contract manufacturing effective in helping them maintain and even increase market share. Any number of overseas contract manufacturers in almost all industries offer their production facilities to American companies. They generally have no interest in establishing themselves as competitors and are seeking instead to supplement their own production schedules.

A U.S. equipment manufacturer that exports machines to Western European countries and is faced with a declining market share because of protective European Union (EU) tariffs can turn to a contract manufacturer in Belgium, for example, that could produce enough inventory to meet EU market needs. The U.S. company, rather than selling a high-tariff "made-in-the-USA" product, would instead be selling a Belgian-made product duty-free throughout EU markets.

The U.S. company could continue to book orders directly from its customer base or dealer organization in individual European countries. The difference is that the equipment would be shipped from Belgium and invoiced in Belgian francs. Initial remittances from a German customer, for instance, would be in deutsche marks and converted into Belgian francs for deposit in a commercial account in Belgium.

These funds, after expenses, would be subject to Belgian income taxes as well as Belgian remittance taxes should the U.S. firm decide to convert its profits into dollars for remittance back to the United States.

Because Belgium and the United States have bilateral treaties against double taxation, all income and remittance taxes paid to the Belgian government on taxable earnings would be eligible for U.S. foreign tax credit. Thus, the amount of tax paid to Belgium would not have to be paid again to the United States.

Establishing a Foreign Branch Office to Manage the Local Market

It would ultimately be preferable for the U.S. company to establish a more permanent presence in the EU, especially once market share increases. A simple branch office, managed by a local national (a sales manager type) with assistance from a home office representative, might initially suffice. The company's EU office would then coordinate relations with the contract manufacturer, manage the daily administrative tasks of billing and collections, handle banking, and in general manage all field operations, including sales and marketing.

Tax Ramifications

The disadvantage of the branch office concept for a small firm is mainly financial by virtue of the branch office's affiliation with the parent organization. It is not separated from the parent and/or U.S. tax law. Therefore, its Belgian income is treated in the United States as part of the parent's worldwide income and is subject to federal income taxes. The foreign tax credit helps reduce the tax burden a little, assuming a tax treaty exists (there is one with Belgium), but some taxes may nevertheless have to be paid.

Further, a branch office in many countries is not treated under the same tax laws that apply to corporations and can have the effect of creating needless additional tax burdens for the branch office in the foreign market.

Business Incorporation Abroad

Rather than establishing a branch office, the U.S. company would be better off (and it would prove no more expensive) forming a subsidiary corporation in the overseas country. The subsidiary would be treated under the same laws as other locally chartered corporations. In Belgium, and many other (but not all) countries, the foreign parent would be allowed to own 100% of the subsidiary's shares, which would give it legal and operational control.

The tax ramifications of owning a foreign "sub," as overseas subsidiaries are often called, would be to separate its earnings from the parent's worldwide income. This happens because the sub would be considered under U.S., Belgian, and international law as an independent legal entity or "persona," with the right and obligation to have its own set of financial documents (i.e., balance sheets, income statements, cash flow statements, and annual reports).

Corporate income taxes in Belgium are generally lower than those on branch offices, which are taxed as unincorporated businesses at the personal tax rate. Belgian corporate income taxes would not be picked up for U.S. federal income tax purposes. Remittances consisting of dividends and other earnings would be subject to the foreign tax credit. However, no remittance tax would be imposed by the host government as long as no remittances are made.

Sourcing U.S. Production with Foreign Contract Manufacturers

The utilization of foreign-based, low-cost, and high-quality production by U.S. companies has long been a cornerstone of the strategy of both big and small businesses. It long ago stimulated the Mexican-American Macquiladora program, which eventually led to the creation and expansion of the North American Free Trade Association. It is probably safe to say that most imports to the United States are the output of carefully designed and produced products manufactured to U.S. standards primarily to meet U.S. market needs and wants.

The U.S. equipment company that went contract manufacturing shopping in Europe in order to remain competitive there might have to do the same thing in order to survive in the United States, given the amount of excellent and low-cost foreign competition. A contract manufacturer in Mexico, perhaps an existing dealer or distributor, might offer to do the U.S. company's production in Mexico on contract, first to better penetrate the Mexican market and second to sell back in the United States.

CONCLUSION AND SUMMARY

Turnkey agreements and management contracts are often used on behalf of foreign clients by companies that specialize in the design and construction of complex facilities by weaving together skills and resources from a number of different industries spread around the world. Turnkey contractors typically are involved in the construction of hotels, airports, and petrochemical plants, which require a marriage of many different technologies. Once the contractor completes the project and trains the personnel to run it, the new facility is turned over to the foreign client for operation.

Contract manufacturing agreements are used by companies as a quick and ready means of accessing foreign markets without making a fixed asset investment in plant and equipment. Exporters that enjoy comfortable overseas market niches may be suddenly awakened by the fact that their favorite markets have formed a trade bloc with high import restrictions against their goods. Other companies that traditionally produce all their products within the United States for domestic sale may suddenly discover that rising labor, material, and overhead costs are pricing them out of their home markets. They may contract with a manufacturer in a lower cost country to produce goods there for export to and final sale in the United States.

A manufacturing company that begins to supplement its domestic operations by exporting or importing and then goes on to develop alternative approaches to maintaining its operations will find that it has gone international, whether or not it planned to. It has evolved into a business whose functions and parts have become highly interdependent with companies outside the United States.

At some point in the company's ongoing growth, it will notice that even a number of well-placed contract manufacturing arrangements will not provide an effective answer to emerging issues such as the protection of intellectual property, warranty and liability obligations, research and development, new product growth, and long-term market expansion and management.

It will then become necessary to consider more alternative strategies. In the meantime, contract manufacturing may be viewed as a low-cost, low-risk first step to test the waters prior to making a major foreign investment.

KEY TERMS AND CONCEPTS

Contract manufacturing agreement. The typical arrangement calls for a contract manufacturer to produce a fixed amount of inventory from given specifications at a negotiated total cost. A 50% prepayment of the total cost is often required; the balance is payable on completion of the production run. Contract manufacturers can agree to warehouse and sometimes distribute the finished run upon receipt of shipping instructions from the contracting firm.

Turnkey agreement. Commonly used in emerging markets during the design, procurement, assembly, and construction phases of a capital project. They are also widely used for complex industrial projects throughout the world. Companies that have the critical skills needed to coordinate the building of large capital projects (e.g., steel mills, petrochemical refining and processing facilities, resort and housing developments, commercial air terminals, etc.) become known as turnkey contractors.

QUESTIONS

15.1 A small New Jersey manufacturer of industrial solvents that has been successfully selling its products in Western Europe through import distributors in the region's major cities is about to be priced out of the market by rising transport costs and high import taxes. Discuss the following:

a. The main points to be negotiated between the New Jersey company and a local contract filler somewhere in Western Europe.

b. The organizational structure of the contract manufacturing arrangement in terms of the New Jersey company's European production and warehousing, its distribution, and the flow of funds from transactions.

15.2 Describe and explain the nature, purpose, and structure of a turnkey project. Discuss its advantages and disadvantages for all parties to the transaction.

CHAPTER 16

International Licensing and Franchising

INTRODUCTION

In this chapter, the international transfer of technology and know-how through arrangements called licensing and franchising agreements is explored. These agreements are contracts by which owners of intellectual property such as patents, trademarks, trade names, and copyrights are able to temporarily rent, through a lease or license, their rights to those assets to a licensee in return for a fee or royalty.

THE BUNDLE OF INTELLECTUAL ASSETS

Business executives normally think of assets as cash, inventories, accounts receivables, buildings, desks, motor vehicles, and a host of other tangible items that have a known purchase cost and a book value for accounting purposes. They are also familiar with the notion of "goodwill" as an asset. A company's goodwill is part of its intangible asset base, an amorphous mass of "intellectual properties" that is the real stuff that makes the business's tangible assets works. Any company that has survived for a number of years will have marketable and protectable "intellectual properties" or intangible assets. In the case of high-profile brands like Coke, protecting the company's intellectual properties can be more important than safeguarding its tangible assets from theft and vandalism.

The Corporate "Goodwill" Basket

These "goodwill" assets, or intellectual properties as they are more aptly called, consist mainly of patents, trademarks, trade names, copyrights, know-how, and so-called "curbside" recognition and appeal to which companies can claim ownership.

Once a business owner recognizes that the fruit of hard labor is a steady cash flow based on achieving hard-won market share, maintaining that market position, in part by legally protecting that "goodwill" basket, becomes a more important concern.

Intellectual Assets

As stated above, these are the patents, trademarks, trade names, and copyrights that encompass a company's technology, know-how, and position in the market.

Business Name

The mere act of initially registering a trade or business name at the city, county, or state level for tax purposes also protects against the infringement of that name without the consent of the business owner. Should a business ever contemplate becoming a player in the national marketplace, trade name registration in Washington, D.C. would be appropriate. Once that is done, it is possible to obtain trade name protection in other countries through a similar process.

Company/Product Logos and Names

Similar to the overall business name are the symbols and derived names that are used as identifiers for a company and its specific products. Sometimes referred to as trade names, they are usually called trademarks.

Hence, the Coca-Cola Company is a trade name and a trademark, because of its unique shape and spelling. So too are the words Coke and Diet Coke. The Coca-Cola Company and all its products would not be where they are today were it not for the zeal with which corporate executives and their legal staff guard these assets globally.

Copyrights

These are the word, shape, and symbol combinations that appear on labels and packaging. They should be protected against infringement nationally and internationally by registering them in all areas where the company plans to enter markets.

Patents

These are the inventions and unique innovations that a company possesses which distinguish its products from all others. Market-oriented companies like Coca-Cola, Nestle, and Disney do not rely as much on patent protection as do product- and technology-oriented companies such as Westinghouse, IBM, and Hewlett-Packard. Crossover businesses like Microsoft depend on patent, trademark, trade name, and copyright protection.

There are three types of patents: utility (product) patents, design patents, and process patents. A product patent protects an invention and the idea(s) behind the invention. Patents are also available for innovations that expand the use or application of the original device. Hence, a four-legged seating element with a backrest, the whole thing being called a "chair" and never having been in evidence before, could be eligible for a product patent. Additional patents could be granted if arms or rockers are subsequently added. The process by which the chair is made, if sufficiently unique, might be eligible for a process patent.

It is more important to protect process patients than product patents, mainly because the process governs the invention. When the Polaroid camera was developed, it was covered by more than 300 distinct process patents that took Eastman Kodak over 25 years to decipher. When Kodak finally succeeded and introduced its own instant camera in time for the U.S. bicentennial in 1976, it was saddled with a lawsuit that years later cost it over $900 million, not including legal fees, to settle.

Know-How

This is the magic that makes a company live and prosper. It is the most difficult of all intellectual properties to protect because it describes a company's valued human resources. Short of bringing back slavery, it is virtually impossible to keep people from moving from company to company, even in a small business environment.

All forms of employment contracts exist to keep valuable employees from leaving with trade and technological secrets, and all leave much to be desired. The situation becomes even murkier internationally, and adding the extra element of industrial espionage to the problem defies solution.

INTERNATIONAL LICENSING AGREEMENTS

International licensing is an arrangement whereby a foreign company, called the licensee, leases from a U.S. company (the licensor) the temporary right to use its intellectual properties for the purpose of manufacturing and sometimes selling its products in the foreign country. In return for the license, a fee or royalty is paid to the licensor, distributed throughout the life of the agreement.

Advantages of Licensing Agreements to Licensors

1. The licensor does not have to pay for production start-up costs and bear the risks associated with opening up a new market. The licensee puts up most of the capital necessary to get the overseas operation going.
2. It is an attractive option for smaller undercapitalized firms that lack the resources to finance extensive international investments.
3. It is an equally attractive option for small technology-intensive companies that may be left in a vulnerable position by contract manufacturing arrangements.
4. Licensing is often used in politically unstable areas where investors are unwilling to commit substantial financial resources to a volatile environment. Licensing agreements in such cases are usually on an up-front fee basis.

Disadvantages of Licensing Agreements to Licensors

1. A licensing agreement, especially if with an independent firm overseas, does not give the licensor control over production and marketing. This can be a problem when high quality standards must be maintained and a specific market image must be upheld.
2. The only source of income is a fee or royalty, usually paid over the life of the licensing agreement. This cash flow nowhere approaches the bottom line earnings that would normally be generated through a direct foreign investment.
3. There is the potential of losing know-how to the foreign licensee, which is in a position to absorb the licensor's technology. For example, the RCA Corporation once licensed its color video technology to a number of Japanese companies that quickly assimilated the technology, improved upon it, and then used it to enter the U.S. market.

The Perilous Nature of Licensing Agreements

Licensing agreements have been called "marriages of convenience." They can be temporarily helpful in gaining quick entry into foreign markets for technology-intensive or brand-sensitive companies that are not ready to make the expensive jump into a direct investment.

They are ideally suited for companies whose technology or brand awareness (that curbside appeal alluded to before) is so unique and so powerful that the licensor can unilaterally set the terms of the contract, front-loading it with such a heavy initial payment by the licensee that any breach would be useless.

U.S. companies transferring technology abroad to their wholly owned subsidiaries and other affiliates sometimes feel that licensing agreements can be avoided because they are engaging in a series of "in-house" transactions, the purpose of which is not to create royalty income but bottom line profits from operations. The lack of a licensing agreement in such instances creates a high level of vulnerability.

Thus, if a U.S. company owns a foreign subsidiary in Belgium that wants to produce its products for the European Union (EU) market, a licensing contract would still be in order. It would also make good sense for those intellectual assets to be registered in the EU, not in the name of the subsidiary (even if it is wholly owned by the parent) but by the parent in its own name.

The license, even among affiliates, defines the legal relationship between licensor and licensee insofar as it concerns ownership of the intellectual assets. It also helps determine how royalty revenue is to be treated by the tax authorities in the licensor's country and in the licensee's country.

The foreign subsidiary could be sold off, or it could be nationalized in short order. If the registration of the licensor's intellectual properties was made in the licensee's (sub's) name, those assets would go with the sub to its new owner, and the U.S. company could lose all rights to the use of those properties wherever the former subsidiary had been doing business.

International licensing can be an important component of doing business in other countries. Many business executives may believe that there is no need to guard their intellectual properties when simply selling finished goods overseas from a U.S. manufacturing base. Empirical evidence dictates otherwise. Negative experiences chronicled by U.S. embassies and courts of law in the United States and abroad attest to infringement of designs and products by foreign companies that started an innocent relationship with an American company as a mere import distributor. Consultation with competent legal counsel on the subject of intellectual property protection is recommended before embarking on any international selling adventure.

FRANCHISING

Franchising is similar to licensing, although it tends to involve much longer term commitments. Licensing is pursued primarily by manufacturing firms, whereas franchising is used more by more service-oriented companies such as McDonald's, Hertz, and hotel chains. Trade names, trademarks, and copyrights are more often at issue than patents.

In a franchising agreement, a franchisor sells or leases limited rights for the use of its name, know-how, and international advertising to a franchisee in return for a lump sum payment, a royalty, and a share of the franchise profits.

In contrast to many licensing agreements, the franchisee agrees to abide by strict rules in the conduct of its business. When McDonald's enters into a franchising agreement with a foreign firm, it expects that firm to run its restaurant in a manner that replicates the global corporate image, beginning with its logo and extending to its menu and customer service methodology. Small service companies will probably find franchise contracts more appropriate to their needs than straight licensing agreements.

Advantages. The advantages of franchising as an entry mode are very similar to those of licensing. Specifically, a firm is relieved of the costs and risks of opening up a foreign market on its own. Instead, the franchisee typically assumes those costs and risks. Thus, by using a franchising strategy, a service firm can build up a global presence quickly and at a low cost.

Disadvantages. The disadvantages of franchising are not as apparent in comparison to licensing. Because franchising is used mainly by non-manufacturing companies, not as much attention is paid to establishing and maintaining quality and image standards on a universal level. Only the largest franchises seriously consider the need for coordination of manufacturing and services to achieve experience curve and location curve economies.

CONCLUSION AND SUMMARY

The United States is a net exporter of technology sold as intellectual property. Royalties and fees received from foreigners have been, on average, almost four times those paid out to foreigners by U.S. firms for access to their technology.

Japan is the largest consumer of U.S. technology sold in this manner. While sales of technological know-how contribute positively to the balance sheets of U.S. firms and the U.S. economy in the short term, there has been ongoing controversy regarding the long-term consequences.

The United States has a long-standing tradition of protecting the intellectual property of its citizens. Its courts extend the same due process to the intellectual property claims of most foreign residents litigating claims in the United States. Such equal protection is not offered in many countries. The patents, trademarks, and copyrights of U.S. citizens are at times ignored in other nations, and piracy, product and design counterfeiting, and below-standard replication result in a considerable loss of revenues for American companies and sometimes lead to dangerous quality assurance problems. These problems are worsening despite increased multinational adherence to ISO standards.

Genuine efforts have been made over the years by the General Agreement on Tariffs and Trade and its successor organization, the World Trade Organization, by the Paris Convention for the Protection of Industrial Property, and by the Berne Convention for the Protection of Literary and Artistic Works to develop a multinationally enforceable judicial mechanism to deal with the infringement and theft of intellectual assets. To date, there is no uniform protection available to an individual whose invention, music, art, literary work, or computer software might be replicated and sold in many countries without compensation to the originator.

Property protection in a foreign country frequently is dependent upon the owner meeting the registration requirements of the individual country. Individual applications for patent protection, for example, must be filed in each country in which the patent owner desires protection, unless the country conforms to an international agreement. A foreign patent agent or attorney is usually needed to file an application in another country.

More recent treaties, such as the Patent Cooperation Treaty, allow applicants from member countries to file one standardized international application for use in member countries in which intellectual property protection is desired.

The U.S. Patent Office makes available a list of countries where intellectual property protection is inadequate.

1. Copyrights are inadequately protected in Brazil, China, India, Korea, Indonesia, Malaysia, Singapore, and Saudi Arabia.
2. Patents are unprotected or inadequately protected in Indonesia, Mexico, Thailand, Brazil, India, Korea, the Philippines, Singapore, Saudi Arabia, Taiwan, China, and United Arab Emirates.
3. Trademarks are inadequately protected in Brazil, India, Indonesia, the Philippines, and Thailand.
4. Product piracy and counterfeiting are recurring problems in Taiwan, especially with audiovisual material.

KEY TERMS AND CONCEPTS

Business name. The mere act of initially registering a trade or business name at the city, county, or state level for tax purposes also protects against the infringement of that name without the consent of the business owner.

Company/product logos and names. Similar to the overall business name are the symbols and derived names that are used as identifiers for a company and its specific products. Sometimes referred to as trade names, they are usually called trademarks.

Copyrights. The word, shape, and symbol combinations that appear on labels and packaging. They should be protected against infringement nationally and internationally by registering them in all areas where a company plans to enter markets.

Corporate "goodwill" basket. These "goodwill" assets, or intellectual properties as they are more aptly called, consist mainly of patents, trademarks, trade names, copyrights, know-how, and so-called "curbside" recognition and appeal to which firms can claim ownership.

Franchising agreement. A franchisor sells or leases limited rights for the use of its name, know-how, and international advertising to a franchisee in return for a lump sum payment, a royalty, and a share of the franchise profits.

Intellectual assets. The patents, trademarks, trade names, and copyrights that encompass a company's technology, know-how, and position in the market.

International licensing. An arrangement whereby a foreign company, called the licensee, leases from a U.S. company (the licensor) the temporary right to use its intellectual properties for the purpose of manufacturing and sometimes selling its products in the foreign country. In return for the license, a fee or royalty is paid to the licensor, distributed throughout the life of the agreement.

Know-how. The magic that makes a company live and prosper. It is the most difficult of all intellectual properties to protect because it describes a company's valued human resources. Short of bringing back slavery, it is virtually impossible to keep people from moving from company to company, even in a small business environment.

Patents. The inventions and unique innovations that a company possesses which distinguish its products from all others. Market-oriented companies like Coca-Cola, Nestle, and Disney do not rely as much on patent protection as do product- and technology-oriented companies such as Westinghouse, IBM, and Hewlett-Packard. Crossover businesses like Microsoft depend on patent, trademark, trade name, and copyright protection.

QUESTIONS

16.1 Discuss how technology licensing agreements differ from fast-food franchises.

16.2 Discuss the advantages and disadvantages of licensing agreements from the point of view of licensors and licensees.

16.3 Discuss the approaches a high-technology company might take in protecting itself in markets known for pirating intellectual properties.

16.4 Discuss the steps a company like Walt Disney might take to protect its intellectual assets in countries like China.

CHAPTER 17

Strategic Alliances

INTRODUCTION

This chapter illustrates how businesses can use strategic alliances in an international environment to mutual advantage.

STRATEGIC ALLIANCE DEFINED

Strategic alliances are intercorporate agreements between two or more companies designed to achieve various degrees of vertical and horizontal integration. This vertical–horizontal integration is also possible with wholly owned subsidiaries where expansion takes place through merger, acquisition, and joint ventures.

The distinguishing feature of a strategic alliance lies in its informality. Exchanges of debt and equity are rarely involved, as is the case in joint venture arrangements. Companies are not merged, nor are they acquired. The strategic alliance is a temporary marriage of key human and other resources from the partnering firms to achieve certain synergies that could not occur as quickly were the individual partners to go it alone. Once the objectives have been met, it is normal for the alliance to end.

Vertical Integration

The process of vertical integration establishes control over sources of production (e.g., supplies, technology, financing, labor, and other resources). It can also be used to establish control over distribution, marketing, sales, and after-sales service. Strategic alliances between computer software companies like Microsoft and hardware companies like IBM are common in order to more effectively link technology with information systems to be marketed to end users. They are also common in the aerospace industry, where major contractors like Boeing continually cooperate with primary vendors like United Technologies (Pratt & Whitney) for engines and other components.

Horizontal Integration

This process is intended to achieve market control through understandings or cooperation agreements designed to allocate and maintain market share. Two or more companies that sell in the same market can therefore agree to share the same sales force, the same marketing team, and pool their advertising and promotion funds into a single budgeted campaign. This is commonly done by beverage companies, restaurant chains, and the entertainment industry. Companies are ready for a strategic alliance when they come to believe that a measure of intercorporate cooperation may result in synergies that will more quickly achieve mutual or reciprocating objectives.

Strategic Alliances Are Not for Everyone

There are successful and unsuccessful strategic alliances. A business executive might first want to answer a few questions before entering into such an arrangement.

1. Is the goal being sought attainable without help from others?
2. Is the goal so important to the business that it is worth possibly compromising its future by dealing with outside partners even in a limited environment?

Strategic Alliance Formats

The simple one-time-only import/export transaction is an example of a strategic alliance between a seller in one country and a buyer in another country. There is a mutual objective, some sort of synergy will result, and the alliance will end once all goals have been achieved. The relationship between the two firms might start up again in the future and a new strategic alliance of short duration may be formed, or there may be no further contact.

Strategic alliances are generally of longer duration than a one-time transaction, but they are not intended to be long-term affairs. They are "marriages of convenience." All good strategic alliances have a "divorce clause" in the body of the contract.

Distributorship agreements are strategic alliances, as are licensing, franchise, and contract manufacturing arrangements. Two or more companies sharing in the capitalization of an investment project through corporate joint ventures would be an example of a longer term strategic alliance.

A mutual agreement to merge two enterprises can also be called a strategic alliance of sorts, as was the 1995 merger between Disney and ABC. However, that might be more appropriately described as an outright takeover in which ABC, as a subsidiary, would ultimately be absorbed as an integral part of the parent organization. By rather arbitrary definition, strategic alliances are not supposed to be of long duration.

Making Alliances Work

Four characteristics seem to govern successful strategic alliances: selection of the strategic alliance partner, the organizational structure of the alliance, management style, and harmonization of competing corporate cultures.

Selection of the Strategic Alliance Partner

It is important that prospective partners share a similar vision of what they want to achieve. If two firms approach an alliance with radically different agendas, chances are the relationship will not be harmonious, will not flourish, and will end in discord and litigation.

Strategic alliance parties should contribute equal portions to the resource pool that will produce the synergies that can make the entire joint enterprise successful. Partner inequality in terms of strengths or weaknesses may be fatal to any alliance. In other words, each participant must have valued capabilities that the other not only lacks but also appreciates.

A good strategic alliance partner is unlikely to exploit the alliance for its own ends, using the other's know-how while giving away little in return. In this respect, firms with a reputation for "fair play" probably make the best allies.

To select an appropriate partner, a firm needs to conduct some comprehensive research on potential alliance partners that can meet at least most of the criteria identified.

To increase the probability of selecting a good partner, a firm should:

1. Collect as much pertinent information on potential allies as possible.
2. Collect data from informed third parties, including firms that have had alliances with the potential partners, banks, shipping companies, government officials, and former employees.
3. Get to know the potential partner before making a binding commitment. This should include face-to-face meetings over a period of time to make sure that interests on both sides are indeed mutual.

Organizational Structure

Having selected a partner, the alliance should be structured so that the risk of losing technology and know-how to the other partner(s) is kept to a minimum.

Alliances can be designed to limit technology transfers to those exclusively specified in protocol agreements. No transfers should be allowed unless they are formally included in licensing arrangements and in fee-paid technical service contracts.

Contractual safeguards can be written into an alliance in the form of restrictive covenants for employees in order to minimize "inside" raids on intellectual properties such as patents, trademarks, trade names, copyrights, and other "goodwill" assets by partners.

All partners to an alliance can agree in advance to exchange specified skills and technologies in a mutual "open-house" atmosphere for a given time frame.

The risk of malfeasance by an alliance partner can be reduced if a firm extracts a significant credible commitment (cash in an escrow account) from partners in advance.

Strategic alliance agreements will eventually be couched in any number of structured and legally binding contracts, such as jointly financed and/or managed research and development projects, contract manufacturing, licensing and franchise arrangements, and protocol agreements that provide the umbrellas for broad-based and long-term joint ventures.

Management Style

Once a partner has been selected and an appropriate alliance structure agreed upon, the task facing a firm is to maximize its benefits from the alliance. As in all international business deals, an important factor is sensitivity to cultural differences.

Many differences in management style are due to cultural differences. Business executives, working closely with their counterparts in other countries, need to make allowances and be flexible if cross-cultural relationships are going to work for the mutual benefit of all parties concerned. It goes without saying that a U.S. company can learn as much if not more from a foreign affiliate than the overseas partner can learn from its so-called American "mentor."

The challenge of managing an international alliance successfully seems to be building interpersonal relationships between the firms' owners, managers, and workers. The resulting friendships and collegiality help build trust and create harmonious relations between the two firms.

Moreover, personal relationships foster an informal and often important line of communication between the partners by establishing a "parallel" or unofficial management network. This network can be used to address problems which may be difficult to express in a more formal context.

Harmonization

Disputes occur in all human associations, and they invariably sprout up in strategic alliances. The issue of whether one or another party is right or wrong is irrelevant, and pursuing it to a conclusion too often results in a "lose–lose" scenario for everyone, dooming the alliance to a premature end.

It is unimportant for an intra-alliance dispute to have winners or losers. It is more important to compromise the vested interests of the alliance partners through some process of harmonization.

Binding arbitration by mutually agreed upon third parties is the usual way in which arguments are handled in such situations. Internal committees can also be established through a selection methodology that guarantees impartiality in decision making. Whatever harmonization process is jointly selected, it should be built into the basic agreement that sets up the strategic alliance.

Advantages of Strategic Alliances

Strategic alliances can facilitate entry into a foreign market because the local partner will usually be familiar with the environment. Also, significant cost savings and increased profits can be realized once international synergies are established, as in the case of contract manufacturing and licensing agreements. Finally, a strategic alliance is a way to bring together complementary skills and assets that one of the partners lacks.

Disadvantages of Strategic Alliances

The major and possibly only disadvantage of strategic alliances lies in the vulnerability of a high-technology company to piracy by alliance partners during the course of collaborating on specific projects. It is difficult if not impossible for companies to determine beforehand whether alliance partners have joined forces to genuinely achieve joint objectives or whether the arrangement is merely a smoke screen for the theft of intellectual properties and know-how.

CONCLUSION AND SUMMARY

While the advantages of pursuing a strategic alliance may outweigh the disadvantages, there are some serious concerns. The minority view that strategic alliances give competitors low-cost and below-the-belt access to new technology and markets is not without merit. For example, it has been argued that Japanese successes in the machine tool, semiconductor, and video industries were a consequence of strategic alliances with unwary and overly trusting U.S. companies that initially developed the know-how and technology, only to let them slip into foreign hands through some carelessly negotiated strategic alliances.

KEY TERMS AND CONCEPTS

Horizontal integration. This process is intended to achieve market control through understandings or cooperation agreements designed to allocate and maintain market share.

Strategic alliance. An intercorporate agreement between two or more companies designed to achieve various degrees of vertical and horizontal integration. This vertical–horizontal integration is also possible with wholly owned subsidiaries, where expansion takes place through merger, acquisition, and joint ventures.

Vertical integration. The process of vertical integration establishes control over sources of production (e.g., supplies, technology, financing, labor, and other resources). It can also be used to establish control over distribution, marketing, sales, and after-sales service.

QUESTIONS

17.1 Discuss the use of strategic alliances within the environment of antitrust activity by governments to maintain open and competitive markets.

17.2 Describe and explain, with specific examples, what horizontal integration is.

17.3 Describe and explain, with specific examples, what vertical integration is.

CHAPTER 18

Foreign Investments

INTRODUCTION

In this chapter, foreign direct investments in the form of joint ventures and wholly owned subsidiaries (foreign subs) are examined. The objective is to explore the decision-making process a company should consider before making an often irreversible long-term commitment in another country.

FOREIGN DIRECT INVESTMENTS

Foreign direct investments are investments into other countries with the objective of owning partially or entirely an economic enterprise for the purpose of establishing market share and generating revenue and profits that can ultimately be transformed into stockholders' dividends. They differ from foreign portfolio investments, which are investments into financial instruments such as stocks and bonds where the objective is not to engage in business but to generate dividend income, interest income, and capital gains.

A Matter of Choice

Any company considering a direct foreign investment in which the plan is to own an equity interest (voting common stock) in a foreign enterprise will be faced with the choice of owning either all (wholly owned subsidiary) or some of the outstanding shares, with the balance being held by another corporation. Joint venture companies and wholly owned subsidiaries involve a permanent commitment by a parent to a local business environment. They cannot be as readily terminated as a strategic alliance, which has defined but limited objectives.

In general, companies seeking to capitalize on temporary marketing opportunities, which can evaporate quickly as trends, tastes, and technology change, may be better off with a short-term strategic alliance. Companies that are more fixed asset oriented (pharmaceuticals, chemicals, plastics, paper, petroleum, steel, automobiles, etc.) seem to prefer the more structured joint venture and wholly owned subsidiary routes.

A More Complex Formative Process

The legal process of forming a joint venture or a foreign subsidiary can vary among countries, but it is no more complicated than the act of incorporation might be in any state in the United States. What is more difficult is the decision-making process that must be endured before allocating corporate resources to a foreign direct investment, which by its nature involves a very long-term relationship and commitment.

Host Country Attitudes Toward Joint Ventures and Foreign Subsidiaries

Most industrial countries make few if any distinctions in their preference for one form of investment over another. Japan, Singapore, and a few other developed nations prefer incoming investments to go the joint venture route, with the foreign investor having a minority interest.

This course is followed by a number of emerging economies that restrict foreign investments to a minority interest. This leaves the joint venture as the only way to make a foreign direct investment in many countries today.

The prevailing attitude against wholly owned subsidiaries in many societies is based on the desire to neutralize any possibility of foreign economic domination that might reincarnate their colonial experience. In many of these societies, most of which are former colonies, the general feeling is that unrestricted foreign investments of a wholly owned nature, without participation of local partners, are tantamount to neocolonialism or foreign corporate imperialism.

This host government view of non-national businesses should not deter one from making a minority investment in a country. Many nations aggressively court U.S. foreign investments and have signed non-expropriation treaties with the United States which are duly enforced in international tribunals. These treaties also make the U.S. company's foreign direct investment, even if it only involves a minority interest, eligible for political risk insurance by the Overseas Private Investment Corporation.

Recent history (Chile under Salvador Allende in 1973 and Iran under the Ayatollah Khomeini in 1980) indicates that countries that have violated treaties with the United States have lost judicial decisions in international courts. Censure in these courts often leads to economic sanctions, starting with freezing overseas bank accounts.

It is also not a hard and fast rule that all developing areas discourage wholly owned subsidiaries. Each country must be investigated on its own merits. Many smaller nations, like those in the Caribbean and Central America, are eager for foreign investments and welcome subsidiary operations with lavish tax holidays.

CHARACTERISTICS OF A JOINT VENTURE

A joint venture is a highly structured and formal strategic alliance that involves two or more partners. Sometimes the alliance is strictly voluntary, but often it is mandated by the laws of the host country.

Many governments still insist on owning part of an enterprise that is funded by a foreign-based investment. In China in particular, most manufacturing plants are owned by the central government; hence, a joint venture relationship with the Chinese government is unavoidable. The Beijing government has created special offices throughout China, charging them with the mission of helping foreign companies of all sizes jumpstart their enterprises in the country. Governments of many other countries provide similar services, even where joint ventures are not required.

Equity Distribution

Joint ventures vary in their flexibility and participation by the stockholding partners. There can be two principal partners, each owning 50% of the voting common stock, or there can be several partners. The protocol joint venture agreement can require an equal sharing of the enterprise's capitalization, or the partners may agree to another formula (e.g., one party provides technology and scarce resources and the other(s) supplies labor, management, land, and other needed assets).

Earnings Distribution

Earnings distribution among the joint venture partners is generally but not always determined by each participant's contribution. As in ownership breakdown, distribution formulas vary. Two important factors which influence dividend policy and distribution are local restrictions on remittances (more of a problem in developing areas, where foreign exchange reserves may be limited) and issues of international taxation, not the least of which is the impact of income tax holidays granted by host governments to foreign direct investors.

Joint Ventures and Small Business

Smaller companies that already enjoy a successful distributorship arrangement with a local company overseas will often share a new investment with the distributor, perhaps to take the business to new enterprises or perhaps to jointly participate in building a manufacturing facility in the distributor's market. It is also not unusual for a U.S. company, in order to protect sources being supplied by an overseas contract manufacturer, to invest in the existing foreign business and become a joint venture partner in the process.

This has been the growth experience of Crate & Barrel, a large chain retailer of housewares made mostly in foreign countries. Starting as a single-store outlet in Chicago over 25 years ago, Crate & Barrel has grown into a $500 million global business with franchises all over the world. It controls its supply sources by turning many of its foreign vendors into strategic alliances via the joint venture route.

Advantages of Joint Ventures

There are numerous advantages to establishing joint ventures. A company is able to marshal the joint venture partner's knowledge of the host country's culture, language, and political and business system. When McDonald's decided to expand to Japan, it selected as a joint venture partner a local real estate developer that was also well connected in Japan's food industry. A few years later, when Toys-R-Us followed McDonald's to Japan, it selected the same developer as a partner to give it access to the country's more desirable shopping areas.

The Mennen Company, back in the 1960s, when it was still a minor player in the toiletries industry, turned an import distributorship agreement with a much larger French company called Loreal into a joint venture in France for the purpose of producing and selling Skin Bracer and Speed Stick deodorant in European markets.

The Mennen Company also parlayed initial import/export agreements with distributors in Venezuela, Colombia, and elsewhere in Latin America and the Caribbean first into licensing agreements and then into joint venture arrangements, many of which lasted until the 1994 acquisition of Mennen by Colgate-Palmolive.

Disadvantages of Joint Ventures

There are two major disadvantages concerning the use of joint ventures. First, there is always the risk of losing control of assets dedicated to the investment project to the joint venture partner. This is a fundamental problem with all strategic alliances. Control over dedicated assets, policies, and programs is never as absolute, as in the case of a wholly owned subsidiary.

Second, joint ventures do not always give the joint venture partner the flexibility necessary to wage global commercial wars with other major competitors because the decision-making process to allocate financial resources to specific R&D and marketing targets has to be shared with other partners that may not share the same global objectives.

WHOLLY OWNED SUBSIDIARIES

In some instances, an international business owner would prefer to have full equity participation. It may seem that a wholly owned subsidiary would involve too much of a challenge for a small business, but it may, in fact, represent a more viable alternative as a foreign market entry mode than a strategic alliance.

Small retail/wholesale shops that market reproduction antiques and fine art often own their foreign sources of production outright. It gives them the advantage of controlling their own supply sources in a more absolute fashion. It also gives them the advantage of being able to market the services of the foreign "atelier," as it may be called on a contract manufacturing basis, to other clients.

The machine shop industry is a highly segmented part of the U.S. economy that is dominated by large numbers of small companies doing subcontract work for major accounts like Boeing or General Electric. More frequently than ever, the design and prototype work is done by the machine shop in the United States and then farmed out to small subs abroad where labor and overhead costs are less and skills are high.

Yacht-chartering companies that maintain fleets of vessels in warm-climate countries for the use of their clients from cold-weather locations are generally small companies incorporated in Eastern Seaboard states. Most of their offshore fleets are managed by foreign subsidiaries located in any number of Caribbean or South Pacific countries.

The retail/wholesale outlets that market reproduction antiques and fine art, the machine shops, and the yacht-chartering firms have five qualities in common: they tend to be small, they must keep costs down in order to survive, they serve niche markets in the United States and abroad, quality control is critical, and superior service is of the essence.

If a small company is dependent on all five characteristics, the wholly owned subsidiary route may be not merely a viable alternative—it may be the only way to go.

Foreign Subsidiaries and How They Work

A wholly owned subsidiary abroad comes into existence when a business in Germany, Grenada, the Bahamas, or anywhere else is incorporated in that country, with all of its shares owned by residents (U.S.) domiciled (living) outside the nation of incorporation.

Thus, a U.S. company that owns 100% of the stock of a company in Grenada has a "sub" in that country. The U.S. company takes on the colloquial moniker of "parent." The creation of a foreign sub can be from start-up (e.g., registering and capitalizing a new company in a country). A U.S. firm can also acquire an existing company and use it as a base of operations.

Advantages of a Wholly Owned Subsidiary

There are two major advantages to using wholly owned subsidiaries as an entry mode. First, it preserves and transfers a firm's comparative technological advantage to the foreign area that can offer expanded revenue opportunities by catering simultaneously to its own market as well as to several larger markets through its own export sale of goods and services. Second, a sub gives the parent the tight control over operations in different countries that is necessary in many industries dominated by small businesses.

Disadvantages of a Wholly Owned Subsidiary

The first disadvantage of wholly owned subsidiaries is that the parent must bear the total cost of the sub enterprise. The second is a human resource challenge. Someone has to be selected to manage the local sub, and employees must be hired.

CONCLUSION AND SUMMARY

Large corporations have a natural preference for foreign direct investments in the form of wholly owned subsidiaries. The subsidiary route offers maximum equity ownership and management control in overseas markets. However, certain investments are so large and so complex that they require an association of several companies in order to realize required synergies. Formalized joint venture arrangements are necessary in these cases.

As investments into countries where governments own and operate economic enterprise increase, the joint venture route is the principal alternative to creating a wholly owned subsidiary in such a political environment. Many countries that experienced a negative colonial history wish to avoid what they commonly call a "neocolonial" relationship with foreign investors that might be locally construed as replacing their former colonial overloads. In such cases, a joint venture arrangement with local corporate partners is one way to minimize the onus of possible foreign domination.

KEY TERMS AND CONCEPTS

Foreign direct investment and foreign portfolio investment. An investment into another country with the objective of owning partially or entirely an economic enterprise for the purpose of establishing market share and generating revenue and profits that can ultimately be transformed into stockholders' dividends. Foreign direct investments differ from foreign portfolio investments, which are investments into financial instruments such as stocks and bonds, where the objective is not to engage in business but to generate dividend income, interest income, and capital gains.

Joint venture. A highly structured and formal strategic alliance that involves two or more partners. Sometimes the alliance is strictly voluntary, but often it is mandated by the laws of the host country.

Wholly owned subsidiary. A wholly owned subsidiary abroad comes into existence when a business in Germany, Grenada, the Bahamas, or anywhere else is incorporated in that country with all (better than 75%) of its shares owned by residents (U.S.) domiciled (living) outside the nation of incorporation. Thus, a U.S. company that owns 100% of the stock of a company in Grenada has a "sub" in that country. The U.S. company becomes popularly known as the "parent" and the overseas entity becomes called the "sub." The creation of a foreign sub can be from start-up (e.g., registering and capitalizing a new company in a country). A U.S. firm can also acquire an existing company and use it as a base of operations.

QUESTIONS

18.1 A large U.S.-based telecommunications company wants to become a key player in China's growing markets. It is interested in manufacturing equipment for use in China as well as for export to other countries. It also wants to offer general telecommunication services to individuals, business, and government clients in China. Discuss the possible entry strategies the company should consider.

18.2 A large U.S.-based pharmaceutical company wants to become a key player in China's growing markets. It is interested in producing over-the-counter and prescription pharmaceuticals for consumption in China and other countries. Discuss the possible entry strategies it should consider.

18.3 A major industrial design and engineering company wants to establish itself in Indonesia to gain better access to the markets of Southeast Asia. Discuss the possible entry strategies it should consider.

PART III

Policy and Institutions

CHAPTER 19

Trade Regulation
and Restrictions

INTRODUCTION

In this chapter, the regulatory environment of international trade and its impact on the conduct of international business transactions are examined.

It is generally accepted that national governments have a responsibility to guard their countries' borders. They also have an obligation to raise revenues in the form of taxes to fund their roles as governing bodies. Finally, governments, in promoting and maintaining the common good of the national communities they serve, participate in the regulation and management of economic enterprise.

Large and small companies venturing out into business relationships abroad that are unaware of these laws and government policies impacting trade and investments can suffer significant losses.

EXPORT RESTRICTIONS

Restrictions fall into three categories: export taxes, export quotas, and national security restrictions. The United States is among the few countries that impose a minimum of export restrictions.

Exporters are thus often caught by surprise when informed that there may be a problem with the goods they wish to sell overseas. Unfortunately, they are sometimes brought to task only after the items have been shipped and paid for.

National Security Restrictions

National security restrictions are restrictions and/or general prohibitions on exports of goods whose use abroad is contrary to U.S. policy interests. For example, a general prohibition by the U.S. government against the export sale of RIBS (rigid inflatable boats—small inflatable vessels with hard fiberglass bottoms used by most people as pleasure craft and yacht tenders) is intended to prevent their use for terrorist or military purposes by consumers in designated countries.

The government therefore classifies RIBS as dual-purpose products, and exporters are required to apply for specific export permits from the U.S. Departments of State, Commerce, and Defense. A point of interest is that these three agencies do not always agree with one another. The result is that while one or two departments may approve a sale, the third might not, creating a bureaucratic nightmare and snafu for exporters.

Other government agencies, such as the Department of Agriculture and the Food and Drug Administration, may be called on to rule on certain food and pharmaceutical products whose exportation may be in violation of U.S. laws designed to ration exports of merchandise considered to be in short supply.

The U.S. government also imposes general prohibitions on exports to specific countries, such as Syria, Cuba, and North Korea, to mention a few. An updated list of restricted countries is usually available from any U.S. Department of Commerce district office.

Export controls are randomly and only occasionally exercised by the U.S. Department of Commerce and U.S. Customs at the country's various departure points. It is, therefore, the exporter's obligation to determine ahead of time, through freight forwarders, carriers, and direct prior contact with the appropriate government authority, the need for specific export permits or licenses.

Export Quotas

Export quotas are restrictions on the quantity of product that can be exported out of a country. The purpose of these quotas is to conserve scarce resources by ensuring that enough stocks or inventories are retained to meet domestic needs before meeting foreign demand. The United States imposes relatively few export quotas. Most are found levied on costly and one-of-a-kind specialty products manufactured by the chemical-processing industry for particular uses and customers, where the intent was not to produce and sell for a general global market.

The more general use of an export quota is to allocate supplies of scarce commodities in the global marketplace. Some of these emerge as production quotas, similar to those periodically attempted by the oil-producing countries through OPEC. Others take the shape of voluntary restraints (VOLs), bilateral agreements to restrain exports of certain products between two trading countries. Informal agreements between the United States and Japan in the early 1990s to limit Japanese automobile exports to the United States could be categorized as VOLs.

Export Taxes

Governments do not as a rule tax their own exports, because that reduces their competitiveness in world markets. U.S. taxes on exports have not been an issue because of their rarity. There is also no internationally accepted protocol for the creation and classification of export taxes, as there is for import taxes (import tariffs or duties). In general, export taxes are imposed by governments on an ad hoc basis not so much to prevent exports but to generate revenue or to encourage value-adding changes to a product before exportation.

Brazilian export taxes on coffee exports are a case in point. The Brazilian government imposes low export taxes on many of its exports merely as a mild revenue-producing medium to defray the costs of maintaining port facilities.

However, the tax on green (unroasted) coffee exports is higher than the tax on semi-roasted coffee beans. The intent is to encourage Brazilian exporters to install processing facilities (to dry off and slightly roast the beans before shipment) in distressed parts of port cities. The desired result is to generate economic enterprise in economically depressed areas, where unemployment is traditionally high.

IMPORT RESTRICTIONS

Import restrictions fall into three general categories: taxes, quotas, and restrictions based on product standards or specifications. Taxes on imports are commonly known as import duties or import tariffs and are "value-added" or "price-plus" almost by definition. Import quotas are a restriction on the quantity of product that may be brought into a country. Restrictions based on industry-prescribed and government-sanctioned standards and specifications can actually prevent any quantity of product subject to such scrutiny from being imported.

Import Taxes

Taxes on imports are value-added excise taxes and exist in three formats: a percentage-based value-added tariff, a fixed-rate tariff, and a combination percentage and fixed-rate tariff. The emphasis in the United States is mostly on the first and second formats.

Ad-Valorem (Value-Added) Import Taxes

A percentage-based value-added tax is imposed as a given percentage over either the FOB (free on board) port-of-embarkation selling price of the imported merchandise or the CIF (cost, insurance, and freight) port-of-entry price. The United States generally levies import taxes on the FOB vessel selling price. Most other countries impose their tariffs on the CIF selling price.

If an item has an FOB Vessel, Bremen, Germany, price equivalent of US$100,000 and the United States imposes a 10% import tax, then the tax would amount to $10,000, payable by the importer. If the basis for the duty assessment is CIF New York (FOB Vessel, Bremen plus freight and insurance costs to move the goods from Bremen to New York, assuming these costs amount to $10,000), a 10% import tax on $110,000 CIF New York would be $11,000, payable by the importer. The landed cost (CIF duty paid cost) to the importer would increase from $110,000 in the first case to $111,000 in the second case.

Fixed-Rate Import Taxes

A fixed-rate tariff is a tax imposed on the weight, measure, or volume of the item being brought in. Imported lumber in log, strip, or panel form is usually taxed on a linear foot basis (e.g., $0.10 per foot). Imported fruits and vegetables tend to be taxed on a weight basis (so much per pound or kilo), whereas liquids are usually taxed based on their volume (so much per liter or gallon). In general, low-value goods are taxed on a fixed-rate basis, whereas higher value merchandise (automobiles and computers) are subject to an ad-valorem percentage tax.

Combination Ad-Valorem–Fixed-Rate Import Taxes

These taxes are generally imposed by governments of countries with a low internal or domestic tax base. Import tax revenues are counted on to significantly widen a country's narrow income tax base. Some jurisdictions impose an "either–or" tax, whichever brings in the most tax revenue. Other jurisdictions impose the two taxes simultaneously (i.e., a tax on the weight, measure, or volume of the item plus a tax on its stated value).

Import Tax Systems

There are three basic import tax structures in the world today: single-column, double-column, and triple-column systems. These allow countries to impose different taxes on an import depending on its point of origin. They also permit countries to extend most favored nation (MFN) status to trading partners with which they enjoy friendly economic and political relations.

Single-Column Tariffs

These are now a rarity. A country with a single-column structure imposes a flat tax on an import irrespective of its point of origin. Such a country would have no preferential agreements with other countries or groups of nations.

Double-Column Tariffs

The United States, until its entry into the North American Free Trade Association (NAFTA), was basically a double-column tariff country. It imposed a "general" or "non-preferential" rate on imports originating in countries with which it had no particularly special relationship ("Column One"). It then placed a lower or a "preferential" rate on imports originating in areas with which it enjoyed a "special" or MFN status ("Column Two").

Hence, if product X originated in a "Column One" country, it might be subject to a 30% import levy; if that same product originated in a "Column Two" nation with MFN status, like the United Kingdom, it might hypothetically be subject to a 10% tax.

Triple-Column Tariffs

The United States, and many other industrial and industrializing countries that have formed trade blocs such as NAFTA, MERCOSUR, and the European Union (EU), operate under triple-column tariff systems. Some can even be said to have four-column systems.

Triple-column tariff countries still maintain a non-preferential column (highest duties); they also have a preferential column (lower duties) for friendly, non-trade-bloc nations, and they extend the lowest or sometimes zero taxes on goods produced by other trade bloc member countries. In addition, these countries may extend special duty-free status to many products made in politically friendly Third World countries, thus bringing to life a "fourth" column.

Different bilateral and multilateral tariff agreements, along with globalization of manufacturing, provide importers with opportunities to select foreign suppliers on the basis of lowest cost, lowest import restrictions, highest quality, and best service. For example, the U.S. machinery importer discussed above, bringing in a piece of equipment from Germany at an FOB Bremen price of $100,000, which would be subject to a preferential 10% import tax ($10,000) upon entry into the United States, could consider importing the equipment from the German company's affiliate in Mexico. Because Mexico, the United States, and Canada are all members of NAFTA, no U.S. import tax would apply on the Mexican-made machinery.

Similarly, a U.S. textile goods manufacturer might have trouble exporting to EU countries like France, which impose relatively high import taxes on non-member goods. However, the company could shift production through a contract manufacturing arrangement with a specialty textile producer in an ACP (African-Caribbean-Pacific) Conference country (whose members have duty-free access to EU markets) like Senegal, Barbados, or Sri Lanka. The American company would probably benefit from a lower cost production platform in Senegal and would see that lower cost output enter European markets duty-free, thereby enhancing its competitiveness.

Import Quotas

These restrictions on the quantity of product that can be imported from overseas often create great difficulties for importers that depend entirely on offshore sources for their supplies. The rationale for import quotas stems from a desire to protect domestic producers from being overwhelmed by foreign competition. This is accomplished by dividing market share on an allocation basis.

The U.S. cotton quota imposes quantity limits on foreign cotton-growing countries to protect domestic growers and to allocate market shares as fairly as possible to overseas producers. A problem arises when countries export cotton-polyester blends to U.S. importers. All cotton and cotton blend imports come to a temporary but troublesome halt when cotton quota limits are unintentionally breached.

It is alleged by some commodity-dependent (coffee, cocoa, etc.) exporting countries that import quotas levied by industrial nations are often punitive. Even if not punitive, they have the same effect by severely limiting open market access. Such issues have been repeatedly addressed by organizations like the General Agreement on Tariffs and Trade (GATT) and its successor, the World Trade Organization (WTO), with few tangible results.

Technical Restrictions

Technical restrictions are restrictions imposed by governments on imports that allegedly do not meet local standards. Some are legitimately intended to maintain high quality standards, but many are used as a means of restricting imports, even when the superiority of the imported item can be demonstrated. Europeans have historically made market entry difficult for U.S. telecommunications companies by insisting on technical specifications that can be impossible to meet.

Restrictions based on a product's standards and/or technical specifications are used principally by competing industrial countries.

CONCLUSION AND SUMMARY

Considerable work has been done over the years by GATT and its successor organization, the WTO, to reduce trade restrictions among nations. This has resulted in an approximately 50% lowering of import levies throughout the world. The two major obstacles to barrier-free trade today remain non-tariff restrictions such as quotas and the formation of regional trade groups like the EU, MERCOSUR, and NAFTA, which often erect common tariff walls against imports from non-member countries. A key objective for multilateral trade negotiations in the future may be to reconcile the regional interests of trade blocs with the broader goals of trade without barriers on a global scale.

KEY TERMS AND CONCEPTS

Export quotas. Restrictions on the quantity of product that can be exported from a country. The purpose of these quotas is to conserve scarce resources by ensuring that enough stocks or inventories are retained to meet domestic needs before meeting foreign demand.

Export taxes. Imposed on an ad hoc basis by governments not so much to prevent exports but to generate revenue or encourage value-adding changes to a product before it is exported.

Import quotas. Restrictions on the quantity of product that can be imported from overseas. They often create great difficulties for importers that depend entirely on offshore sources for their supplies. The rationale for import quotas stems from a desire to protect domestic producers from being overwhelmed by foreign competition. This is accomplished by dividing market share on an allocation basis.

Import taxes. Value-added excise taxes. They exist in three formats: a percentage-based value-added tariff, a fixed-rate tariff, and a combination percentage and fixed-rate tariff. The emphasis in the United States is mostly on the first and second formats.

Technical restrictions. Restrictions imposed by governments on imports that allegedly do not meet local standards. Some are legitimately intended to maintain high quality standards, but many are used as a means of restricting imports, even when the superiority of the imported item can be demonstrated.

QUESTIONS

19.1 Discuss, with specific examples, the arguments for and against import taxes.

19.2 Explain how import quotas function and how they can be used to restrain trade among nations.

19.3 Explain, with examples, how import quotas can be used by high-income countries as a political tool to control lower income trading partners.

19.4 Describe and explain, with examples, the structure and rationale of multiple-column tariff systems.

19.5 Describe and explain, with examples, the purpose of export quotas.

19.6 Describe and explain, with examples, the purpose of export taxes.

CHAPTER 20

Investment Restrictions

INTRODUCTION

In this chapter, the regulatory environment of international investments and its impact on the conduct of international business transactions are examined. Beyond governments' responsibility to regulate trade is said to lie an obligation to guide investments into areas of economic activity seen necessary to promote economic growth and development. Governments fulfill this obligation through a mix of fiscal (tax) and monetary (interest rate and exchange control manipulation) policy.

INVESTMENT RESTRICTIONS

Today, countries impose restrictions on both outgoing and incoming investments. They impose restrictions on the types of investments that can be made, as well as investments made by overseas affiliates in third-party nations. Both foreign direct investments and foreign portfolio investments are impacted by government restrictions, many of which conflict with one another.

When Political Relations Sour

A sudden deterioration in bilateral political relations often leads to one country's nationalization without compensation of locally based assets owned or controlled by residents of the adversarial nation. Thus, when

Bayer of Germany had its assets in the United States seized by federal marshals in World War I, it lost its right to the use of the name "Bayer" in the United States. It was not until 1995 that Bayer's control and ownership of the name were firmly re-established.

The U.S. assets of the General Analine & Film Corporation (GAF), another German company, were expropriated at the outset of World War II and never returned. Its equity was subsequently sold by the U.S. government to American residents.

Expropriation or nationalization of foreign-owned assets such as plant and equipment, inventories, accounts receivables, intellectual properties, bank accounts, and private residences is common practice throughout the world when nations begin dueling internationally. Properties may occasionally be restored, but most of the time they are not. The probability of nationalization is one of the more important risk factors to be weighed when engaging in cross-border enterprises.

Regulating Outgoing Investments

Governments tend to classify other countries as either "friendly" or "unfriendly" and "low risk" or "high risk." The United States in particular prohibits investments in countries such as Libya and Cuba, which it regards as definitely "unfriendly."

"Friendly High-Risk" Countries

The United States encourages investments into China, despite the fact that the latter is not particularly "friendly" and carries out policies that often appear at odds with U.S. domestic and foreign policy. Its contradictory posture with China is probably explainable in the sense that long-term U.S. foreign policy objectives seek to preserve a global balance of power by helping China's economy develop and somehow turn that country into an ally.

The United States also encourages investments into Mexico, a practice that started with the Macquiladora program and is now gathering steam under the North American Free Trade Association. The geographical proximity of Mexico makes it important for the United States to partially sponsor Mexico's economic growth and development through industrialization, even though the political risk of doing business may be high, given the unrest and corruption that exist there.

U.S. investments are encouraged in a number of African and Asian countries (Zaire, the Republic of South Africa, and Indonesia), again because the development of these areas is considered important to maintaining long-term political stability in a larger geographic region. U.S. investments are not restricted, even with the prior knowledge that the countries can be easily destabilized.

The same prevailing attitude governs the flow of private investments from the United States to the emerging markets of the former Soviet Union and Eastern Europe. Their economic growth and development are seen as a means of preserving regional peace and stability.

"Friendly Low-Risk" Countries

These include the more mature industrial and post-industrial countries (e.g., the members of the European Union, Canada, Japan, Australia, New Zealand, and a small handful of other nations). No government incentives are needed for these countries, where political risk is generally low (at least since 1945), and, of course, that is where the majority of new investments go each year.

"Unfriendly High-Risk" Countries

These nations include Iran, Iraq, and Libya, with which trade and investments, except under severely circumscribed instances, are prohibited by the U.S. government. A persistent antagonistic relationship with these states makes economic cooperation difficult and hazardous.

"Unfriendly Low-Risk" Countries

Some countries, such as Cuba and Nicaragua, have maintained an adversarial relationship with the United States but do not constitute a significant military or political threat. Investments by U.S. residents into these countries are either prohibited or severely restricted.

Regulating Incoming Investments

The United States imposes little federal regulation on investments from abroad except to issue somewhat ambiguous definitions of what constitutes a "made-in-the-USA" product as opposed to a "foreign-made" product. There have also been attempts to define by statute an "American" company as opposed to an "American subsidiary" of a foreign-based corporation. The general attitude seems to be "live and let live" as long as the incoming investment creates a net economic benefit for the impacted region.

Investment Incentives

Individual states often offer attractive incentives to foreign investors to establish facilities in their locales. These practices lured foreign automobile companies, for example, to build manufacturing plants in the United States, contributing to the economic growth of specific regions.

Investment incentive strategies in the form of tax abatements and holidays are not unique to the United States. They are practiced by most countries. They range from import quota and import tax exemptions on imported raw materials to tax holidays that spare new companies from paying income taxes for a number of years.

Regulation of Profits and Dividends

These are often regulated for the purpose of encouraging investors to plow the fruits of investments back into the local economy. Most countries, including the United States, impose exit taxes on earnings taken out of the host country and remitted back to foreign stockholders, joint venture partners, and licensors. These taxes vary with the nature of the local income earned.

Many countries impose restrictions that impact the exchange rate used to convert a local currency back into the investor's home exchange. These exchange control regulations are most common in countries faced with chronic shortages of hard convertible currencies.

Regulating Portfolio Investments

There are few restrictions on incoming portfolio investments. Naturally, most countries are anxious to receive funding in one form or another. Most of the restrictions are on the repatriation of dividend and interest income and on capital.

High-income countries. Most industrialized countries impose few restrictions on remittances, except for revenue taxes. More stringent restrictions may be imposed when a country experiences temporary foreign currency shortages.

Lower income countries. Lower income countries that are eager to retain the proceeds of portfolio investments within their borders arm themselves with elaborate exchange control restrictions by limiting the amount of money that can be taken out of the country. These restrictions also serve to limit capital flight during a financial panic or period of high inflation.

The Multinational Reach of National Laws

All countries attempt to control the overseas activities of their resident corporations as well as those of their private residents. Larger, more powerful nations like the United States are better positioned to influence the foreign activities of their residents than are smaller, less powerful states.

The practice of carrying the legal weight of U.S. laws beyond national borders goes back to the early days of the republic. In more recent years, it has been reflected in the passage and implementation of a number of laws specifically designed to curtail trade and investments by U.S. companies and their overseas affiliates in areas specifically prohibited by U.S. law. Laws have also been passed to mandate codes of corporate conduct in a variety of practices, ranging from human rights to bribery and environmental degradation.

"Trading with the Enemy" Prohibitions

A 1996 law passed by the U.S. Congress tightened the general embargo on doing business with Cuba. It is the latest in a series of laws enacted by the government to prevent not only American-based companies but all companies throughout the world from doing business with Cuba.

Many countries have protested that the law is arbitrary, capricious, and discriminatory, as well as a possible violation of international law. It is currently being contested within the World Trade Organization. A ruling by that body is expected before the end of 1997.

It should be noted, however, that, viewed from the broader perspective of international affairs over time, the law is no better or no worse than the infamous "Arab embargo" against companies doing business with Israel. The embargo had little effect and has proven over the years to be an embarrassment.

Trade Retaliation Laws

The "Tariff of Abominations" (passed by the U.S. Congress in the 1830s), the Hawley-Smoot Tariff of 1932, and a number of other acts affirm the de-facto right of the United States to retaliate economically against its commercial neighbors. Again, this is a right exercised by all countries that can afford to do so without worrying about retaliation.

The right of retaliation was reaffirmed through the Omnibus Trade and Competitiveness Act of 1988, which was renewed by executive order in March 1994. Briefly, the law mandates economic retaliation against countries that, after negotiation, continue to maintain "unwarranted" trade surpluses with the United States.

"Conduct Unbecoming..."

The United States, like many countries, also attempts to legislate morality and ethics. This was the intent of the Foreign Corrupt Practices Act (FCPA), passed by the Congress in 1977 in the aftermath of the Watergate era.

The FCPA, in amended form, remains on the books today. While it condones "grease" payments by American executives to foreign function-aries to accelerate cargo clearance procedures and other clerical chores, it imposes high criminal and civil penalties on the time-honored practice of bribing foreign government officials in order to obtain a favorable business decision.

Comments about the FCPA by international businesses have been generally negative. The law has been accused of costing U.S. companies billions of dollars in potential revenues due to prospects lost because of an inability to bribe foreign government officials.

It is difficult to determine how much of this commentary is quanti-fiable fact and how much is hyperbole. In all fairness, attempts by foreign residents to influence government decisions in the United States through bribery would at the very least generate scandal, if not an official inquiry followed by high-profile court action. The FCPA's theme can best be summarized as follows: Do not do abroad that which ought not to be done at home!

CONCLUSION AND SUMMARY

Foreign direct and foreign portfolio investments, along with the interna-tional trade of goods and services, are the principal vehicles of economic growth and trade. Their movement also has important political and social consequences apart from their economic ramifications. Therefore, their control by governments is a cardinal feature of the foreign and domestic policies of nations. In general, U.S. foreign policy has been to use commerce as a means of enhancing national power beyond U.S. borders and minimizing foreign influence within U.S. borders. While this posture may betray an overzealous ethnocentric bent, it does seem to fall within a country's right to pursue its own self-interest to maximize its national security.

KEY TERMS AND CONCEPTS

Expropriation/nationalization. A takeover of ownership of foreign-owned assets (such as plant and equipment, inventories, accounts receivable, intellectual properties, bank accounts, and private residences) by a host government.

Regulating incoming investments. The United States imposes little federal regulation on investments from abroad except to issue somewhat ambiguous definitions of what constitutes a "made-in-the-USA" product as opposed to a "foreign-made" product. There have also been attempts to define by statute an "American" company as opposed to an "American subsidiary" of a foreign-based firm.

Regulating outgoing investments. Governments tend to classify all other countries as either "friendly" or "unfriendly" and "low risk" or "high risk." The United States in particular prohibits investments in countries such as Libya and Cuba, which it regards as definitely "unfriendly."

QUESTIONS

20.1 The manager of the foreign subsidiary of a U.S.-based company makes a sizable contribution to the election campaign of a local politician in the host country. Discuss the situation in terms of a possible violation of local law as well as the Foreign Corrupt Practices Act.

20.2 Discuss the protection a U.S.-owned foreign investment may have in a country that suddenly nationalizes all industries.

20.3 Discuss how realistic an objective a company's globalization efforts may be in view of individual nations seeking to control trade and investments to meet their own particular ends.

CHAPTER 21

U.S. Policies:
Taxation and Related Programs

INTRODUCTION

U.S. trade and investment policies have tended to encourage the nation to export, import, invest overseas, and invite investments from abroad. The general official attitude has been, since the country's beginnings, that trade and investments are good for the economy in an overall long-term sense. This chapter analyzes U.S. government policies and programs embodied in a number of tax laws that specifically support private sector involvement in international trade and investments.

INTERNATIONAL TAXATION:
WHO PAYS TAXES TO WHOM?

Corporate residents of a country, like private residents, pay income taxes and a number of other types of taxes, ranging from use and sales taxes to property taxes. How much in total taxes is paid and to whom the taxes are paid depend largely on where the business is located and where a specific transaction takes place.

The Concept of Residency

Who pays taxes to whom is determined by the concept of residency. The expression "resident" in the United States has nothing to do with citizenship, although citizenship is used in courts as prima facie evidence to establish one's residency. Residency refers to an individual's or a business's physical domicile, or where one "lives" for most of a calendar year. The term "most of the calendar year" is understood in many countries to mean more than 180 days or more than 270 days, depending on the type of tax treatment being sought.

The U.S. Worldwide Income Rule

Under U.S. law, a resident of the United States must pay taxes on all income earned in the United States and in other countries. In other words, a U.S. resident must pay federal income taxes on worldwide income.

A U.S.-based company that consummates an export sale to a customer in a foreign country will pay, with exception allowed by law, the same tax is if the sale were made to a customer located in the United States. Therefore, Hoffman LaRoche, a pharmaceutical company in New Jersey and a wholly owned subsidiary of its Swiss parent, would pay the same income taxes on a sale to its parent as Johnson & Johnson, an American-owned company, would if it sold something to Hoffman LaRoche in Switzerland. Both Hoffman LaRoche and Johnson & Johnson are residents of the United States, and their shipments to Switzerland are recorded as exports from the United States to Switzerland. Profits on these sales are normally subject to payment of U.S. federal income taxes.

Taxation of Foreign Branch Offices

Companies often open unincorporated offices, called branch offices, overseas before capitalizing a formal subsidiary or joint venture corporation. While these offices may be taxed by the host government as a local resident, they are nevertheless treated as part of the U.S. company's American persona. This means that the foreign branch's income is subject to U.S. federal income taxation, just as it would be in the foreign country.

A foreign branch that is merely an unincorporated business abroad is considered in the same manner as an unincorporated business in the United States, either as a sole proprietorship or a partnership. It has no separate identity from that of its owner. It merely fills out a tax form (Schedule C for proprietorships) which is appended to the owner's personal 1040 income tax return. Different forms are needed to report taxable foreign branch income, but the net effect is the same. Foreign branch operating revenues are taxed as part of the U.S. company's worldwide earnings. If the U.S. company is a corporation, its foreign branch earnings become part of its U.S. corporate tax return.

Taxation of Foreign Subsidiaries and Joint Ventures

The formation of a foreign subsidiary, or a joint venture, in a foreign country creates an entirely different taxation scenario for a U.S. company. A new legal persona in another country has "come to life," so to speak. It bears no relationship to the U.S. parent or joint venture partner except through equity participation and perhaps through the lease of intellectual assets.

A U.S. firm's worldwide income in the case of its foreign direct investments in overseas subsidiaries and joint ventures takes the form of dividends, royalties, service and franchise fees, etc. This foreign source income is, of course, subject to U.S. taxation. However, the operating revenues of the local enterprise are taxed only by the host government, which may also impose a special remittance tax on those cash flows claimed by the U.S. owners or partners for repatriation back home.

Tax Treaties and Double Taxation

It is useful to remember that all firms doing business in other countries are vulnerable to double taxation unless a bilateral tax treaty is in place. Foreign branch offices are most obviously affected because their taxable income could be payable twice, in the host country and again in the United States.

Thus, an American branch office in Belgium can pay a 30% income tax there, not to mention a remittance tax on repatriated after-tax earnings, and then find its earnings also subject to taxation by the U.S. Internal Revenue Service (IRS). Fortunately, Belgium and the United States have a bilateral tax treaty in place. This allows the U.S. company to apply for a foreign tax credit to offset the taxes paid in Belgium. With some luck and creative accounting, the company's final and total tax bill might be no higher than if it were doing business only in the United States.

Tax Treaties

The U.S. government does not have tax treaties in place with all countries. Further, each tax treaty is individually tailored as opposed to crafted from a general template. Consequently, it is necessary for companies and their tax specialists to have a working knowledge of the particulars of a foreign country's tax laws and the international taxation relations that exist between that nation and the United States.

Tax Incentive Programs

There are both direct tax incentives and indirect tax incentives to encourage U.S. firms to engage in international business. Direct incentives are intended to promote increased U.S. exports and are couched in the Foreign Sales Corporation Act of 1983.

Indirect incentives impact both U.S. exports and foreign direct investments and are more in the form of tax-subsidized programs designed to reduce international business risk than in the form of discounts on income tax rates.

The United States Agency for International Development program, for instance, makes it possible for smaller companies to export to developing areas that are friendly to the United States without having to worry about non-payment, because all monies are fully funded through congressional appropriations.

The Export-Import Bank of the United States offers small business exporters political and credit risk insurance on their shipments to overseas customers. It also provides at or below market loans to specific direct foreign investments.

The Small Business Administration arranges for low-cost loans to small businesses to help them finance export inventories and foreign receivables.

The Overseas Private Investment Corporation enables small companies with foreign assets committed to wholly owned subsidiaries, joint ventures, and other strategic alliances to insure those assets against expropriation by a host government.

In addition, many countries offer individualized tax incentive programs to attract and keep foreign investments. Many of the smaller developing nations offer corporate income tax holidays of up to 25 years, along with duty-free status for materials that must be imported to fuel an investment.

Foreign Tax Havens

As the saying goes, "There is no free lunch." Many small countries, like the Bahamas, position themselves as tax havens. Summarily, they offer tax-free status to individuals and businesses that invest and take up residency there. The theory is that by establishing subsidiaries in foreign tax havens, U.S. companies can conduct tax-free business through their subs. In practice, it is taken to the extent that the subs often receive and process income from affiliates elsewhere that would otherwise remit funds directly back to the U.S. parent.

The IRS does not recognize tax havens per se. Furthermore, tax havens usually have no tax treaty with the United States, which creates a double problem for a U.S. firm opening a sub in a tax haven.

The first problem occurs when a company is unable to unequivocally answer the following question: Is the reason for the incorporation in the tax haven to conduct a legitimate revenue-generating economic enterprise there, or is it to avoid or evade U.S. taxes? The position of the IRS is that it will not tax income generated by U.S. subs in tax havens if they are conducting legitimate business.

Consequently, foreign direct investments in businesses like hotels, tourism, finance, banking, restaurants, yacht chartering, retail–wholesale trade, franchises, car rentals, etc. are treated as any other foreign-source income generated by overseas subs or joint ventures. The income is treated as income from any foreign sub, and only stockholder remittances are subject to U.S. taxation.

The IRS will seek to capture a sub's total income for taxation if the sub and/or its parent cannot show any local economic activity except for some office functions designed to launder funds.

The second problem is twofold and occurs because of the absence of a tax treaty with the United States. Tax havens tend to hold and manage Euro-currency accounts, which must be invested if they are not to turn stale (generate no income).

Interest paid on loans made to a resident U.S. company from an offshore tax haven that enjoys no tax treaty with the United States is subject to a flat tax of 30% before it is remitted from the United States.

Use and excise taxes in tax havens are high, acting as proxies for the missing income taxes. When sufficiently high, parent companies try to offset the cost by applying for U.S. foreign tax credit in order to deduct these charges from their U.S. income taxes. The tax credit may not be available, however, if no tax treaty exists between the tax haven and the United States.

Taxation of Foreign-Earned Income Subject to Currency Changes

U.S. companies earning income from the use of their assets and investments abroad report their transactions as follows: Income statement items are calculated at the average foreign exchange rate for the fiscal year. Balance sheet items are calculated at the end-year foreign exchange rate. Companies therefore suffer foreign exchange transaction losses and gains, even with the best forward contract hedges. These gains and/or losses must be reported even though no physical remittance is made.

Whether or not taxes must be paid on foreign exchange gains, or deductions taken for losses, is a subject for discussion and negotiation between a company and the IRS. The rule is that all earnings that have been scheduled for remittance back to the United States in accordance with a company's stated financial plan must be shown on all relevant tax documents, as they are subject to taxation. The issue of whether the unremitted earnings (perhaps kept in the host country due to foreign exchange problems) will be taxed or tax deferred is separate from the issue of full disclosure and accounting.

Frequent Changes in Law Mandate Ongoing Consultation

This section is not intended as a primer for all businesses engaged in the various enterprises of international trade and investments. It is intended to provide a brief overview of the general issues of international taxation that must be considered as a cost of doing business in any form with other countries. The discussion is not a substitute for consultation with international tax experts when doing business overseas.

FREE TRADE ZONES AND DUTY-FREE CUSTOMS (IN-BOND) AREAS

Free trade zones, or FTZs as they are commonly called, have been in existence for thousands of years. They were used by the Greeks and Egyptians in pre-biblical times. FTZs can be found in many countries, including the United States, and are used to reduce, defer, or eliminate the payment of import taxes. They are used by small and large companies to maintain a competitive cost and price advantage in U.S. and overseas markets. This section examines FTZs, along with duty-free or in-bond facilities, which exist to help importers and exporters reduce their international transaction costs.

Free Trade Zones Defined

An FTZ is described as a geographical enclosure within the customs area of a country (that is to say, within the United States) into which goods may be imported without the payment of import taxes.

Once in this "zone," goods may be stored, processed, and/or transformed so as to change their nature and description. The appropriate import tax is levied on the final character of the item as it leaves the FTZ.

If this same merchandise is shipped out of the zone directly to another country, without ever entering the customs authority of the United States, it is exempted from U.S. customs duties and other ordinarily applicable excise taxes. The import restrictions of the country of ultimate destination would apply instead.

What Companies Can Do in a Free Trade Zone

FTZs in the United States allow companies that utilize the facilities to engage in a number of activities, such as re-export, warehouse, test and examine, salvage, relabel, repackage, demonstrate, display/sell, repair, destroy, assemble, and manufacture. These are a few of the functions that can be carried out in an FTZ. In principle, any function that a company may perform at its factory may be performed in an FTZ. In fact, however, FTZs in the United States are used mainly for storage and processing.

For example, the major automobile importers routinely bring their vehicles into large designated FTZs for warehousing prior to final distribution to area dealers. This serves to defer payment of import taxes until a dealer delivery is imminent.

Food importers also avail themselves of FTZs. A prime example would be an importer of Brazil nuts and fruit. The import taxes on these items are levied on a weight basis (i.e., so much per 100 kilos). Thus, if these items were to be imported directly into the United States (and assuming a tariff of $1.00/kilo), a 200-kilo bag of the nuts and fruits would be subject to a $200 tax. Nut importers install drying ovens in FTZs, thereby reducing the weight of their imports by as much as 50%. The duty cost of the product is hence reduced by half, which is a substantial savings to importers.

Free Trade Zones and Their Origins in the United States

Congressional legislation on FTZs extends back to 1896. The first comprehensive law, the Foreign Trade Zones Act, was passed by Congress in 1934. It was designed to boost employment in major port cities.

The act has been amended several times and has been expanded and liberalized in the process. There are presently about 196 general-purpose zones and 259 subzones in the United States. The customs value of goods passing through U.S. FTZs in 1995 was over $130 billion. Most U.S. FTZs are privately operated and are accessible to all interested users. A freight forwarder or customs broker can easily handle all application details on behalf of a client.

Free Trade Zones in Other Countries

Most countries have FTZs in one form or another. Sometimes they are called free trade areas or free ports. In all cases, they describe a geographical area in which goods may be kept, and even business transacted, in a tax-free environment.

The largest FTZ in the Western Hemisphere is the Panama Free Trade Zone in the city of Colon at the Atlantic end of the Panama Canal. Almost 600 companies, of which about 500 are American, have warehousing and processing facilities located in the Panama FTZ. Over 90% of the goods enter the FTZ by ocean freight, and 95% leave via airfreight, a testament to the magnitude of the processing and manufacturing activity that takes place.

Alternatives to Free Trade Zones in the United States

FTZ operators frequently complain that their facilities are underappreciated and underutilized. Indeed, FTZs are used principally by importers of motor vehicles and agricultural products. One of the reasons often cited is lack of awareness that FTZs exist. Another reason is the distance between a company's main facility and an FTZ.

The real reason may be that under many new laws passed by Congress in recent years, companies are allowed to import goods directly into their own warehouses without paying customs duties if the merchandise is intended for re-export, or they can pay all customs charges and then apply for a refund of the taxes paid if the same goods are subsequently re-exported. This process is known as a duty drawback. Finally, the global trend toward import tax reduction under the continuing General Agreement on Tariffs and Trade (GATT)/World Trade Organization (WTO) accords is gradually rendering the FTZ concept obsolete.

The In-Bond Warehouse Concept

Under U.S. law, a company may obtain permission from U.S. Customs to bring imported merchandise into its own facilities without paying duties if those goods are not intended for domestic consumption and are intended for eventual shipment to another country.

This practice is followed by many companies in chemical-processing industries, pharmaceutical/healthcare industries, and textiles. It is also practiced by some machinery and equipment manufacturers that source their components globally, assemble in the United States, and then export some of their finished goods overseas. No import taxes are levied as long as the imported merchandise is eventually shipped abroad.

Duty Drawbacks

It is also possible to apply for a refund of customs charges levied if the imported merchandise is eventually re-exported. Companies often import goods that are not originally intended for re-export, but as time passes, the goods may ultimately be shipped to an overseas affiliate or customer.

Under existing law, companies have the right to apply for a "drawback" or refund of the customs duties paid. The amount refunded is about 90 to 95% of the monies paid out, including customs brokerage fees.

Reduced Import Restrictions

The governments of most countries are beginning to take the view that many tariffs, quotas, and other types of import restrictions hinder economic growth and development in the long term. Trade bloc agreements notwithstanding, countries have thus generally cooperated with one another and with the GATT and its successor organization, the WTO, to gradually ease trade restrictions.

Tariffs and other restrictions that remain tend to surround entire trade bloc areas and are designed more to redirect trade than to stifle it. Automobiles imported into the United States are a case in point.

Import taxes on European- and Japanese-made vehicles were once as high as 25%, shrinking to between 5 and 10% in the 1960s and 1970s. Today, they are 2%. However, a long-term North American Free Trade Association (NAFTA) objective is to establish a protective tariff on motor vehicles that are not produced within the NAFTA region with at least 70% local content. The result is that foreign vehicle producers have been rushing to establish production facilities in North America.

Goods originating in Third World countries are another example. The output of most developing areas enjoys duty-free or reduced duty access to the markets of industrial nations through either bilateral trade agreements or multilateral treaties negotiated through the former GATT. Even when import taxes are imposed, they tend to be low and non-restrictive.

The Future of Free Trade Zones

It is probable that FTZs as they exist today may change in the early part of the next century. Concepts of international logistics involving transport, distribution, and materials management and handling are rapidly moving from port-to-port to warehouse-to-warehouse structures. The transportation industry's vision of the future is trade and commerce without borders, where government policing and revenue gathering will be reorganized closer to corporate shipping and receiving centers. Many of these centers are situated away from sea and air ports of entry.

THE FOREIGN SALES CORPORATION ACT OF 1983

The United States, like many other countries, has sought for many years to provide tax subsidies for the exporting community. These efforts over the past 50 years have resulted in the passage of a number of tax laws that were originally intended to benefit small business. Many of these laws were found to be either unconstitutional or in violation of international agreements. However, the Foreign Sales Corporation Act (FSCA), passed by the U.S. Congress in 1983, is still on the books and active. It offers small business exporters some significant tax advantages.

Origins of the Foreign Sales Corporation

The United States has been involved in an ongoing dispute with its trading partners concerning its periodic attempts to artificially stimulate corporate exports by enhancing their profitability through income tax reduction on bottom line earnings. These disputes go back to the 1950s, when the government passed the Western Hemisphere Trading Corporation Act, and continued throughout the 1970s, when the law was replaced by the Domestic International Sales Corporation Act in 1971, which in turn was replaced by the FSCA in 1983.

The Western Hemisphere Trading Corporation

In the 1950s, the U.S. Congress passed a law known as the Western Hemisphere Trading Corporation (WHTC) Act. It allowed U.S. corporations to deduct from federal taxation a portion of export earnings on revenues generated from sales made outside the United States but within the Western Hemisphere (North and South America and the Caribbean).

The law was awkward, as it forced companies to first make a "paper" sale to a change-of-title point somewhere offshore (like Bermuda or the Cayman Islands), with the "transfer agent" in that location making the final sale, including title transfer to the "ultimate consignee" (importer) at the goods' final destination. The U.S.-based exporter would therefore ship to the transfer point at cost plus a very low markup to the transfer agent, who would resell the goods at a higher markup to the real buyer at the final destination. Federal income taxes would be assessed on the transfer agent's export earnings, with a deep incentive discount applied as called for under the law.

The Domestic International Sales Corporation

The WHTC approach was replaced in 1971 by the Domestic International Sales Corporation (DISC). This allowed a U.S. company to establish a corporate subsidiary (it could use the parent's location and address) whose worldwide export sales would be eligible for a 50% tax deferral on bottom-line export earnings. This deferral became a write-off if the taxable earnings were spent in the next fiscal period on export promotion and/or other export-related activities.

The DISC law also allowed a DISC subsidiary to make loans back to the parent (called producers' loans) ostensibly for the purpose of increasing export inventories. It remains unclear at this time if there was ever a binding requirement for the parent to repay those obligations, many of which remained on the books until the law was changed in 1983.

The legality of the DISC, from the point of view of international trading agreements between the United States and major trading partners like Canada and the GATT nations, was bitterly contested from the start. The argument was that a DISC constituted an export subsidy prohibited under the GATT.

In August of 1983, after much pressure from the GATT Council, the administration submitted a proposal to replace the DISC with an offshore entity known as a foreign sales corporation (FSC). Congress passed the proposal in June 1984, and it was signed into law in July 1984. The first major provision of the FSCA was to forgive the taxes on previously tax-deferred DISC income, laying to rest forever the issue of the unrepaid producers' loans, along with all other unpaid taxes on now permanently tax-deferred income.

The Foreign Sales Corporation

The question as to whether WHTC and DISC provisions constituted a prohibited export subsidy under GATT has not been resolved.

How the Foreign Sales Corporation Works

In order to conform with the requirements of the FSCA, a U.S. exporter must be a stockholder of a business entity that is incorporated outside the United States but in a territory of the country (the U.S. Virgin Islands, but not Puerto Rico). This office must be managed outside the United States and perform certain economic processes (meeting selling activity and direct cost test requirements) outside the United States. It must specifically elect to be an FSC (have a corporate charter statement to that effect) and must meet the basic foreign presence requirements defined in the FSCA.

This means an FSC must prove that it is an active business in the territory where it is incorporated. Finally, its stockholders must be involved in exporting and/or export-related activities. If all these conditions are met, a portion of the FSC's earnings from the sale of exports will be exempt from U.S. tax.

Location of Foreign Sales Corporation Offices

An FSC must be created and maintain an office outside the United States, such as in a U.S. possession or country that has an acceptable "exchange of information" agreement with the United States. The list of qualifying areas includes Guam, American Samoa, the Commonwealth of the Northern Mariana Islands, and the U.S. Virgin Islands. Puerto Rico is not included because of its special commonwealth status with the mainland.

Management of Offices Outside of the United States

All board of directors and shareholder meetings must take place outside the United States in the territory of the FSC. It may have no more than 25 shareholders at any given time during the taxable year, nor may it issue or have preferred stock outstanding at any time during the taxable year.

An FSC must have at least one member of the board who is not a resident of the United States. The principal bank account of the FSC must be maintained outside the United States at all times during the taxable year, and a permanent set of books must reside in the foreign location. Also, all disbursements, such as legal fees, dividends, officer salaries, etc., must be drawn from the account that is maintained outside the United States.

Performance of Economic Processes

There are two categories of foreign economic process requirements that must be satisfied. Both may be performed by an FSC or on its behalf by subcontract.

Selling. The first category encompasses selling activities. An FSC is required to solicit, negotiate, and engage in activities that produce foreign trading revenue. In other words, it must not only be credited with the sale of goods and services for export outside of its territory, but it must show that it is actively involved in the solicitation, negotiation, and processing of those sales.

The "direct cost" test. The second category involves a direct cost test where an FSC must demonstrate for each transaction that generated foreign trade income that 50% or more of the total cost incurred by the FSC for advertising and sales, order processing and delivery, issuing invoices and receiving payment, and assuming credit risk is attributable to activities performed by the FSC outside of the United States.

Taxation of Foreign Sales Corporations

In an attempt to persuade FSCs to utilize the U.S. Virgin Islands, Guam, the Northern Mariana Islands, or American Samoa, the FSC legislation contains a provision that prohibits the governments of these possessions from imposing any tax on FSC foreign trading income.

However, this inducement can be misleading. For example, FSCs in the U.S. Virgin Islands are not subject to local income taxes. However, they are subject to a Virgin Islands 10% withholding tax on distributions of Virgin Islands source income. On a positive note, there are many cases where an FSC's foreign trade income would not be considered predominantly of Virgin Islands source; therefore, the dividends the FSC pays to its shareholders could and very often do avoid the Virgin Islands withholding tax.

Tax-Exempt Portion of Foreign Trading Income of Foreign Sales Corporations

A total of 34% of foreign trading income generated by an FSC is today exempt from federal income taxes. This exemption is due to the foreign trade income being classified as foreign-source income, which is not connected to business in the United States and, therefore, not subject to federal tax.

Pricing Rules

Two pricing rules are used to determine the exempt income amount:

1. If the amount of income is based on the transfer price (or commission) actually charged but subject to the "arm's-length" pricing rules under Section 482 of the FCPA, then 34% of the income derived from the foreign trade will be exempt from U.S. federal income tax.
2. If the income of the FSC is derived using special administrative pricing rules, then the exempt foreign trade income is 17/23 of its 23% of combined profits. This latter alternative allows an FSC to utilize "safe-haven rules" if it performs all of the activities mandated in the foreign economic process requirements. This means that, as distinguished from the economic process test, some functions (like solicitation of foreign sales) may be performed from the "safe-haven" (partially tax-exempt) office in the United States.

U.S. Taxation of Non-Exempt Foreign Trading Income of a Foreign Sales Corporation

The non-exempt portion of income that utilized the "arm's-length" method is not specifically covered in the FSC rules and therefore will be taxed according to the rules that apply to foreign corporations with U.S. activities. The portion of income from an FSC that utilized the safe-haven rules will be subject to U.S. tax. The new rules treat this income as U.S. source income connected with trade or business conducted through permanent establishment of an FSC within the United States. By classifying the income in this manner, it is subject to U.S. tax as normal business income.

Distributions to Shareholders/Dividends Received from a Foreign Sales Corporation

Distributions to shareholders must be made out of foreign trade income first (not, for example, out of investment income). Any distribution that is made from foreign trade income is considered to be connected to trade or business conducted through an establishment of the shareholders within the United States. These distributions, therefore, are generally subject to federal income tax.

A 100% dividends-received deduction is allowed to domestic corporations with regard to amounts distributed from an FSC out of earnings and profits. In essence, there would be no corporate-level tax on exempt foreign trade income and only a single-level corporate tax (at the FSC level) on foreign trade income not considered exempt.

Implications for Multinational Corporations

The existing FSC legislation allows business the choice of operating under an FSC umbrella while maintaining a measure of control from stateside offices under the so-called "safe-haven" rules discussed above. Major companies like AT&T have taken advantage of FSC law in recent years.

It seems clear that the FSC offers some very definite tax advantages. A number of banking and corporate groups have formed FSCs in the past and reserve equity positions for new exporter-stockholders from time to time as permitted under FSC stockholder rules. These FSCs have offices and staff in place and offer marketing and selling services which a small business exporter may not have developed yet.

Forming a Foreign Sales Corporation

An election must be filed with the IRS in order for a business in the U.S. Virgin Islands, for example, that is incorporated to operate as an FSC to be treated as one for tax purposes. This election may be filed at any time at least 90 days before the beginning of a new tax year. The election requires the written consent of all stockholders, as they are all deemed to have a vested interest in the management of the FSC.

Comparing FSCs with DISCs and a Future Glimpse

There is little doubt that DISC was a cleaner act in terms of its intent and application. In some ways, FSCs are a throwback to the old WHTCs, which were indeed clumsy to manage from both an administrative and accounting viewpoint. An FSC's tax-exempting benefits are somewhat better than those of a DISC, because they provide a permanent tax deduction and not merely a temporary deferral of taxes due, which often required creative accounting to make them permanent.

In any case, FSCs have now survived longer than DISCs and have not yet been challenged by U.S. trading partners through the WTO, which absorbed GATT in 1996.

CONCLUSION AND SUMMARY

Consultation with tax specialists as part of the preparation for doing business in other countries can make the difference between losing and making money from international operations. There are as many tax codes as there are nations, each with its own particular impact on business transactions. Therefore, conflicts in the interpretation of these codes are inevitable, even when tax treaties exist.

A few corporate executives aggressively seek low-tax areas or so-called tax havens in which to base their companies' higher profit businesses. This practice is known as "treaty shopping" and is looked upon with increasing disfavor by the tax authorities of many countries. Governments generally encourage economic enterprise to seek profitable activities that increase the tax base and are more reluctant than ever to sanction businesses whose main goal may be tax avoidance or outright tax evasion.

KEY TERMS AND CONCEPTS

Export-Import Bank of the United States (Ex-Im Bank). This quasi-government bank offers large and small business exporters political and credit risk insurance on their shipments to overseas customers. It also provides at or below market loans to specific direct foreign investments.

Foreign Sales Corporation Act of 1983. This U.S. law provides a tax incentive to corporations that conduct export operations from offices based in offshore possessions such as the U.S. Virgin Islands and Guam.

Foreign tax haven. A country or region offering an income-tax-free environment.

Free trade zone (FTZ). A geographical enclosure within the customs area of a country (that is to say, within the United States) into which goods may be imported without the payment of import taxes.

Overseas Private Investment Corporation (OPIC). A government-chartered insurance company that enables companies with foreign assets committed to wholly owned subsidiaries, joint ventures, and other strategic alliances to insure those assets against expropriation by a host government.

Residency. Who pays taxes to whom is determined by the concept of residency. The term "resident" in the United States has nothing to do with one's citizenship. Residency refers to an individual's or a business's physical presence in an area for a prescribed time period.

Small Business Administration (SBA). This government agency arranges for low-cost loans to small business to help them finance export inventories and foreign receivables.

Tax treaties and double taxation. All firms doing business in other countries are vulnerable to double taxation unless a bilateral tax treaty is in place. Foreign branch offices are most obviously affected because their taxable income could be payable twice, in the host country and again in the United States.

United States Agency for International Development (USAID). The USAID program makes it possible for smaller companies to export to developing areas that are friendly to the United States without having to worry about non-payment, as all monies are fully funded through congressional appropriations.

U.S. worldwide income rule. Under U.S. law, a resident of the United States must pay taxes on all income earned in the United States and in other countries. In other words, a U.S. resident must pay federal income taxes on worldwide income.

QUESTIONS

21.1 A large U.S.-based corporation is contemplating a long-term foreign direct investment in the European Union region. Carefully plot the organizational structure it should pursue in terms of the impact of taxes on its activities.

21.2 Describe and explain, with examples, the nature of international tax treaties and how they might affect a U.S. corporation doing business in many countries.

21.3 Describe and explain how a U.S. corporation might organize itself to take advantage of the Foreign Sales Corporation Act.

21.4 Discuss how the concept of residency and the worldwide income rule can impact the multinational organizational structure of U.S. companies.

CHAPTER 22

U.S. Trade and Investment Support Organizations

INTRODUCTION

In this chapter, the roles played by key U.S. government organizations in assisting business in doing business overseas are examined. The focus is on four support groups: the Overseas Private Investment Corporation, the Export-Import Bank of the United States, the Small Business Administration, and the United States Agency for International Development.

THE OVERSEAS PRIVATE INVESTMENT CORPORATION

What It Is and How It Started

The Overseas Private Investment Corporation (OPIC) was created by Congress in 1969 as a quasi-private–public corporation. Its mission was to insure the foreign direct investments of U.S.-based corporations against losses from host government acts of property expropriation (nationalization). The level of insurance is on 80% of the book value of assets at the time of expropriation. OPIC insurance covers political events such as the inability to convert local currency into dollars; expropriation, nationalization or confiscation by a foreign government; or political violence (war, revolution, civil strife, or insurrection).

Additionally, from Argentina to Poland to Zimbabwe, OPIC offers valuable assistance to U.S. firms planning projects around the world.

OPIC has assisted U.S. investors in making profitable investments in over 100 developing countries. It encourages investment projects that will help the social and economic development of these countries. At the same time, it assists the U.S. balance-of-payments equilibrium through the generation of profits returned to the United States as well as the creation of U.S. jobs and exports.

The organization was established by Congress in 1969 and began operations in 1971 as a self-sustaining government agency. Starting with funding of $106 million, OPIC's reserves have grown to more than $1.5 billion, which it uses primarily for two purposes: to provide financing for U.S. investments and projects through direct loans, loan guarantees, and equity investments and to provide U.S. firms with investment insurance against political risks.

Qualifications

Eligible enterprises include processing, manufacturing, storage, mining, forestry, fishing, agricultural production, energy development, tourism, hotel construction, equipment maintenance, and distributorship facilities. OPIC generally does not provide financing for projects that involve housing or infrastructure development.

OPIC Programs

OPIC's direct loan and guarantee programs provide medium- and long-term funding and permanent capital to international investment projects that involve significant equity and management participation by U.S. companies. OPIC's award of financing is based upon the economic, technical, and financial soundness of a project. Project sponsors must show an adequate cash flow to cover operational costs, to service all debts, and to provide a return on investment.

Direct loans. Through direct loans, U.S. investors may obtain financing for smaller projects. Loans for such projects typically range from $500,000 to a maximum of $6 million. Direct loans may only be used to finance projects sponsored by or which significantly involve small businesses.

Loan guarantees. OPIC offers loan guarantees for larger projects, which can involve small companies or major corporations. Loan guarantees range from $2 million to as large as $50 million. Terms of direct loans and loan guarantees generally provide for a final maturity of 5 to 12 years following an appropriate grace period, during which only interest is payable. The length of the grace period depends upon the time required for the project to generate a positive cash flow.

Seed capital. OPIC may also provide capital for a project through stock investments and the purchase of a project's debentures convertible to stock. These investments increase a project's capital base, which helps project sponsors obtain more debt capital to finance the project. OPIC's equity investments typically range from $250,000 up to $2 million, but may be larger depending upon the particular project. U.S. companies of any size are eligible to receive financial assistance under the equity investment program. However, because equity investments usually involve greater risk, OPIC is very careful in selecting which projects it will finance.

Coverage. OPIC policies can cover up to 90% of the investment in an eligible project. It is OPIC's policy to offer insurance only for new investments that involve the expansion or modernization of an existing plant or equipment or the acquisition of additional working capital to expand an existing project. Eligible investors are citizens of the United States; corporations, partnerships, and/or other organizations founded under U.S. laws (and substantially owned by U.S. citizens); any state or territory of the United States; or foreign businesses which are at least 95% owned by sponsors eligible under the above requirements.

Pre-investment services. OPIC also offers pre-investment services to assist U.S. companies in assessing foreign market potential. In 1996, OPIC agreed to provide political risk insurance to a U.S. financial management firm that intends to invest in a number of Soviet enterprises.

OPIC's Current Economic Involvement

OPIC is often seen as a governmental agency that places a drain on the U.S. economy. In actuality, OPIC is a highly profitable entity with earnings over $100 million per year. During its history, OPIC has accumulated earnings of over $1.2 billion and has enough reserves to cover 20% of all of its potential liabilities as an insurer.

Risk. OPIC does what no private risk insurer is willing to do: finance and/or insure high-risk foreign investments. By insuring American foreign investments for up to 20 years, OPIC gives these long-term projects the security needed to generate meaningful economic development in emerging areas. As a point of reference, most of OPIC's projects are located in some of the poorest developing countries in the world.

While many people may agree that the U.S. government needs to be involved in assisting U.S. businesses to compete overseas, some are worried about the procedures that are in place. The loan requirements used by OPIC are very similar to those of any bank doing business within the United States.

The problem arises when a borrower defaults on a OPIC loan. Because OPIC is a governmental agency, the taxpayers must suffer the loss. Therefore, OPIC has come under much scrutiny for its risky loan practices.

Problems. One such investigation found that a huge shipment of Israeli arms that ended up in the hands of the Medellin drug cartel was apparently financed with $1.3 million in loans secured through OPIC. The investigation showed that an alleged Antiguan melon farmer and former Israeli soldier secured these funds supposedly for his melon farm, but instead engineered an arms deal.

THE EXPORT-IMPORT BANK OF THE UNITED STATES

The Export-Import Bank of the United States (Ex-Im Bank) is a quasi-independent U.S. government agency that aids in financing and insuring the foreign sale of U.S. goods and services.

Origins

The Ex-Im Bank was established in 1934 by presidential order and was reorganized in 1945. Its mission has changed over the years from supporting U.S. foreign-aid-financed exports through a system of credit and political insurance programs to supporting private sector exports that benefit the domestic economy.

The use of Ex-Im Bank financing has been influential in helping U.S. firms to boost exports, especially to developing nations. At the same time, its mission is to work with U.S. businesses in identifying, insuring, and financing foreign direct investment projects that will both create jobs and foster economic growth in the United States. In other words, an important criterion for Ex-Im Bank involvement is that a project must benefit both the overseas country as well as the U.S. economy.

Objectives

The Ex-Im Bank's mission is to create jobs through exports. It has several programs available to assist both small and large U.S. companies engaged in international trade and investments. These programs include a Working Capital Guarantee Program, export credit insurance to protect foreign receivables, and medium-term and long-term direct loans and guarantees to finance capital goods and service exports which may require long repayment terms. The Ex-Im Bank gives priority to small and medium-sized businesses so that they can maximize their involvement in foreign countries.

The bank complements and does not compete with private banks. It does so by taking on risks not ordinarily accepted by private sector banks and insurance companies. For example, it will provide political risk insurance coverage for investments in and shipments to politically unstable countries where the enterprise is seen as beneficial to both the impacted area and the United States. It will also assume a measure of the credit risk if it is satisfied that there is reasonable assurance of repayment.

General Ex-Im Bank Programs

The Ex-Im Bank has a number of direct loan programs for exporters, with terms that are intended to compete with and counter the export trade subsidies provided by other governments.

Direct financing. It provides direct financing to creditworthy foreign buyers when private financing is unavailable.

Insurance. It may offer credit and political-risk-based non-payment insurance (payment guarantees) on individual investment projects and export transactions as incentives to private sector banks to extend short-, medium-, or long-term financing.

Export support. The bank supports U.S. export sales worldwide. Its focus is nevertheless on those developing nations with rapidly growing economies. It also concentrates, often in concert with the World Bank, on investment projects in some of the poorest and neediest countries that share common foreign policy objectives with the United States.

Export financing. The bank will finance the export of all types of goods and services, including commodities and consumables. It does not finance the sale of military and/or military-related goods and services.

Qualifications. The product or the service must be at least 50% of U.S. content to qualify for Ex-Im Bank support. Two current goals are to increase the export of environmental goods and services and to expand the number of small businesses using Ex-Im Bank programs.

Financial Assistance without Foreign Aid

The Ex-Im Bank does not dispense foreign aid; nor is it an economic development agency. However, its programs often help U.S. exporters participate in development projects. The Ex-Im Bank will co-finance or provide payment guarantees on projects in conjunction with the United States Agency for International Development and the World Bank, as indicated above.

Specific Programs

The Ex-Im Bank provides financing support for U.S. exporters through working capital guarantees, export credit insurance, loan guarantees, and direct loans.

Working Capital Guarantee Program

The Export Trading Act of 1982 allowed the Ex-Im Bank to establish a financing program to guarantee loans to U.S exporters. This became known as the Working Capital Guarantee Program.

Over 100 working capital guarantees are extended to small and medium-sized companies each year by the Ex-Im Bank. Products that have been shipped under the program include semiconductor test equipment, wood products, agricultural products, and metal-processing equipment.

In general, many small business exporters tend to be highly leveraged. Even with a proven ability to sell and ship goods against letters of credit from overseas buyers, many exporters find it difficult to obtain credit.

This lack of collateral and the perceived risks of foreign business by lenders reduce an exporter's ability to borrow money. This makes it more difficult for the exporter to finance inventories and extend trade credit to foreign customers.

Ex-Im Bank's Working Capital Guarantee Program addresses this problem by reducing a lender's risk through the bank's loan repayment guarantee to the lender if the exporter (borrower) ends up being unable to repay the obligation. With sufficient working capital, exporters are in a better position to take advantage of vendor discounts, shipment consolidations, and other benefits that come from being sufficiently capitalized. The final result is improved operating margins and the ability to extend credit to customers abroad.

The guarantee covers 90% of the principal and interest on commercial loans to creditworthy companies that need funds to buy or produce U.S.

goods and services for export. The Ex-Im Bank will process loan requests for $833,334 and above. The Small Business Administration processes loans for lesser amounts on behalf of small businesses.

The loan repayment guarantee transaction may be approved for a single sale or a series of sales under a revolving line of credit. Its terms are typically 12 months, but may be extended for a total of 2 years. Ex-Im Bank requires that the borrower's assets be secured, usually in the form of inventory of exportable goods and/or accounts receivables on goods or services already exported or other forms of collateral.

There is an up-front $100 application fee. The bank then charges the guaranteed lender an up-front facility fee of 0.5% on the loan amount and a quarterly usage fee of 0.25% on the disbursed amount.

The total cost of the loan is similar to the cost of a regular commercial loan. This is because the funds are disbursed to the exporter not by the Ex-Im Bank but by the private bank with which the exporter normally deals. These Ex-Im Bank guaranteed loans are usually priced at the prime rate plus 1 to 3% or more, depending upon the exporter's credit rating.

Export Credit Insurance

Export credit insurance policies protect exporters and their lenders against both the political and commercial (credit) risks of a foreign buyer defaulting on payments. This program was begun in 1960 by an association known as the Foreign Credit Insurance Association (FCIA), created as a joint venture between the Ex-Im Bank and private insurance companies. The FCIA was dissolved some years back, and its functions were absorbed by the Ex-Im Bank.

Political-risk loss categories include war, currency inconvertibility, central bank failure, blocked currency accounts, import license revocation, acts of terrorism, etc. Credit risk categories include non-payment by the buyer due to insolvency or default. With export credit insurance, exporters are in a better position to extend payment terms to their foreign customers.

Insurance policies are available for single or multiple transactions. They can also be obtained for equipment leases. The political risk side of the policy can cover up to 100% of an exporter's invoice value. The credit or commercial risk side of the policy may cover up to 90% of an exporter's invoice value.

These insurance policies are generally of a short-term nature and enable exporters to grant payment terms to foreign customers for up to 180 days on sales of consumer goods, raw materials, equipment, and spare parts. Insurance policies on bulk commodities, consumer durables, and capital goods enable exporters to offer payment terms of up to one year to their foreign customers.

Capital Goods Insurance

Capital goods transactions that are large (over $1 million) may be insured for up to five years under Ex-Im Bank's medium-term policy. Insurance coverage for longer periods of time and/or for very large transactions is available by special negotiation.

Ex-Im Bank uses the same country risk classifications adopted by the Organization for Economic Cooperation and Development. These classifications are the basis for determining the Ex-Im Bank's maximum acceptable exposure on each transaction or set of transactions to individual countries. Ex-Im Bank loan guarantee and risk insurance coverage programs have thus far stayed within the ten-year range.

Commercial Bank Medium-Term Guarantees

These loan repayment guarantees are available directly to exporters, their foreign customers, and/or their banks. The guarantees cover loans of up to five years and are usually in excess of $1 million. In actuality, Ex-Im Bank prefers to be involved in transactions over $10 million.

This guarantee program to U.S. exporters and to foreign buyers of U.S. goods and services covers 100% of principal and interest against political and commercial risks of non-payment. It covers the sale of capital items such as truck and construction equipment, scientific apparatus and medical equipment, food-processing machinery, project-related services including industrial and architectural design and building plans, and goods (computers) related to the performance of project-related services. It can also be used to extend medium-term credit to buyers of U.S. capital goods and services through banks in certain foreign markets.

Direct Loans

Direct loans provide foreign buyers with competitive fixed-rate financing for their purchases in the United States. Ex-Im Bank's loans and guarantees cover 85% of the contract price, with 100% of that portion financed.

The foreign buyer is required to make a 15% cash payment. The fees charged by the Ex-Im Bank for its programs are based on the risk assessment of the foreign buyer or guarantor, the buyer's country, and term of the credit. Ex-Im Bank's fees are highly competitive with those charged by the export credit agencies of other exporting countries.

The Application Process

The Ex-Im Bank conducts an in-depth credit review which takes approximately two months. This cycle may be shorter or longer depending on how complete a submitted application is and Ex-Im Bank's backlog. Information required is similar to that requested by most banks. An applicant, whether domestic or foreign, is usually asked to submit three years of financial statements, resumes, credit references, and business plans with the completed application form.

When reviewing an application, the Ex-Im Bank considers three factors: the viability of the transaction itself, the ability of the applicant to perform, and the reliability of the source of payment.

A company may apply directly to obtain a preliminary commitment for a guarantee from the Ex-Im Bank and then use it to shop for the lender that offers the best terms, or the applicant's bank may obtain the guarantee. Certain lenders, experienced in dealing with the Ex-Im Bank, have the enabling authority to make commitments on behalf of the Ex-Im Bank.

Recent Ex-Im Bank Activities

Recent Ex-Im Bank efforts have included loan guarantees for a large computer sale to Russia in 1992. This involved $32 million in loan guarantees for six large mainframe computers intended to improve safety at Russia's nuclear power plants. The exporter was Control Data Systems of Minneapolis, Minnesota.

Ex-Im Bank also provided loan guarantees for the completion of a nuclear power reactor in the Czech Republic in 1994. This transaction was somewhat controversial, as the loan guarantees were intended to allow Westinghouse Electric Company to complete a Soviet-designed nuclear power plant.

Opponents of the loan guarantee cited nuclear safety and environmental concerns as reasons to oppose the deal. However, the export market is the only market for U.S. manufacturers of nuclear power equipment because no nuclear power plants have been constructed in the

United States since 1978. Westinghouse was to supply $334 million in instruments, nuclear fuel, and control equipment.

The Ex-Im Bank's Future

The U.S. Congress has been threatening to abolish the Ex-Im Bank since the 1980s. It was earmarked for extinction in 1981 as part of a federal budget-cutting process and continues to survive similar threats today. Congressional funding of Ex-Im Bank activities in 1994 was $1 billion. It fell to $800 million in 1995, and its budget remained more or less unchanged in 1996 and 1997. With the current interest in smaller government through privatization, plans for the bank's extinction as a public sector institution are continually being discussed by the Congress.

THE U.S. SMALL BUSINESS ADMINISTRATION

What It Is and How It Works

The Small Business Administration (SBA) was created in 1953 as a federal agency to help small businesses raise operating capital. Over the years, it has become the government's major source of support for small business and small business issues.

The SBA today offers existing and prospective small businesses two financing channels. The first is through a direct lending program in which the SBA makes a direct loan to a firm. The second is through a guaranteed loan program in which the SBA provides loan repayment guarantees to financial institutions that make loans to small business.

SBA and Ex-Im Bank Cooperation

According to the Ex-Im Bank, small businesses account for 96% of all U.S. exporters but only 30% of the dollar volume of the nation's exports. These small companies have export growth potential but need working capital.

The SBA is trying to meet those financing needs with its own Working Capital Program in coordination with the Ex-Im Bank. The SBA and Ex-Im Bank have divided the support finance market, with the SBA handling the smaller loans so that the Ex-Im Bank can focus on the larger transactions. Hence, the Ex-Im Bank handles transactions over

$833,333, which represents the largest loan amount the SBA can cover with a 90% guarantee.

The SBA Loan Guarantee Program for Exporters

The guaranteed loan program is specifically intended to provide financing to small businesses. The program helps reduce the risk taken on by the primary lender (the exporter's bank) and also allows the SBA to leverage its congressionally appropriated funds.

Known as the SBA 7(a) Loan Guaranty Program, it is of long-term assistance to small businesses when other funding sources are unavailable on reasonable terms through normal lending channels. Private lenders, usually banks or large corporate financing companies, make loans that are guaranteed up to 90% by the SBA.

The borrower then makes loan payments to the lender, which feels more secure with a government repayment guarantee in hand. This program promotes small business formation and growth. Many small business loans made by private lenders are arranged in this manner, and the financial services branches of major corporations like AT&T have become important sources of funding for small business.

Small Business Loan Objectives

Most SBA loans made under the 7(a) Loan Guaranty Program are to meet small business porter needs as listed below:

- Purchase inventory and material
- Purchase furniture, fixtures, machinery, and equipment
- Purchase or construct business premises
- Construct leasehold improvements
- Purchase a business
- Repay existing trade payables or other debt
- Provide working capital
- Provide receivables financing

The SBA can guarantee up to $833,000 or up to 70 to 90% of a loan. There is one exception, which needs Ex-Im Bank concurrence. Export sales that generate loan guarantees can be as high as $1,250,000. Interest rates on SBA-guaranteed loans generally do not exceed 2.75% over the prime lending rate.

The Contract Loan Program

In addition to its regular programs, the SBA has designed specialized programs to meet specific needs of the small business community. The Contract Loan Program helps small businesses in the short-term financing of labor and material costs of specific assignable contracts. Each contract loan finances one contract. Eligible businesses are small construction, manufacturing, and service contractors that provide a specific product or service. Exporters can avail themselves of this program if they are engaged in building or fabricating one-of-a-kind tailor-made machinery, devices, or equipment for overseas customers. For example, this program would be well suited for machinists.

Seasonal Lines of Credit

The Seasonal Line of Credit Program helps small businesses to finance increased receivables and inventory needs that result from seasonal upswings in business activity. Small businesses that have seasonal loan requirements are eligible. Small business exporters can be ideal candidates for this program.

The Small General Contractor Loan Program

This program is intended for financing the construction or renovation of residential and commercial buildings for sale. Construction contractors and home builders are eligible. Contractors that specialize in smaller construction projects in foreign countries, particularly if the projects involve low-cost housing developments, would be suitable for the contractor loan program.

The Export Working Capital Program

This is an export-specific program to assist small business in financing the manufacture or purchase of goods and services for the export or development of a foreign market. Lenders often consider export working capital loan requests too small and risky compared to longer term domestic loans. The Export Working Capital Program (EWCP) replaces the SBA's Export Revolving Line of Credit and can support single transactions or multiple sales.

Under the program, the SBA guarantees up to 90% (as high as $750,000) of a private sector loan. Guarantees can be extended for pre-shipment working capital, post-shipment capital, or a combination of the two. A pre-shipment guarantee is used to finance the production or acquisition of goods or services for export; a post-shipment guarantee is used to finance receivables resulting from export sales. EWCP loans are generally for a 12-month term but may be renewed twice, up to a total of 36 months. Collateral can include export inventory, foreign receivables, assignments of contract or letter-of-credit proceeds, domestic receivables, and in some cases personal guarantees.

When reviewing an EWCP application, the SBA considers the viability of each transaction, the reliability of the payment sources, and the exporter's ability to perform. The applicant must have been in business for at least one year. The loans cannot be used to expand overseas, to acquire fixed assets, or to pay existing debt. The program is mainly designed to help small companies that have not yet established a long-term banking relationship with lenders or a track record as an exporter.

The program in large was modeled after California's export finance program. It also works with the Ex-Im Bank to eliminate confusion and duplication and to simplify the application process. As a result, the SBA and Ex-Im Bank have divided the export finance market. The SBA now extends guarantees of $833,000 or less and the Ex-Im Bank handles all guarantees over that amount. The two agencies have developed a joint export loan application form and coordinated other program elements such as fee and interest rate policies.

An advantage of the EWCP is that a business can apply directly to the SBA for a preliminary commitment. Under the old system, only lenders could request an SBA guarantee. With a preliminary commitment in hand, a small business owner is in a better position to find a lender willing to extend credit.

Other SBA Programs

- *The International Trade Loan Program.* Assists small companies engaged in or preparing to engage in international trade and small businesses adversely affected by competition from imports. This program is useful for importers as well as exporters.
- *The Qualified Employee Trust Program.* Designed to allow a trust to relend funds to its employer firm or to permit employees to buy the employer concern.
- *The Pollution Control Loan Program.* Designed for the purpose of planning, designing, or installing a pollution control facility for the

applicant's own business. It can also be used to fund pollution control equipment sales to foreign countries.

- **The Low Documentation Loan Program (Low-Doc).** Involves loan requests of $100,00 or less. The one-page application used in this program relies heavily on the strength of a small company's credit history. This is an excellent program for a tiny start-up firm.
- **The Green Line Program.** Used for short-term working capital needs of small businesses. This program uses inventories and receivables to collateralize loans.
- **The Vietnam-Era and Disabled Veterans Loan Program.** Allows U.S. war veterans to apply for direct loans to establish a small business or expand an existing small business. The ceiling for these direct loans is $150,000.
- **The Handicapped Assistance Loan Program.** Enables disabled and handicapped businessmen to finance their business activities.
- **The Women's Loan Program.** Specifically targets female business owners.

In all the above cases, the SBA provides liquidity so that the guaranteed portion of the loan can be traded in the secondary markets (i.e., between investment banks and finance companies).

Eligibility

In order to be eligible for SBA assistance, firms must be for-profit organized and fall within a standard size, based on the average number of employees over the previous 12 months of operation or based on sales averaged over a 3-year period. In manufacturing, a company is considered a small business if it has less than 1,500 employees. (The usual maximum for eligibility is 500 employees.) In the wholesale trades, a small business is defined as having fewer than 100 employees. In services, average annual receipts may not exceed $14.5 million, depending on the specific industry. In retailing, average annual receipts may not exceed $21 million, again depending on the specific industry. In construction, average annual receipts may not exceed $17 million, depending on the type of industry. In agriculture, average annual receipts may not exceed $7 million, depending on the specific industry.

Loan terms depend on the use for which the proceeds are intended and the ability of the business to repay. Working capital loans have maturities of up to ten years. Fixed asset financing (i.e., purchase or major renovation) can be for up to 25 years. Most SBA-guaranteed loans are for up to five years. Direct loans made by the SBA are for five years.

UNITED STATES AGENCY FOR INTERNATIONAL DEVELOPMENT

What It Is and How It Started

The United States Agency for International Development (USAID) was created by Congress in 1961 and charged with the mission of combating communism by promoting economic development. USAID's initial mission was to provide loans and grants to developing areas that were friendly to the United States. During the Cold War, the feeling was that economic aid could help stem the expansion of communism by promoting democracy through economic growth. The communist threat à la the Soviet Union is long gone, but the fundamental mission of USAID remains largely unchanged. It is still to provide loans to friendly developing areas to encourage economic growth.

Today, it administers U.S. foreign economic and humanitarian assistance programs in more than 100 countries in the developing world, including Central and Eastern Europe and the newly independent states of the former Soviet Union. It is the federal government's lead agency in providing foreign aid. Congress appropriated about $4 billion in 1995. The administration requested $4.2 billion for USAID for fiscal 1996. USAID currently employs 3,500 people worldwide. At the end of the Vietnam War, it employed 17,000 personnel, more than half of whom were stationed in Asia (which contains more than half of the world's poor).

Five USAID Objectives for the 1990s

1. Protecting the environment
2. Building democracy
3. Stabilizing world population growth
4. Encouraging broad-based economic development
5. Providing humanitarian assistance

Protecting the environment and controlling population growth are new USAID targets. The pursuit of democracy and general development have been goals of the agency since its inception.

Protecting the environment. USAID environmental programs support two strategic goals: reducing long-term threats to the global environment, in particular, loss of biodiversity and climate change, and promoting and sustaining economic growth locally, nationally, and regionally by addressing environmental, economic, and development practices that impede development.

Globally, USAID programs focus on reducing the sources of greenhouse gas emissions and on promoting innovative approaches to the conservation and sustainable use of the planet's biological diversity. The approach to national environmental problems differs on a country-by-country basis, depending upon a particular country's environmental priorities. Country strategies may include improving agricultural, industrial, and natural resource management practices that play a central role in environmental degradation; strengthening public policies and institutions to protect the environment; holding dialogues with country governments on environmental issues and with international agencies on the environmental impact of lending practices and the design and implementation of innovative mechanisms to support environmental work; and environmental research and education.

Building democracy. The agency's strategic objective in this area is to help countries make the transition to democracy. Programs focus on some of the following problems: human rights abuses; misperceptions of democracy and free market capitalism; lack of experience with democratic institutions; the absence or weakness of intermediary organizations; non-existent, ineffectual, or undemocratic political parties; disenfranchisement of women, indigenous peoples, and minorities; failure to implement national charter documents; powerless or poorly defined democratic institutions; tainted elections; and the inability to resolve conflicts peacefully.

Stabilizing world population growth. USAID contributes to a cooperative global effort to stabilize world population growth and to support women's reproductive rights. These programs vary with the particular needs of individual countries and the kinds of approaches that local communities initiate and support. Most USAID resources are directed to the following areas: support for voluntary family planning systems, reproductive healthcare, needs of adolescents and young adults, infant and child health, and education for girls and women.

Encouraging broad-based economic development. USAID promotes broad-based economic growth by addressing the factors that enhance the capacity for growth and by working to remove the obstacles that stand in the way of individual opportunity. In this context, programs concentrate on strengthening market economies, expanding economic opportunities for the disadvantaged in developing areas, and building human skills and capacities to facilitate broad-based participation.

Providing humanitarian assistance. USAID provides humanitarian assistance that saves lives, reduces suffering, assists victims in returning to self-sufficiency, and reinforces democracy. Programs focus on disaster prevention, preparedness, and mitigation; timely delivery of disaster relief and short-term rehabilitation equipment, supplies, and services; preservation of basic institutions of civil governance during disaster crises; support for democratic institutions during periods of national transition; and raising local capabilities to anticipate and manage disasters and their aftermath.

How USAID Works

USAID offices are usually located at American embassies in designated countries where joint U.S. and local programs are already under way to bring about change within USAID's objectives. The local USAID office generally functions under the auspices of the American embassy but reports to the USAID assistant administrators for one of the four geographic bureaus (Africa, Asia and Near East, Europe and the New Independent States, and Latin America and the Caribbean). These bureaus are housed in the U.S. Department of State, of which USAID is part.

USAID has three functional groupings: AID missions, representative AID offices, and AID sections of the embassy. The missions are located in countries in which the U.S. economic assistance program is major, continuing, and usually involves multiple types of aid in several sectors. Each mission is headed by a mission director, who has been delegated program planning, implementation, and representation authority.

Offices of the AID representative are located in countries where the economic assistance program is moderate, declining, or has limited objectives. The offices are usually headed by an AID representative, who also has been delegated authority for program implementation and representation.

AID sections of the embassy are located in countries where the assistance program is nominal or is being phased out. Program planning and implementation authorities are delegated to the chief U.S. diplomatic representative, who is assisted by the AID affairs officer.

Overseas program activities that involve more than one country are administered by regional offices. These offices may also perform country organizational responsibilities for assigned countries. Generally, the offices are headed by a regional development officer.

Development Assistance Coordination and Representative offices provide liaison with various international organizations and represent U.S. interests in development assistance matters. Such offices may be only partially staffed by agency personnel and may be headed by employees of other federal agencies.

Importance to Business

Implementation of USAID programs is required by law to give priority to small businesses, known in USAID parlance as "contractors." Almost all USAID programs involve the export of goods and services to developing areas where U.S. economic assistance funds have been committed.

Once a development project has been articulated in the form of an action plan with an approved budget (a low-cost housing and shopping complex, for example), the entire program is put out for competitive bids, with interested businesses invited to tender offers. The bidding format is announced through government publications and SBA mailings that circulate among small businesses, as it is government policy to give preference to small and minority-owned firms. The payment terms on these USAID contracts, once awarded, are always against an irrevocable confirmed letter of credit. Payment can be made at the end of contract performance, but very often is made on a percentage of completion basis.

Financial and Political Issues

What is interesting about the program is that USAID-appropriated funds rarely leave the United States. Payment for goods bought by foreign importers and financed by USAID loans is generally made directly to exporters. Loan repayment must be made by the foreign importer to USAID either in U.S. dollars or in another acceptable currency.

The net result of the overall USAID program is that it helps meet three federal government objectives: it contributes to the economic development of countries friendly to the United States, it helps meet U.S. foreign policy goals for specific regions in the world, and it helps increase U.S. exports.

CONCLUSION AND SUMMARY

U.S. government programs designed to stimulate exports and investments through the use of public funds loaned or granted to foreign countries have come under increasing scrutiny and criticism in recent years. USAID in particular has been attacked by the Congress. Originally created as a temporary government agency, it is believed by many to have outlived its usefulness. At the very least, suggestions have been advanced for its privatization.

In recent years, a series of scandals have emanated from USAID. There are many diverse opinions about what should be done with the agency. Many people criticize the agency's goals and objectives, including those who run it. Many also criticize the agency's lack of a verification system to ensure that the funds provided to countries are actually used to fulfill their real requirements.

Many feel that USAID is important symbolically for the United States but that its contribution to the economic growth of other countries is at best marginal. This leads many American citizens to wonder whether investing abroad is worth it when there are so many problems at home.

There are two diverse opinions as to the purpose of foreign aid. The first is that many see foreign aid as a noble undertaking for humanitarian reasons to help the poorest countries grow and become industrialized societies. The opposing argument is that foreign aid is a way of buying the allegiance of strategically located countries such as Israel and Egypt, which are located near oil-producing countries. It is interesting to note that about half of all USAID funding each year goes to Egypt and Israel.

KEY TERMS AND CONCEPTS

Export-Import Bank of the United States (Ex-Im Bank). A quasi-independent U.S. government agency that aids in financing and insuring the foreign sale of U.S. goods and services. The Ex-Im Bank was established in 1934 by presidential order and remains active today.

Overseas Private Investment Corporation (OPIC). This insurance and investment financing company was created by Congress in 1969 as a quasi-private–public corporation. Its mission was to insure the foreign direct investments of U.S.-based corporations against losses from host government acts of property expropriation (nationalization).

United States Agency for International Development (USAID). This agency was created by Congress in 1961 and charged with the mission of combating communism by promoting economic development. USAID's initial mission was to provide loans and grants to developing areas that were friendly to the United States. During the Cold War, the feeling was that economic aid could help stem the expansion of communism by promoting democracy through economic growth. The communist threat à la the Soviet Union is long gone, but the fundamental mission of USAID remains largely unchanged. It is still to provide loans to friendly developing areas to encourage economic growth.

U.S. Small Business Administration (SBA). The SBA was created in 1953 as a federal agency to help small businesses raise operating capital. Over the years, it has become the government's major source of support for small business and small business issues.

QUESTIONS

22.1 Describe and explain the functions of the Overseas Private Investment Corporation, which has been around since 1969. Is it serving any useful purpose today? Is it self-supporting? Should it be changed? If so, to what? Should it be discontinued? If discontinued, should something else take its place? If so, what?

22.2 Describe and explain the functions of the United States Agency for International Development, which has been around since 1961. Is it serving any useful purpose today? Is it self-supporting? Should it be changed? If so, to what? Should it be discontinued? If discontinued, should something else take its place? If so, what?

22.3 Describe and explain the functions of the Export-Import Bank of the United States, which has been around since 1934. Is it serving any useful purpose today? Is it self-supporting? Should it be changed? If so, to what? Should it be discontinued? If discontinued, should something else take its place? If so, what?

CHAPTER 23

International Systems and Organizations

INTRODUCTION

The trend toward international economic cooperation through the creation of trade blocs, euphemistically called the "regionalization" of trade and investments, is reviewed in this chapter. The roles played by international organizations, such as the World Bank and the International Monetary Fund, in assisting nations to grow their economies through international trade and investments are also examined.

TRADE BLOCS

An awareness of the problems and opportunities presented by nations forming trade blocs can go a long way in helping international businesses to globally maximize market share and earnings. Nations often create new and larger trading areas that are easier to penetrate than the traditional single-nation market. An overview of trade blocs, how they work, and how they are used to advantage by importers and exporters is provided in this section.

The Trade Bloc as a Working Concept

A trade bloc can be loosely defined as a group of two or more nations that agree to a common policy with regard to goods imported from outside the member countries. A common policy may also be established with regard to goods produced within the region. Today, most trade blocs are partial rather than comprehensive. That is to say, they do not cover all goods and services produced outside or inside the trade bloc area.

The ultimate objective of any trade bloc is to achieve a measure of economic integration (i.e., to achieve resource, production, and market synergies, which many economic and political scholars and leaders believe might not be possible otherwise). The more limited goal, which some trade blocs have gone a long way toward meeting, is trade without borders.

Economic Integration

The idea of economic integration is to merge the economic activities of member countries to accelerate the processes of growth and development by maximizing market size, production capacity, and technological advancement. Trade blocs are often seen as a stepping-stone on the path toward economic integration. Trade blocs are also formed to protect countries from what they may perceive as overwhelming foreign influence and competition.

The Stepping-Stones of Economic Integration

The oldest surviving trade bloc in the twentieth century is the European Union (EU). Its origins can be traced to the Belgium-Luxembourg Free Trade Association, formed in the early 1920s. This free trade group expanded in 1949 with the entry of the Netherlands to become a customs union called Benelux, which in 1957 was absorbed into the European Economic Community (EEC), or European Common Market as it was known in the United States. The EEC started with 6 member countries and has expanded to include 13 nations in its present form as the EU.

The EU reveals the stepping-stones upon which it has built its influence, power, and survivability. It began as a free trade association, grew into a customs union, and evolved into a larger and relatively comprehensive economic union. This procedural outline has been used as a basis for trade bloc agreements elsewhere in the world with varying degrees of success.

Free Trade Association

A free trade association (FTA), based on the Belgium-Luxembourg model, is an association of two or more countries that agree to engage in duty-free or borderless trade for goods produced within the association area. The member nations, however, maintain their own customs regulations and specific tariff structures against non-member imports.

Thus, if product X of U.S. origin is imported into Luxembourg, it might be subject to a 20% import tax. If the same product from the same source is imported by Belgium, it might only be subject to a 10% import tax.

Customs Union (The Benelux Model)

A customs union incorporates the concept of an FTA as indicated above. In addition, member countries agree to a common tariff structure against non-members. In the Benelux model, which added the Netherlands to the Belgium-Luxembourg association, all three countries would hypothetically set or "harmonize" their duties on product X of U.S. origin at perhaps 15%.

Economic Cooperation Agreements

A unique characteristic of those Western European countries that eventually formed the EEC was their creation of two parallel agreements prior to creation of the EEC. The first was the Schumman Plan or European Coal and Steel Community (ECSC) of 1949. The ECSC's mission was to encourage its members to pool resources and cooperate in the mutual development of their iron and steel industries. The second was the European Atomic Energy Community of 1954 (EURATOM). Its mission was to help member countries develop nuclear energy for peaceful purposes. For a while, the EEC, the ECSC, and EURATOM maintained separate structures and were known as the "communities." They were merged into the EEC in the 1970s.

Economic Integration Association or Common Market

A common market, as in the case of the EEC, incorporates all the features of an FTA and a customs union. It also allows for the free mobility of production factors such as labor, capital, and technology. These targets have been at least partially reached by the European member countries.

Economic Regionalism Today

There are a number of functional regional trade blocs in the world today that are moving to integrate their economies beyond the point of just forming a customs union. The oldest in existence is the EU.

The European Union

The EU is the expansion of the original EEC that came to life with the Treaty of Rome in March 1957. The old EEC had six members: Belgium, France, West Germany, Italy, Luxembourg, and the Netherlands.

These countries were also members of the ECSC and EURATOM. A few years later, these three "communities," as they were called, were merged into the EEC, which by that time had become known as the European Community.

Membership increased in 1973 to nine countries with the addition of Denmark, Ireland, and the United Kingdom. Greece joined in 1980, and Spain and Portugal followed in 1985. The EC changed its name in 1992 to the European Union. Austria joined in 1995, followed by Sweden and Finland. More nations are expected to join within the next few years.

Caribbean Common Market

The Caribbean Common Market (CARICOM), which consists of the English-speaking West Indian nations, was formed in 1974 and is an outgrowth of the Caribbean Free Trade Association of 1965. It is, despite its name, a modified FTA. Not all products produced within the region are covered by the treaty.

North American Free Trade Association

The North American Free Trade Association (NAFTA) came into existence in 1993 as a free trade association among three countries: Canada, Mexico, and the United States. Maligned as a source of future unemployment and economic distress for the United States, it has in fact led to increased trade and investments for the three participants. Further, the rising unemployment that was predicted never materialized. NAFTA remains a free trade association at this time, with plans for becoming a customs union by the end of the century.

Other Latin American countries have expressed interest in joining NAFTA. It should be noted that the United States has been the more reluctant partner in expanding NAFTA. Chile in particular has been seeking entry into NAFTA almost from its inception. In late 1996, it finally signed a bilateral trade treaty with Canada, in a way bypassing the United States.

MERCOSUR

MERCOSUR (MERCOSUL in Brazilian Portuguese) is the South American term for the "Southern Cone Common Market." It is actually a free trade association consisting of Argentina, Brazil, Paraguay, and Uruguay. Chile, Bolivia, and a few other South American countries have expressed interest in joining MERCOSUR, which is probably one of the few trade association success stories in Latin America and the Caribbean.

The region has had a long history with FTAs. Two FTAs were formed in 1960: the Latin American Free Trade Association (LAFTA) and the Central American Common Market (CACM). LAFTA included ten South American nations (all the countries in the area with the exception of Guyana, Surinam, and French Guyana) plus Mexico.

The CACM included all the Central American countries with the exception of Belize and Panama. It discontinued operations in 1969. LAFTA developed several subgroups, the most noteworthy of which was the "Andean Six," which included Venezuela, Colombia, Ecuador, Peru, Chile, and Bolivia. LAFTA was reconstituted in the 1980s as the Latin American Integration Association (LAIA). This ten-member group included the original LAFTA countries except for Mexico.

The early shortcomings experienced by Latin American countries may be due to the fact that their integration plans were too ambitious. MERCOSUR appears to be successful because it follows a go-slow pattern of development, with the more limited goal becoming an effective free trade association before becoming a customs union and eventually a common market.

Operating on the same premise as MERCOSUR are the relatively new free trade accords negotiated between Venezuela and Colombia. The goal there is also to grow into an FTA before considering the more difficult processes of creating a customs union or common market.

Association of Southeast Asian Nations

The Association of Southeast Asian Nations (ASEAN) was formed with the mission of creating an FTA for its members, which consist of Brunei, Indonesia, Malaysia, the Philippines, Thailand, and Singapore. The member countries have consulted and met repeatedly over the years. Other area nations have expressed interest in seeing ASEAN expand, but it has still to realize its original objective of becoming a fully operational FTA.

Using Trade Blocs to One's Advantage

Trade blocs are important to the international trading community. In general, trade blocs offer the advantage of enlarging market size for outside suppliers once a workable entry strategy can be devised. They also offer greater flexibility by expanding sourcing horizons for companies that depend on materials from a number of different countries in order to manufacture their final products.

Germany, for example, is a source for textile machinery, supplies, and chemical raw materials for almost all wearing apparel producers in the world. Germany exports machinery to the United States, but German companies also produce the same machinery through international affiliates in Argentina, Brazil, and Mexico.

A U.S. apparel manufacturer can now shift its equipment sourcing from Germany to, say, Mexico, a NAFTA member. Indeed, there would probably be a decisive cost advantage in terms of freight and insurance charges and import tax reductions if the textile equipment and related materials could be brought in from Mexico instead of from Germany.

A U.S. garment manufacturer, now purchasing textile equipment from Mexico, may also have been eyeing EU finished goods markets with envy and with some bitterness about the high protective trade bloc tariffs. However, some concerted research would indicate several opportunities.

A contract manufacturing arrangement with a European company (often used by small companies) would enable the U.S. company to leapfrog into the EU without having to contemplate an expensive licensing agreement or investment. All sourcing can then be done in the European theater, and all customers would be supplied from a European source. The U.S. firm would become a Euro "player," bypassing the EU's protective tariffs.

Another approach for the same U.S. garment manufacturer, and one which would provide even greater advantages, would be to enter into a similar production contract with a fabricator in a Third World country that has duty-free access to EU and U.S. markets. Such a nation could be the Ivory Coast, one of about 70 nations which, as former European colonies and members of the African-Caribbean-Pacific (ACP) Conference, have been granted duty-free access to European markets. Most ACP members also have duty-free access to U.S. markets. An Ivory Coast source of textile production would gain market entry into Europe as well as the United States.

Should the U.S. firm decide to make a modest foreign direct investment in the Ivory Coast, perhaps forming some sort of strategic alliance with the local contract manufacturer, it would probably find increased profits in the form of income tax holidays, offered by many developing countries to attract entrepreneurial investments.

Finally, a small U.S. equipment manufacturer would probably discover considerable cost and market size advantages by relocating some of its production to Mexico, a NAFTA member along with the United States and Canada. This would make it possible for that same equipment, now made in Mexico, to be sold in the United States and Canada duty-free, as well as in the growing Mexican market.

It is interesting to note that often the immediate beneficiaries of trade blocs are not the huge multinational corporations but the smaller and more agile companies that target niches in the global marketplace.

THE WORLD BANK

The World Bank is well known among large multinational firms throughout the world. They follow its activities closely because, whatever their own political and economic convictions, World Bank funding activities in developing areas average US$10 billion each year, representing lucrative supply and performance contracts to the business communities of many countries. This section details the mission and operation of the World Bank and how it can be of importance to the business community.

Mission

While the mission of the World Bank is to lend monies to Third World countries for economic development purposes, and although the World Bank is dependent on high-income countries for its capitalization, the fact remains that the allocation of these funds to specific projects means business with a guaranteed payment structure to companies selected as corporate vendors and contractors. This reality does not escape the eyes of business.

Indeed, as part of the World Bank effort to stimulate growth by encouraging the development of small business enterprises (cottage industries) in many areas, it also seeks vendor/contractor participation among small businesses located in high-income countries, Hence, smaller companies have just as good a chance of being selected through a bidding process to take part in a World Bank–financed project as does a much larger multinational corporation.

Composition of the World Bank

The World Bank group includes the International Bank for Reconstruction and Development (IBRD), the International Development Association (IDA), the International Finance Corporation (IFC), the Multilateral Investment Guarantee Agency (MIGA), and the International Commission for Settlement of Investment Disputes (ICSID).

The main lending arm of the World Bank is the IBRD. It is also the bank's executive center and houses all its major administrative and decision-making offices. The IDA is the World Bank affiliate that makes loans to the world's poorest countries. The mission of the IFC is to help finance private sector projects through a combination of loans and private sector equity investments. The role of MIGA is to provide investment guarantees to the private sector on their loans and equity investments which have been approved by the World Bank for specific projects in individual nations. MIGA also offers investment policy advice and provides consulting services to economic planning officials and to private investors crafting investment projects in coordination with officials in those country. The ICSID offers mediation, arbitration, and conciliation services between private sector investors and their national government counterparts when disagreements among the parties occur.

The International Bank for Reconstruction and Development

The IBRD is the World Bank's nerve and operations center. It is "owned" by member countries. Each member makes an annual monetary contribution in its own currency, based on its relative economic standing among all other member nations. Thus, high-income countries like the United States and Japan contribute a larger percentage of the IBRD's capital than do poorer countries like Mozambique and Bangladesh. About 180 countries are now members of the World Bank group.

This initial annual capitalization is augmented by a pledge to the bank of additional sums known as "callable" capital. The bank then uses the combination of its "paid-in" and "callable" capital as guaranteed collateral for more funds that are obtained by selling bonds through bond markets. The buyers of these bonds can be private sector investors and/or various national government agencies that may wish to hold IBRD paper to attractively fringe a "politically correct" portfolio.

The IBRD has a governance presided over by a president, who is selected by the bank's major contributors. The president, to date, has always been a resident of the United States. The major role of the IBRD is to manage the finances of the World Bank group, to develop and establish overall policy and direction, to coordinate political and economic relations with member countries, to coordinate the policies and programs of other World Bank affiliates charged with more specific missions, and to make direct loans on approved industry development projects.

The International Finance Corporation

The IFC was established in 1956 to further economic growth in its developing member countries by promoting private sector investment. It is all too commonly referred to as the World Bank's "hard loan" window, a bit of a misnomer because the IFC makes equity investments in addition to maintaining a direct loan portfolio.

Although the IFC is part of the World Bank, it functions autonomously, with its own articles of agreement, shareholders, staff, and financial structure. Capital is provided by its member states, who determine IFC policies and activities. The majority of funds used for its lending activities are sourced through "triple-A"-rated bond issues in international financial markets throughout the world.

IFC goals call for encouraging what it feels are sound private sector projects in Third World areas. Its approach is to raise a combination of debt and equity financing on behalf of private entrepreneurial companies seeking to take advantage of market opportunities in given countries. It also provides consulting and technical assistance to businesses and governments. The IFC will also make direct loans to public-sector-owned enterprises if it is clear that the intent is to privatize the venture as soon as possible. Finally, the IFC serves as a clearinghouse, bringing together investment opportunities, foreign and domestic private capital, and experienced management.

The IFC is unique among international lending institutions in that it makes equity as well as loan investments and is permitted to make commitments without government guarantees. Loans issued by the IFC are made at the market rate of interest. Debt maturities conform with project requirements, which range from 5 to 15 years. Loans can be denominated in a client's currency of choice. In most cases, however, loans are denominated in hard (convertible) currencies like the dollar, yen, or deutsche mark.

The IFC is presently beginning to move away from direct loans in favor of equity investments. It is placing more emphasis on quasi-equity investments such as subordinated loans, convertible debentures, and preferred stock. It is also expanding into the arena of small business development programs by encouraging smaller scale equity investments in rural communities.

The International Development Association

The IDA was created in 1960. Country members of the IDA are also members of the World Bank. The IDA is often called the World Bank's "soft loan window" because of its long-term loans made at very low or nominal rates of interest to the poorest of developing countries. These loans have highly flexible repayment arrangements and are provided for the purpose of stimulating investment and economic development and encouraging foreign trade.

The IDA does not have its own staff, officers, or buildings. The staff and officials of the IDA are the staff and officials of the IBRD. The IDA is simply a "window" of the bank. It is essentially "legal fiction," a separate account and set of books within the IBRD and not a different institution. The elaborate emphasis on the separate nature of the IDA is said to be necessary to assure the capital markets from which the IBRD borrows that their funds would not be endangered by the soft loans made by the IDA.

Much of the IDA's activity is concentrated on infrastructure development (e.g., road construction and transport facilities; health and educational facilities; energy, power, and light generation; telecommunications; etc.).

Although the IBRD and the IDA finance the same type of projects and select countries according to the same standards, there are some differences between the two. The IBRD and IDA transfer resources to different groups of countries (some are called "blend" countries because they receive a blend of IBRD loans and IDA credits).

The IBRD would more likely concentrate its resources in a country like Brazil, bankrolling projects leading to industrialization, capital stock expansion, employment, and income generation in the country's depressed northeast. The IDA would instead focus on building roads and healthcare delivery centers in Bolivia.

The Multilateral Investment Guarantee Agency

MIGA, a relatively new affiliate, opened its doors in 1988. It is a form of international insurance agency. Its purpose is to guarantee investments recommended and backed by the World Bank against failure for credit and political risk reasons. It is similar in this regard to the thrust of the Export-Import Bank of the United States. The intent of a MIGA investment guarantee is to help make projects in Third World areas attractive to private sector investors. A MIGA guarantee can also make it easier for a private company to secure financing without working under the IFC umbrella.

Specifically, MIGA insures investments made by foreign investors against losses caused by political risks. This guarantee program protects investors from currency transfer difficulties, expropriation, war and civil disturbance, and investment-related breaches of contract by host governments.

In addition to new projects, the agency can cover expansion investments, privatization acquisitions, and the financial restructuring of existing projects already registered with MIGA. No minimum investment is required for MIGA coverage. This is attractive to smaller businesses seeking to plant more modest investments in developing areas and makes the MIGA guarantee program a viable alternative to using USAID and Ex-Im Bank facilities.

MIGA also provides promotional and advisory services to assist member countries in creating a responsive investment climate to attract private investments. To acquaint the international business community with specific opportunities that exist in developing countries, the Policy and Advisory Services (PAS) department organizes periodic investment-promotion conferences that promote dialogue among interested private investors, local business managers, and policymakers. The advisory services of the PAS are carried out through the Foreign Investment Advisory Services (FIAS) coordinating group, which provides member governments with advice on laws, policies, regulations, programs, and institutions that affect investment flows. The FIAS is jointly operated by MIGA and the IFC.

The International Commission for Settlement
of Investment Disputes

Misunderstandings and disputes between vendors, investors, host governments, and the World Bank institutions are channeled through the ICSID. The smallest World Bank affiliate, it operates through special committees that consist of representatives from the other World Bank group members.

The ICSID seeks to encourage greater flows of international investment by providing facilities for the conciliation and arbitration of disputes between governments and foreign investors. To further its investment-promotion objectives, the ICSID also carries out a range of research and publication activities in the field of foreign investment law.

Some Observations

Of all the national and international organizations involved in giving motive and direction to international trade and investments, the World Bank group appears to be the best organized and has the best and most comprehensive programs. It also seems to be in the best position to live up to its potential as the premier institution qualified to mobilize and allocate financial, human, technical, and material resources to bring about economic growth and development in Third World areas. This involvement means an ever-expanding number of trade and investment opportunities for big and small business.

THE INTERNATIONAL MONETARY FUND

The purpose of this section is to explain the influence of the International Monetary Fund (IMF) on trade and investments. Successfully guessing and second-guessing the short-term movement of foreign exchange rates very often depends on how one interprets and forecasts not only the foreign currency trading activities of central banks but also IMF participation in stabilizing exchange rates.

International traders and business executives sometimes confuse the IMF with the World Bank because both have their origins in the formation of the United Nations in 1944. In many ways, the IMF has a more immediate impact on trade and investments than does the World Bank, which is primarily a funding organization. How IMF operations can affect day-to-day market decisions in international business and trade is the focus of this section.

History and Objectives

The framework of the IMF was laid down at the Bretton Woods Conference in July 1944. The IMF was established in December 1945 to promote international monetary cooperation, to facilitate the expansion and balanced growth of international trade, and to promote stability in foreign exchange. IMF objectives as set out in its Articles of Agreement are:

1. To promote international monetary cooperation
2. To facilitate the balanced growth of international trade
3. To promote stable exchange rates
4. To eliminate cross-border currency restrictions
5. To create standby currency reserves

How the IMF Works

The IMF is modeled after the U.S. Federal Reserve. In the United States, a bank may join the "Fed" by opening an "account." This account is a deposit with the Federal Reserve that permits the new member bank to borrow from the Fed at a specified rate of interest, called the "discount" rate, or from other member banks within the system at the "federal funds rate."

The procedure for joining the IMF is similar. A country joins the IMF through its central bank by opening up a deposit in its own currency. Based upon the size of its deposit and its borrowing limit, a member country may now borrow short term from the IMF in any available currency.

Funds borrowed from the IMF are repaid; repayment arrangements vary from country to country and from situation to situation. In general, funds may be used for any purpose stated within the IMF mission guidelines.

The IMF permits deficit members to buy with their local currencies some of its holdings of convertible exchange. These deficit countries are expected to buy back, with gold or other acceptable securities, the local currencies originally sold to the IMF. This buy-back provision requires

IMF consent, which is given only after a country is able to demonstrate that it has resolved its balance-of-payments problems.

How a Country Joins the IMF

A country applies for membership by providing full financial disclosure about its national accounts statistics. Many countries have been able to do this without difficulty. Other nations, especially those with previously closed economies, like the republics of the former Soviet Union, have experienced disclosure problems mainly due to the fact that complete and accurate data had never been gathered.

The deposit or "subscription" by a member country can be in the home currency or in a mix of reserve currencies. It can also be denominated in monetary gold (this now rarely occurs). This deposit gives the member country the right to borrow (draw) at its discretion up to 200% of its "subscription." The funds borrowed may be denominated in any currency available to the IMF. This is known as a drawing right or 200% quota. Additional funds may be borrowed by separate petition.

IMF members borrow by exchanging their own currencies for convertible currencies of other member countries. A member country may draw 100% of its quota from the IMF at any time. This is called a reserve tranche. It can also borrow up to another 100% of its quota. This is called a credit tranche. Thus, a member country can conceivably borrow on a no-questions-asked basis (with minor exceptions) up to 200% of a given quota in convertible currencies. IMF member country quotas are reviewed every five years to determine whether they should be increased to accommodate the growth of the world economy.

Special Drawing Rights

An interesting feature of the IMF is its special drawing rights (SDRs), created in 1969. SDRs were created as an add-on artificial reserve asset for IMF member countries. SDRs expanded a country's international reserve assets by the amount of its annual allocation. The total allocation of SDRs was treated the same as currency credits among central banks to aid a country in financing temporary balance-of-payments deficits.

The value of the SDR was originally equal to one U.S. dollar when the first units were issued in 1970. In mid-1995, a single SDR bought $1.50. This underscores the downward drift of the U.S. dollar in international monetary markets in the past 25 years.

Achieving Currency Stability and Balance-of-Payments Equilibrium

Achieving and maintaining cross-border currency price stability is a cornerstone objective of the IMF. Its focus is on those countries with ongoing merchandise trade deficits, general current account deficits, and overall balance-of-payments deficits. Each and all of these conditions contribute to exchange rate instability.

A continuing merchandise trade deficit will generate short-term pressure upon a currency to devalue or float downward, because a nation may experience more demand for foreign currencies than it experiences for its own.

A country's current account includes a host of other international transactions, such as foreign travel, transportation, services, returns on investment and other business and royalty income, some military expenditures, and transfer payments, along with the merchandise trade balance. When the current account is in deficit over the long term, it usually means that there will be continuing pressure upon a currency to devalue.

A country's overall balance-of-payments position includes all current account transactions plus so-called autonomous capital account transactions. These consist of the net of foreign direct investments, foreign portfolio investments, and selected government-to-government loans, grants, and currency swap arrangements.

When a nation's overall balance-of-payments position is in long-term deficit, and if that deficit is large relative to the size of the economy, its currency may experience a very long-term negative float that can run for decades. The United States has been in this position since 1970.

What this means is that a country's balance of payments can run the gamut from partial to total disequilibrium. The role of the IMF is to help bring a nation's balance of payments back to an equilibrium or balanced position where there will be no enduring strains upon its currency.

For example, if the root problem is a temporary trade deficit, then no action other than having a country borrow foreign currencies within its automatic quota may be necessary to maintain exchange rate stability. If the problem centers around the current account balance, some longer term (standby) arrangements may be called for to help sustain the currency. However, if the problem covers a range of economic activities that affect all parts of the balance of payments, then even longer term and deeper financial involvement by the IMF, in participation with its more stable members, will be required, as was recently the case in Russia and Mexico.

Importance of the IMF to
the International Business Community

History clearly indicates that individual nations, in an era of business globalization, cannot easily cope alone with the tasks of maintaining exchange rate stability. Unless cross-border currency prices remain predictable and stable over the long term, it becomes unnecessarily complex and clumsy for exporters to figure out how to price their offerings, how much to collect, where and when to collect, and what currency to accept.

The same problems exists for importers but in reverse. Without a stable exchange rate, calculating one's landed cost (CIF duty-paid cost) can turn into a recurring nightmare.

IMF activities in helping countries maintain exchange rate stability are highly public events in the daily press. Companies that do business or plan to do business in areas impacted by IMF policies can reasonably expect their currencies to remain stable at least for the duration of those programs and can consequently adjust payment and shipping/selling terms accordingly.

Governance

There are approximately 172 members. Each member contributes to the IMF's general resources according to its quota, which is generally based on its relative economic and financial importance in the world economy.

The highest authority of the IMF is exercised by the Board of Governors. Each member country is represented on the board by a governor and an alternate governor. Normally, the Board of Governors meets once a year, but the governors may vote by mail or other means between annual meetings. The Board of Governors has delegated many of its powers to the executive directors. However, the conditions governing the admission of new members, adjustment of quotas, election of executive directors, as well as certain other important powers remain the sole responsibility of the Board of Governors. The voting power of each member of the Board of Governors is related to its quota in the IMF.

The 24-member Board of Executive Directors, which is responsible for the day-to-day operations of the fund, is in continuous session in Washington, D.C. under the chairmanship of the fund's managing director (currently Michael Camdessus). Similar to the Board of Governors, the voting power of each member is related to its quota in the fund, but in practice the executive directors normally operate by consensus.

Maintaining Stability in a Multiple-Currency Floating Rate System

Perhaps the toughest job of the IMF was overseeing the international exchange rate system. Until 1971, all exchange rates were set in contract with the IMF and could not be altered until a meeting of the board. At that time, a country could argue for a change in existing rates.

Even after several of the major currencies started using various floating rate systems, there were still major debates over how the fund would treat these rates. Members were pursuing a variety of exchange rate arrangements, but the majority did not have a floating rate.

The major problem at the time was that members frequently changed their exchange rate arrangements; without the (contractual) obligation to inform the IMF of their latest arrangements, it was difficult for the IMF to even keep abreast of the arrangements being followed, let alone consider their fairness.

By 1976, most of the exchange rate issues had been solved. The provisions of Article II of the Second Amendment of the Articles of Agreement resolved the question of members notifying the IMF of their exchange arrangements by obliging them to do so. The matter of having the IMF classify exchange rate arrangements also became less sensitive. By this time, member governments had more or less decided how they were going to respond to the new regime of floating rates and were making changes to their exchange arrangements less frequently.

With 1994 marking the fiftieth anniversary of Bretton Woods and the creation of the IMF, it was a good time to look at the future of the IMF. The disappearance of the fixed exchange rate system between 1971 and 1976 deprived the IMF of its major role as the monitor of international exchange. Since that time, it has struggled to develop a new identity and role in international financial markets.

SPECIAL DRAWING RIGHTS

SDRs were created as a reserve asset by the IMF in 1970. It is the right of a country holding SDRs to access resources from the IMF equivalent to its book entries. The origins of the SDR arose during the crisis in the international monetary system that began to emerge in the 1960s, when the volume of trade expanded much faster than production of gold. Under the Bretton Woods Agreement, countries could hold reserves in the form of either gold or U.S. dollars. The fear was that the United States would not be able to sustain and manage large deficits, and a serious liquidity crisis could result. SDRs were therefore created as an additional reserve asset to complement existing reserves of U.S. dollars and gold and to expand the international community's liquidity.

SDRs are the unit of accounting for all transactions between the IMF and its members, as well as an international reserve asset. Also, SDRs are used to settle international transactions between the central banks of member countries of the IMF.

SDRs were allocated to member countries on the same quota basis as membership. Holding SDRs gives the bearer the option and the flexibility to acquire foreign exchange from other members of the IMF.

The value of the SDR was originally fixed in terms of gold, with one fine ounce of gold equivalent to 35 SDRs (or US$1 = 1 SDR). In 1974, this valuation was replaced by a system that utilized a weighted average of 16 international currencies, commonly referred to as a "basket." This "basket" was made up of the currencies of the 16 IMF members whose share of world exports of goods and services exceeded 1% between 1967 and 1972. Changes were made in this "basket" to reflect the changing proportions of world trade. This arrangement, which lasted until 1980, calculated the SDR on a daily basis.

Despite daily recalculation, this valuation system suffered from many problems. In particular, many of the currencies in the "basket" were not traded actively in the international market, which made actual weighting extremely difficult. In an attempt to remedy this situation, a new "basket" was introduced in 1980. The new "basket" consisted of the currencies of the five countries (U.S. dollars, German marks, Japanese yen, French francs, and British pounds) with the largest share of world exports of goods and services. Today, the value of the SDR is determined by the prevailing market value of the currencies adjusted according to their basket weights. Since the 1980 valuation, the basket weights of the deutsche mark and the yen have increased, while the weight of the U.S. dollar has decreased.

The basic objective of creating SDRs was for Third World countries and other impoverished nations to benefit the most from their distribution. They were to be used as a mechanism to finance aid to meet the needs of developing countries. However, many of these nations contend that SDRs should be linked not to quotas but rather to the actual needs of the IMF member countries.

The majority of the industrialized nations, including the United States, feel that the SDR's primary function is to create international reserves and liquidity. These wealthier nations believe the use of SDRs as an aid-financing mechanism would result in excess liquidity in the worldwide economy. An additional concern is that aid would be extremely difficult to monitor if it were channeled through the SDR mechanism.

Although SDRs were intended to be a major reserve asset, they comprise less than 10% of the world's international financial resources. In fact, no SDRs have been allocated since the 1980s. This means that access to SDRs has become increasingly restricted as IMF membership has swelled to include all the new nations that have joined in the past 20 years.

CONCLUSION AND SUMMARY

It has been suggested that the IMF and the World Bank should either be dissolved or returned to their original purposes. However, the volatility in foreign exchange markets and the development needs of many nations seem to suggest that these organizations still have important roles to play. The IMF is still needed to provide exchange rate stability, and the World Bank continues to route funding to the neediest societies.

The future shape and power of the IMF may depend in many ways on how successful it will be in settling the current impasse regarding the continued creation and distribution of SDRs. Greater use of SDRs would go a long way toward addressing the urgent financing needs of much of the world. In fact, the IMF's managing director, Michael Camdessus, is currently lobbying the membership for a new allocation of SDRs, as well as an increase in the maximum amount a member nation can borrow.

KEY TERMS AND CONCEPTS

Customs union (the Benelux model). A customs union incorporates the concept of a free trade association. In addition, member countries agree to a common tariff structure against non-members.

Economic integration. The idea of economic integration is to merge the economic activities of member countries to accelerate the processes of growth and development by maximizing market size, production capacity, and technological advancement. Trade blocs are often seen as a stepping-stone on the path toward economic integration.

Economic integration association or common market. A common market, as in the case of the European Economic Community, incorporates all the features of a free trade association and a customs union. It also allows for the free mobility of production factors such as labor, capital, and technology.

Free trade association (FTA). An FTA, based on the Belgium-Luxembourg model, is an association of two or more countries that agree to engage in duty-free or borderless trade for goods produced within the association area. The member nations, however, maintain their own customs regulations and specific tariff structures against non-member imports.

International Monetary Fund (IMF). Its charter was laid down at the Bretton Woods Conference in July of 1944. The fund itself was established in December 1945 to promote international monetary cooperation, to facilitate the expansion and balanced growth of international trade, and to promote stability in foreign exchange.

Special drawing rights (SDRs). These were created as a reserve asset by the International Monetary Fund in 1970. It is the right of a country holding SDRs to access resources from the fund equivalent to its book entries.

Trade bloc. A trade bloc can be loosely defined as a group of two or more nations that agree to a common policy with regard to goods imported from outside the member countries. A common policy may also be established with regard to goods produced within the region.

World Bank. The mission of the World Bank is to lend funds to Third World countries for economic development purposes. Although the World Bank is dependent on high-income countries for its capitalization, the fact remains that the allocation of these funds to specific projects means business with a guaranteed payment structure to companies selected as corporate vendors and contractors.

QUESTIONS

23.1 Describe and explain the operation of the World Bank. Discuss how it can be used by multinational companies seeking overseas business opportunities.

23.2 Describe and explain the operation of the International Monetary Fund. Discuss how it can be used by multinational companies in planning trade and investment strategies.

23.3 Define and then discuss the differences between a free trade zone, a free trade association, a customs union, and a common market.

23.4 Discuss the objectives of the European Union. Will they be met? If so, by when?

23.5 Discuss the similarities and differences between NAFTA and MERCOSUR.

23.6 Some regional associations have failed, while others are still in existence. Discuss the reasons why.

Glossary

Accounts receivable. Business assets consisting of financial obligations due from others (e.g., an exporter's invoiced sale to a foreign buyer).

Ad-valorem tax (also known as a value-added tax [VAT]). An excise tax on the selling price of goods and services. All sales taxes are by definition VATs. The European Union has among the highest VATs in the world. Import taxes based on a percentage of an item's invoiced value are also called VATs.

All-risk insurance. Insurance that provides warehouse-to-warehouse coverage on shipments moving from an exporter's facility to that of a foreign buyer (importer). This type of policy can cover both ocean freight and airfreight shipments, as well as most defined risks, including general average risks.

ASEAN (Association of Southeast Asian Nations). A limited free trade association that consists of Brunei, Indonesia, Malaysia, the Philippines, Singapore, and Thailand. Not all products produced within the area are traded free of all import restrictions. Other Southeast Asian countries have recently applied for membership.

Balance of payments (BOP). A systematic recording of all international transactions that occur between residents of one nation and residents of all other nations. A nation's balance-of-payments position is the annual change in its international reserve assets and/or the annual change in foreign official claims on its own monetary assets (international reserves).

Bill of exchange. A draft, written as a check on behalf of a foreign buyer (importer) by a seller (exporter). The draft contains all the instructions to the exporter's and the importer's banks as to who pays whom, how much, where, and when. When the draft is signed by the foreign buyer upon its bank's receipt of the shipping documentation, the buyer accepts an obligation to pay for the goods on the date specified in the draft.

Bill of lading. A common carrier's receipt for goods placed on board an outbound vessel.

Charter party. The party that owns a particular cargo while it is on board an ocean vessel in transit between the exporter and importer.

Clean collection. Shipping documents that include only a bill of lading, draft, and/or invoice sent by an exporter directly to a foreign buyer, bypassing the international banking collection system.

Clean, on board ocean bill of lading. A common carrier's specific receipt for an exporter's invoiced goods placed on board an outbound vessel. These receipts cover no other goods, as might be the case with consolidation shipments.

Consignment import. Goods shipped by an exporter to an import agent where title stays with the exporter.

Copyright. Proprietary rights granted by a government to writers, artists, and other creators of original written, musical, oral, cinematic, video, and computer-designed works.

Correspondent relationship. An arrangement between two banks in which one agrees to represent the other for specific types of transactions. In international trade, the exporter's bank is often a correspondent of the importer's bank. The exporter's bank becomes known as the remitting bank because it has the obligation of sending the exporter's documentation to the importer's bank for collection. Hence, the importer's bank becomes known as the collecting bank. The documentary collection process would be almost impossible to implement if international banks did not have correspondent relationships.

Customs broker. Represents the importer in clearing imported merchandise through local customs at the importing port of entry. It also arranges for the payment of all import tariffs and charges and the transport of the goods to the buyer's facility. The customs broker represents the importer in much the same way as a freight forwarder represents an exporter. Large customs brokers and freight forwarders tend to be part of the same multinational transport and customs service companies.

Dirty float. A process in international monetary markets in which foreign currency prices change relative to one another directly as a result of central bank intervention.

Documentary collection. As distinguished from a clean collection, all shipping documents (bill of lading, draft, invoice, etc.) become part of the international banking collection process.

Draft. A bill of exchange, written as a check on behalf of a foreign buyer (importer) by a seller (exporter). A draft contains all the instructions to the exporter's and the importer's banks as to who pays whom, how much, where, and when. When the draft is signed by the foreign buyer upon its bank's receipt of the shipping documentation, the buyer accepts an obligation to pay for the goods on the date specified on the draft.

Dual-purpose product. A product that can be used for military as well as peaceful purposes. Such products usually require specific export licenses by both the U.S. Departments of Commerce and Defense.

European Union (EU). A free trade association of 15 nations that functions as a customs union and as a single borderless integrated economic community with its own supranational government. The member countries are Austria, Belgium, Denmark, Finland, France, Germany, Greece, Ireland, Italy, Luxembourg, the Netherlands, Portugal, Spain, Sweden, and the United Kingdom. Most other European countries, plus Russia and Turkey, have petitioned for membership.

Explicit warranty. A warranty is explicit when a manufacturer includes a written statement describing what guarantees it offers in the event of product performance failure and for how long a period of time those guarantees are good. Any warranty disclaimers (e.g., "goods sold as is," etc.) should always be in writing.

Export letter of credit. The flip side of an importer's letter of credit. When a letter of credit is opened by an importer in favor of an exporter and received by the beneficiary exporter, it becomes an export letter of credit.

Fixed rate tariff. An import tax on the weight, measure, or volume of product imported (e.g., $1.00 per pound on bulk items, $0.50 per foot on lumber, or $10.00 per gallon of alcohol).

Floating exchange rate. A process in international monetary markets in which foreign currency prices change relative to one another, free of central bank intervention and subject only to the global supply of and demand for specific currencies. Many countries, including the United States, have had their currencies on the "float" since 1971.

Foreign direct investment (FDI). A U.S. investment into other countries, with the objective of owning partially or entirely an economic enterprise for the purpose of establishing market share and generating revenue and profits that can ultimately be transformed into stockholders' dividends. Summarily, they are made to grow a business.

Foreign-earned income. Income earned from an individual's or a company's exports to other countries. It may or may not be treated as regular or foreign-source income for taxation purposes, depending on the application of the foreign sales corporation tax and other incentives offered by the U.S. government.

Foreign exchange rate. Also called the foreign currency price and the cross-border exchange rate, it is the price of one currency stated in terms of another.

Foreign portfolio investment. Investment into financial instruments such as stocks and bonds in which the objective is not to engage in business but to merely generate dividend income and capital gains.

Foreign Sales Corporation Act (FSCA). A federal law that allows U.S. exporters to exempt part of their export earnings from income taxes if their sales are made by an FSCA-approved subsidiary located in an offshore possession of the United States.

Foreign-source income. Income earned in foreign countries by U.S. residents (individuals and corporations). It is usually subject to U.S. federal income taxes.

Forward foreign exchange rate. The price of a foreign currency quoted for delivery at a future date.

Free float. A process in international monetary markets in which foreign currency prices change relative to one another, free of central bank intervention and subject only to the global supply of and demand for specific currencies. Not many countries, including the United States, have their currencies on a free float. The currencies of most industrial countries are on a "managed float."

Free trade area. A geographic area within the customs jurisdiction of a country in which goods may be bought and sold free of all import duties (taxes) and other restrictions.

Free trade association (FTA). An association of two or more countries in which the member nations agree to engage in free trade for goods produced within the association region.

Free trade zone (FTZ). A geographic area within the customs jurisdiction of a country in which goods may be imported, warehoused, and processed. Import taxes are levied on the final nature and description of the goods as they leave the zone.

Freight forwarder. A broker who is to an exporter what a travel agent is to a traveler. The freight forwarder's function is to arrange for the transportation of goods from the exporter's warehouse to the importer's port of entry and/or warehouse destination. It is also the responsibility of the freight forwarder to prepare all export and shipping documentation on behalf of the exporter and then to present the documents to an international bank for collection.

General Agreement on Tariffs and Trade (GATT). See World Trade Organization.

General average claim. A claim by a common carrier (ocean) against all charter parties (shippers) on a specific voyage resulting from damage to the vessel or from its loss.

Goodwill. A marketable asset, especially when one wants to sell a business and when the enterprise is small and local. Goodwill alone becomes less marketable when an enterprise grows large. The problem is that no individual or firm can legally claim exclusivity to goodwill. A company's goodwill must therefore be complemented by specific and legally protectable intellectual assets such as patents, trademarks, trade names, and copyrights.

Hard currency. Money, in order to be an acceptable medium of international exchange, must have "currency." This means it must have three characteristics: it must be universally acceptable, it must be freely convertible, and it must be stable over the long term. These features make it a hard currency, such as the Japanese yen, the Dutch guilder, the Swiss franc, or the German deutsche mark.

Horizontal integration. A process intended to establish control over the competition via strategic alliance, joint venture, merger, and acquisition.

Implicit (implied) warranty. If no written warranty is offered and if there is no written disclaimer, then courts in many countries usually hold the manufacturer liable on the principle of implied warranty, which means that a full warranty is in force for a "reasonable" time. See also Explicit warranty.

Import letter of credit. A bank's written promise to pay a fixed sum of money on behalf of a company (foreign importer) to a beneficiary (an exporter) by a certain date, subject to specific performance (show proof of shipment) by the beneficiary. The importer's bank (collecting bank) sends the letter of credit to its correspondent bank (the exporter's remitting bank), which then forwards it to the exporter. Any letter of credit opened by an issuing bank on behalf of an import buyer can be considered an import letter of credit.

Intangible assets. All the intellectual assets that protect a company's goodwill as reflected in the image and personality the firm conveys to the trade, competitors, and customers. See also Goodwill; Intellectual assets.

Intellectual assets. The patents, trademarks, trade names, and copyrights that identify goods and services as originating with a specific producer. This means that no one else in a given jurisdiction may copy those intellectual assets without the express permission of the owner. While infringements occur routinely in the United States, they are often more flagrant in many other countries.

International collection. A bank collection made by the international banking system on behalf of a seller (exporter). The exporter's bank becomes the remitting bank, and the buyer's (importer's) bank becomes the collecting bank.

International liquidity position. A country's "quick cash" position, which consists of foreign exchange (currency) reserves and reserves on deposit with the International Monetary Fund. These are the funds immediately available to a country, allowing it to discharge its international payables.

International Monetary Fund (IMF). An international bank owned by over 180 member countries whose objective is to assist member countries in achieving and maintaining exchange rate stability and balance-of-payments equilibrium.

International reserve assets. Assets owned by countries which consist of foreign exchange reserves, reserve positions with the International Monetary Fund, monetary gold stocks (not normally used today), and special drawing rights (also not widely used today).

Inventory. A business's assets, which consist of its stock of raw materials, orders in the works, and finished goods waiting to be sold and turned into accounts receivables.

Irrevocable confirmed letter of credit. Has the same features as an irrevocable letter of credit with the additional condition that payment to the exporter will also be guaranteed (confirmed) by the exporter's bank.

Irrevocable letter of credit. An issuing bank's written promise (guarantee of payment) to pay a fixed sum of money on behalf of a company (foreign importer) to a beneficiary (an exporter) by a certain date, subject to specific performance (proof of shipment) by the beneficiary. The importer's bank (collecting bank) sends the letter of credit to its correspondent bank (the exporter's remitting bank), which then forwards it to the exporter. This letter of credit cannot be canceled by the issuing bank prior to its indicated expiration date as long as the exporter (beneficiary) complies with its terms. The word "irrevocable" must appear on the document.

Joint venture. A highly structured and formal strategic alliance involving two or more partners. Joint ventures vary in their flexibility and participation by the stockholding partners. There can be two principal partners, each owning 50% of the voting common stock, or there can be several partners. The protocol joint venture agreement can require an equal sharing of the enterprise's capitalization, or the partners may agree to another formula (e.g., one party provides technology and scarce resources, and the other(s) supplies labor, management, land, and other assets).

Letter of advice. The remitting (exporter's) bank's covering letter accompanying an original letter of credit forwarded by same to the exporter for action.

Letter of credit (L/C). A bank's written promise to pay a fixed sum of money on behalf of a company (foreign importer) to a beneficiary (an exporter) by a certain date, subject to specific performance (proof of shipment) by the beneficiary. The importer's bank (collecting bank) sends the letter of credit to its correspondent bank (the exporter's remitting bank), which then forwards it to the exporter.

Licensing agreement. Written contract in which the owner (licensor) of an intellectual asset such as a patent, trademark, trade name, or copyright gives permission to another party (licensee) to use that asset to produce and/or market the licensor's prescribed goods and services in a given area for a stated period of time. The licensee in return pays the licensor an amount of money, known as a royalty.

Managed float. A process in international monetary markets in which foreign currency prices change relative to one another, subject to the global supply of and demand for specific currencies and subject to some central bank intervention to limit volatility in short-term foreign exchange rate fluctuations. Most industrial countries, including the United States, engage in a managed float.

Marine risk insurance. Insurance that provides warehouse-to-warehouse coverage on shipments moving from an exporter's facility to that of a foreign buyer (importer). The can cover both ocean freight and airfreight shipments.

MERCOSUR (Southern Cone Common Market). A free trade association that consists of Argentina, Brazil, Uruguay, and Paraguay and may soon include Chile. It is gradually transforming itself into a customs union.

North American Free Trade Association (NAFTA). A limited free trade association that consists of Canada, Mexico, and the United States. As of February 1996, not all goods produced within the area are traded free of import duties or other restrictions.

Open cargo policy. A marine risk insurance policy that covers an approximate number of shipments to a number of different destinations over an annual period.

Particular average claim. A claim by a common carrier (ocean) against a charter party (shipper) resulting from damage to the vessel or from its loss that the carrier believes may have been due to the negligence of the shipper.

Patent. A written covenant issued by the United States government and by many other governments to the inventor of a unique device or invention. The covenant restricts all other residents in a given national jurisdiction from replicating the unique device without the inventor's express permission for a specific period of time.

Process patent. A patent that protects the process(es) used to create a product from infringement. Process patents can be more important than product patents to inventors. The Polaroid Land camera owes its market survival in its long struggle with Kodak to the strength of its process patents.

Product liability. Liability incurred by a manufacturer and its agents when its product causes damage to people and property when in use in the United States or any other country.

Product patent. A patent that protects an invention from infringement.

Product warranty. A manufacturer's guarantee that its product will perform as claimed anywhere it is used for a reasonable period of time.

Purchasing power parity theory. Based on Say's law of "one price," it suggests that differences in inflation rates among nations will impact currency exchange rates. Summarily, between two trading partners, the one with the higher relative rate of inflation will see its currency drop in value in the short term against that of its trading partner.

Receivables. See Accounts receivable.

Revenue forecasting. A sales forecast, usually for a full operating year, based on estimated billings or invoices. Reported revenues are the basis upon which income taxes are levied.

Revocable letter of credit. A letter of credit that can be revoked by an importer and/or the importer's bank at any time before the exporter's documents are submitted to the remitting bank for payment. Revocable letters of credit are rarely used today in international trade.

Shipper of record/exporter. The export seller in an import–export transaction whose name appears on all documentation as the party transferring title to merchandise shipped to the foreign buyer or ultimate consignee/importer.

Sight draft. In a sight draft shipment, shipping documents are released to the buyer (drawee) upon payment of the draft. This term of payment is often called D/P (documents against payment) or CAD (cash against documents). It means that the importer's bank will not release the shipping documents to the importer until payment has been rendered.

Soft currency. This type of currency is in low demand and tends to be unstable. Its softness can be camouflaged by pegging it to a hard currency to maintain exchange stability. It then moves in tandem with the harder currency with which it is linked. Thus, the Dominican Republic peso is said to float in the same direction as the U.S. dollar and would be an example of a soft but pegged currency. Countries like Brazil and Mexico are considered to be soft currency countries.

Special drawing rights (SDRs). Created in 1969 and first circulated in 1970 by the International Monetary Fund, they were intended to increase the liquidity of trading nations. Inability of IMF member countries to agree on the allocation system has prevented expansion in the use of SDRs.

Spot foreign exchange rate. The price of one currency stated in terms of another quoted for immediate delivery.

Strategic alliance. An agreement between two or more companies to combine complementary resources in order to achieve economies of scale and market synergies. The agreement can be formal or informal and generally involves processes of vertical and horizontal integration. Vertical integration establishes control over resources, production, and distribution. Horizontal integration provides control over the competition. Two or more companies are ready for a strategic alliance when they believe that cooperation may more quickly achieve mutual or reciprocating objectives.

Time draft. In a time draft shipment, shipping documents are released to the buyer (drawee) upon the importer's promise to pay the draft on a designated future date. That date is stated on the face of the draft. This means that the importer's bank will release the shipping documents to the importer once the draft has been accepted.

Time letter of credit. A letter of credit, usually irrevocable and confirmed, whose proceeds are payable to a beneficiary (exporter) at a specified future date, generally several weeks or months after shipment has been made.

Trade bloc. A generic term for a free trade association or a customs union through which member countries agree to establish a common tariff wall or other restrictions against imports originating outside the trade bloc area. MERCOSUR and the European Union are examples of successful emerging trade blocs.

Trans-shipments. A practice by international carriers that involves off-loading and reloading goods from a ship or airplane before it reaches its final destination.

Treaty shopping. A practice used by individuals and businesses to establish residency outside of the United States in national jurisdictions that have no income taxes or whose taxes are significantly lower than those in the United States. Once a popular practice, it is now in disfavor with the Internal Revenue Service. The IRS's current position seems to be that if the main reason an individual or company establishes residency overseas is to take advantage of a tax haven environment, its income generated through that jurisdiction will be taxed as regular U.S. income under the worldwide income rule.

Ultimate consignee/importer. The importer and foreign buyer to whom exported goods are invoiced and whose name and address appear on all import–export shipping documentation.

Unconfirmed letter of credit. An issuing bank's written promise to pay a fixed sum of money to a beneficiary (an exporter) on behalf of a foreign importer by a certain date, subject to specific performance (proof of shipment) by the beneficiary. While the document may be irrevocable by the issuing bank, it places no obligation on the exporter's bank to pay the exporter.

Value-added tax (VAT). An excise tax on the selling price of goods and services. All sales taxes are by definition VATs. European Union countries have among the highest VATs in the world. Import taxes based on a percentage of an item's invoiced value are sometimes also called VATs.

Vertical integration. A process intended to establish control over resources, production, and distribution via strategic alliance, joint venture, merger, and acquisition.

Warranty. A promise by the issuer that certain actions will result in other predictable events (e.g., that a sewing machine will sew cloth, etc.). A product warranty is a promise by a manufacturer that its product will perform as stated in published literature. A warranty can be explicit or implicit (implied).

World Bank. Also known as the International Bank for Reconstruction and Development, the World Bank is an international bank owned by its members (about 180 nations), whose mission is to make long-term loans to developing countries for economic development purposes.

World Trade Organization (WTO). The successor to the General Agreement on Tariffs and Trade (GATT). The mission of the WTO is to promote economic growth and development through non-discriminatory international trade and investments. While GATT could pass resolutions against member countries, it had limited sanctioning power. Judgments made by special WTO panels against individual members must now be implemented or disposed of by appeal to the entire WTO within 18 months. The WTO's dispute settlement panel, at its maiden 1996 meeting in January, declared that U.S. gasoline standards were discriminatory because more reformulation time was given to U.S. producers than to foreign competitors such as Venezuela and Brazil (the two countries that made the initial complaint) to meet U.S. environmental standards.

Worldwide income rule. Under U.S. law, a resident of the United States must pay U.S. federal income taxes on income earned in the United States as well as on income earned anywhere else in the world, unless exceptions are allowed by law or by international treaty.

Yaounde Conference. The original name for a group of about 70 countries, formerly colonies of European nations, that have associate membership in the European Union, which gives them duty-free access to its markets. The name was subsequently changed to the Lome Conference and finally to the African-Caribbean-Pacific (ACP) nations.

Abbreviations and Acronyms

ACP	African-Caribbean-Pacific Conference
ASEAN	Association of Southeast Asian Nations
Benelux	Belgium, Netherlands, and Luxembourg Customs Union
BOP	Balance of payments
CACM	Central American Common Market
CAD	Cash against documents
C&F	Cost and freight
CARICOM	Caribbean Common Market
CIF	Cost, insurance, and freight
COD	Collect on delivery
D/A	Documents against acceptance
DISC	Domestic International Sales Corporation
DM	Deutsche mark
D/P	Documents against payment
ECSC	European Coal and Steel Community
EEC	European Economic Community
EMS	European Monetary System
EMU	European Monetary Union
ETC	Export trading company
EU	European Union
EURATOM	European Atomic Energy Community
Ex-Im Bank	Export-Import Bank of the United States
FAS	Free alongside ship or vessel
FCIA	Foreign Credit Insurance Association
FCPA	Foreign Corrupt Practices Act
FDI	Foreign direct investment

FOB	Free on board
FOR/FOT	Free on rail/free on truck
FPI	Foreign portfolio investment
FSC	Foreign sales corporation
FSCA	Foreign Sales Corporation Act
FTA	Free trade association
FTZ	Free trade zone
FX	Foreign exchange
GATT	General Agreement on Tariffs and Trade
GDP	Gross domestic product
GNP	Gross national product
IBRD	International Bank for Reconstruction and Development
ICC	International Chamber of Commerce
ICSID	International Commission for Settlement of Investment Disputes
IDA	International Development Association
IFC	International Finance Corporation
IMF	International Monetary Fund
LAFTA	Latin American Free Trade Association
LAIA	Latin American Integration Association
L/C	Letter of credit
MERCOSUR	Southern Cone Common Market
MFN	Most favored nation
MIGA	Multilateral Investment Guarantee Agency
NAFTA	North American Free Trade Association
OPIC	Overseas Private Investment Corporation
SBA	Small Business Administration
SDR	Special drawing right
SWIFT	Society for Worldwide Interbank Financial Telecommunication
USAID	United States Agency for International Development
VAT	Value-added tax
VOL	Voluntary restraint
WHTC	Western Hemisphere Trading Corporation
WTO	World Trade Organization

APPENDIX

The U.S. Balance of Payments

U.S. International Transactions (millions of dollars)

Line	(Credits +; debits −)[1]	1964	1965	1966	1967	1968	1969	1970	1971	1972	1973	1974	1975	1976	1977
1	Exports of goods, services, and income[1]	40,165	42,722	46,454	49,353	54,911	60,132	68,387	72,384	81,986	113,050	148,484	157,936	172,090	184,655
2	Goods, adjusted, excluding military[2]	25,501	26,461	29,310	30,666	33,626	36,414	42,469	43,319	49,381	71,410	98,306	107,088	114,745	120,816
3	Services[3]	7,840	8,824	9,616	10,667	11,917	12,806	14,171	16,358	17,841	19,832	22,591	25,497	27,971	31,485
4	Transfers under U.S. military agency sales contracts[4]	2,086	2,465	2,721	3,191	3,939	4,138	4,214	5,472	5,856	5,369	5,197	6,256	5,826	7,554
5	Travel	1,207	1,380	1,590	1,646	1,775	2,043	2,331	2,534	2,817	3,412	4,032	4,697	5,742	6,150
6	Passenger fares	241	271	317	371	411	450	544	615	699	975	1,104	1,039	1,229	1,366
7	Other transportation	2,076	2,175	2,333	2,426	2,548	2,652	3,125	3,299	3,579	4,465	5,697	5,840	6,747	7,090
8	Royalties and license fees[5]	1,314	1,534	1,516	1,747	1,867	2,019	2,331	2,545	2,770	3,225	3,821	4,300	4,353	4,920
9	Other private services[5]	651	714	814	951	1,024	1,160	1,294	1,546	1,764	1,985	2,321	2,920	3,584	3,848
10	U.S. Government miscellaneous services	265	285	326	336	353	343	332	347	357	401	419	446	489	557
11	Income receipts on U.S. assets abroad	6,824	7,437	7,528	8,021	9,367	10,913	11,748	12,707	14,765	21,808	27,587	25,351	29,375	32,354
12	Direct investment receipts	5,106	5,506	5,260	5,603	6,591	7,649	8,169	9,160	10,949	16,542	19,157	16,595	18,999	19,673
13	Other private receipts	1,256	1,421	1,669	1,781	2,021	2,338	2,671	2,641	2,949	4,330	7,356	7,644	9,043	11,057
14	U.S. Government receipts	462	510	599	636	756	925	907	906	866	936	1,074	1,112	1,332	1,625
15	Imports of goods, services, and income	−29,102	−32,708	−38,468	−41,478	−48,671	−53,998	−59,901	−66,414	−79,237	−98,997	−137,274	−132,745	−162,100	−193,764
16	Goods, adjusted, excluding military[2]	−18,700	−21,510	−25,493	−26,866	−32,991	−35,807	−39,866	−45,579	−55,797	−70,499	−103,811	−98,185	−124,228	−151,907
17	Services[3]	−8,619	−9,111	−10,494	−11,863	−12,302	−13,322	−14,520	−15,400	−16,868	−18,843	−21,379	−21,996	−24,570	−27,640
18	Direct defense expenditures	−2,880	−2,952	−3,764	−4,378	−4,535	−4,856	−4,855	−4,819	−4,784	−4,629	−6,032	−4,795	−4,895	−6,823
19	Travel	−2,211	−2,438	−2,657	−3,207	−3,030	−3,373	−3,980	−4,373	−5,042	−6,526	−6,960	−6,417	−6,856	−7,451
20	Passenger fares	−642	−717	−753	−829	−885	−1,080	−1,215	−1,290	−1,596	−1,790	−2,095	−2,263	−2,568	−2,748
21	Other transportation	−1,817	−1,951	−2,161	−2,157	−2,367	−2,455	−2,843	−3,130	−3,520	−4,694	−5,942	−5,708	−6,652	−7,972
22	Royalties and license fees[5]	−127	−135	−140	−166	−186	−221	−224	−241	−294	−385	−346	−472	−482	−604
23	Other private services[5]	−327	−461	−506	−655	−668	−751	−827	−255	−1,043	−1,180	−1,262	−1,551	−2,006	−2,190
24	U.S. Government miscellaneous services	−415	−457	−613	−661	−631	−686	−576	−592	−689	−640	−722	−769	−911	−951
25	Income payments on foreign assets in the United States	−1,783	−2,086	−2,481	−2,747	−3,378	−4,869	−6,515	−5,435	−6,572	−9,655	−12,084	−12,664	−13,311	−14,217
26	Direct investment payments	−629	−657	−711	−821	−876	−848	−875	−1,164	−1,284	−1,610	−1,331	−2,234	−3,110	−2,834
27	Other private payments	−802	−942	−1,221	−1,328	−1,800	−3,244	−3,617	−2,428	−2,604	−4,209	−6,491	−5,788	−6,681	−8,641
28	U.S. Government payments	−453	−489	−549	−698	−702	−777	−1,024	−1,844	−2,664	−3,836	−4,262	−4,542	−4,520	−6,542
29	Unilateral transfers, net	−4,240	−4,583	−4,955	−6,294	−6,629	−6,735	−6,156	−7,402	−8,544	−6,913	−7,249	−7,075	−6,646	−5,226
30	U.S. Government grants	−3,227	−3,444	−3,802	−3,844	−4,256	−4,259	−4,449	−5,589	−6,665	−6,748	−7,293	−6,101	−3,519	−2,990
31	U.S. Government pensions and other transfers	−399	−463	−499	−571	−537	−537	−611	−696	−770	−915	−909	−1,068	−1,250	−1,378
32	Private remittances and other transfers[6]	−614	−677	−655	−879	−836	−909	−1,096	−1,117	−1,109	−1,250	−1,017	−906	−917	−859

Line	Item														
33	U.S. assets abroad, net (increase/capital outflow (−))	−9,560	−6,716	−7,321	−9,767	−10,977	−11,566	−9,337	−12,476	−14,497	−22,674	−34,745	−30,703	−61,260	−34,766
34	U.S. official reserve assets, net[7]	171	1,225	570	53	−870	−1,179	2,481	2,349	−7	158	−1,467	−849	−2,558	−375
35	Gold	125	1,665	571	1,170	1,173	−967	787	866	547					−118
36	Special drawing rights	266	−94	537	−94	−870	−1,034	−851	−249	−703	9	172	−66	−78	−121
37	Reserve position in the International Monetary Fund		−346	−538	−1,023	−1,173	822	389	1,350	153	−33	−1,265	−466	−2,212	−294
38	Foreign currencies	−220						2,156	382	−1	182	−30	−317	−268	158
39	U.S. Government assets, other than official reserve assets, net	−1,680	−1,605	−1,543	−2,423	−2,274	−2,230	−1,589	−1,884	−1,558	−2,644	366	−3,474	−4,214	−3,693
40	U.S. credits and other long-term assets	−2,382	−2,463	−2,513	−3,638	−3,722	−3,489	−3,293	−4,181	−3,819	−4,638	−6,001	−5,941	−6,943	−6,445
41	Repayments on U.S. credits and other long-term assets[8]	720	874	1,235	1,005	1,386	1,200	1,721	2,115	2,086	2,596	4,826[14]	2,475	2,596	2,719
42	U.S. foreign currency holdings and U.S. short-term assets, net	−19	−16	−265	209	62	89	−16	182	165	−602	541	−8	133	33
43	U.S. private assets, net	−8,050	−6,336	−6,347	−7,386	−7,833	−8,206	−10,229	−12,940	−12,925	−20,388	−33,643	−35,380	−44,498	−30,717
44	Direct investment	−3,760	−6,011	−6,418	−4,805	−6,295	−6,960	−7,590	−7,618	−7,747	−11,353	−9,052	−14,244	−11,949	−11,690
45	Foreign securities	−677	−759	−720	−1,308	−1,569	−1,549	−1,076	−1,113	−618	−671	−1,854	−1,357	−8,885	−6,460
46	U.S. claims on unaffiliated foreigners reported by U.S. nonbanking concerns	−1,108	341	−442	−779	−1,203	−126	−696	−1,229	−1,054	−2,383	−3,221			−1,940
47	U.S. claims reported by U.S. banks, not included elsewhere	−2,505	93	233	−495	233	−670	−667	−2,980	−3,506	−6,980	−19,516	−13,532	−21,368	−11,427
48	Foreign assets in the United States, net (increase/capital inflow (+))	3,643	742	3,661	7,379	9,928	12,702	6,359	22,970	21,461	18,388	35,341	17,170	34,018	53,219
49	Foreign official assets in the United States, net	1,660	134	742	3,451	−774	−1,301	6,908	26,879	10,475	6,026	10,546	7,027	17,693	36,816
50	U.S. Government securities[9]	432	−141	−672	2,261	−769	−2,343	9,459	26,570	8,470	641	4,172	5,563	9,892	32,538
51	U.S. Treasury securities[9]	434	−134	−1,527	2,222	−798	−2,269	9,411	26,576	8,213	59	3,270	4,658	9,319	30,233
52	Other[10]	−2	−7	−1,548	39	29	−74	−74	−8	257	582	905	905	573	2,308
53	Other U.S. Government liabilities[11]	298	65	21	83	−15	251	−456	−610	182	936	301	1,517	4,627	1,400
54	U.S. liabilities reported by U.S. banks, not included elsewhere	930	210	113	21	10	792	−2,075	819	1,638	4,126	5,818	−2,158	969	773
55	Other foreign official assets[12]			742	1,106					185	323	254		2,205	2,105
56	Other foreign assets in the United States, net	1,983	607	4,333	3,928	10,703	14,002	−650	−3,909	10,986	12,362	24,796	10,143	20,326	16,403
57	Direct investment	−222	415	425	698	807	1,263	1,464	357	949	2,800	4,760	2,603	4,347	3,728
58	U.S. Treasury securities and U.S. currency flows	−146	−131	−356	−135	136	−68	81	−24	−39	−216	1,797[14]	4,090	4,090	2,434
59	U.S. securities other than U.S. Treasury securities	−85	−358	906	1,016	4,414	3,130	2,189	2,289	4,507	4,041	378	2,503	1,284	2,437
60	U.S. liabilities to unaffiliated foreigners reported by U.S. nonbanking concerns	75	178	476	564	1,475	792	2,014	369	815	1,005	1,844	219	−678	1,086
61	U.S. liabilities reported by U.S. banks, not included elsewhere	1,818	503	2,882	1,765	3,871	8,886	−6,298	−6,911	4,754	4,702	16,017	628	10,990	6,719
62	Allocations of special drawing rights							867	717	710					
63	Statistical discrepancy (sum of above items with sign reversed)	−607	−457	629	−205	438	−1,516	−219	−9,779	−1,679	−2,654	−2,558	4,417	8,955	−4,099
	Memoranda:														
64	Balance on goods (lines 2 and 16)	6,801	4,951	3,817	3,800	635	607	2,603	−2,260	−6,416	911	−5,505	8,903	−9,483	−31,091
65	Balance on services (lines 3 and 17)	−779	−287	−877	−1,196	−385	−616	−349	957	973	989	1,213	3,501	3,401	3,845
66	Balance on goods and services (lines 64 and 65)	6,022	4,664	2,940	2,604	250	−9	2,254	−1,303	−5,443	1,900	−4,292	12,404	−6,082	−27,246
67	Balance on investment income (lines 11 and 25)	5,041	5,350	5,047	5,274	5,990	6,144	6,233	7,272	8,192	12,153	15,503	12,787	16,063	18,137
68	Balance on goods, services, and income (lines 1 and 15 or lines 66 and 67)[13]	11,063	10,014	7,987	7,878	6,240	6,135	8,486	5,969	2,749	14,053	11,210	25,191	9,982	−9,109
69	Unilateral transfers, net (line 29)	−4,240	−4,583	−4,955	−5,294	−5,629	−5,735	−6,156	−7,402	−8,544	−6,913	−9,249	−7,075	−5,687	−5,226
70	Balance on current account (lines 1, 15, and 29 or lines 68 and 69)[13]	6,823	5,431	3,031	2,563	611	399	2,331	−1,433	−5,795	7,140	1,962	18,116	4,295	−14,335

Line	1996	1995	1994	1993	1992	1991	1990	1989	1988	1987	1986	1985	1984	1983	1982	1981	1980	1979	1978
1	1,055,233	991,490	854,158	771,387	743,358	722,557	700,455	642,921	550,620	449,272	400,842	382,740	395,850	351,306	341,436	380,928	344,440	287,965	220,516
2	612,069	575,871	502,396	456,832	440,352	416,913	389,307	352,120	320,230	250,208	223,344	215,915	219,926	201,799	211,157	237,044	224,250	184,439	142,075
3	236,764	218,739	197,248	186,711	177,154	164,236	147,824	127,142	111,024	98,553	86,312	73,155	71,168	64,307	64,079	57,354	47,594	39,692	36,353
4	14,647	13,756	12,166	13,471	12,387	11,135	9,932	8,564	9,284	11,106	8,549	8,718	9,969	12,524	12,572	10,720	9,029	6,981	8,209
5	69,908	63,395	58,417	57,875	54,742	46,385	43,007	36,205	29,244	23,553	20,385	17,762	17,177	10,947	12,393	12,913	10,588	8,441	7,163
6	20,557	19,125	17,083	16,611	16,618	15,854	15,298	10,557	8,976	7,003	5,582	4,411	4,067	3,610	3,174	3,111	2,591	2,156	1,603
7	27,216	27,412	24,941	23,050	22,616	23,331	22,745	21,106	19,811	17,471	15,784	14,574	13,809	12,590	12,317	12,560	11,618	9,971	8,136
8	29,974	27,383	22,661	20,304	19,656	17,819	16,634	13,818	12,146	10,183	8,113	6,676	6,177	5,778	5,603	7,284	7,085	6,184	5,885
9	73,569	66,850	61,093	54,517	50,294	47,024	39,540	36,204	30,709	28,701	27,303	20,035	19,255	18,192	17,444	10,250	6,276	5,439	4,717
10	893	818	887	883	841	690	668	587	664	526	595	878	714	666	576	517	398	520	620
11	205,400	196,880	154,510	129,844	125,852	141,408	163,324	153,659	129,366	100,511	91,186	93,679	104,796	65,200	86,200	96,529	72,606	63,834	42,088
12	98,890	90,349	70,911	61,241	51,912	52,198	53,740	55,368	52,092	39,608	31,968	30,547	31,262	26,950	23,922	32,543	37,146	39,182	25,456
13	102,856	101,836	79,488	63,495	66,826	81,186	94,072	92,638	70,571	55,592	52,806	57,633	68,267	53,418	58,160	50,300	32,898	23,356	14,788
14	4,654	4,895	4,101	5,108	7,114	8,023	10,512	5,653	6,703	5,311	6,413	5,499	5,227	4,832	4,118	3,680	2,562	2,295	1,843
15	-1,163,450	-1,086,531	-948,849	-825,020	-764,342	-733,335	-757,758	-720,189	-662,876	-593,416	-529,356	-484,047	-474,203	-377,573	-355,804	-384,196	-333,774	-281,657	-229,870
16	-803,239	-749,431	-668,349	-689,441	-636,458	-490,981	-498,337	-477,365	-447,189	-409,765	-368,425	-338,088	-332,418	-268,931	-247,642	-265,067	-249,750	-212,007	-176,002
17	-156,634	-147,036	-135,472	-126,403	-120,255	-121,195	-120,019	-104,185	-99,965	-92,349	-81,806	-72,862	-67,748	-54,973	-61,749	-45,503	-41,491	-35,689	-32,189
18	-10,681	-9,890	-10,292	-12,202	-13,835	-16,409	-17,531	-15,313	-15,604	-14,950	-13,730	-13,108	-12,516	-13,067	-12,460	-11,564	-10,651	-8,274	-7,352
19	-48,739	-46,053	-43,782	-40,713	-38,552	-35,322	-37,249	-33,416	-32,114	-29,310	-25,913	-24,558	-22,913	-13,149	-12,394	-11,479	-10,397	-9,413	-8,475
20	-15,776	-14,433	-12,885	-11,313	-10,556	-10,012	-10,531	-8,249	-7,729	-7,283	-6,506	-6,444	-5,735	-6,003	-4,772	-4,487	-3,607	-3,184	-2,896
21	-28,453	-28,249	-27,255	-25,746	-24,894	-25,204	-25,168	-22,260	-20,969	-19,057	-17,817	-15,643	-14,643	-12,222	-11,710	-12,417	-11,790	-10,906	-9,124
22	-7,322	-6,503	-6,560	-4,819	-6,089	-4,035	-3,135	-2,628	-2,601	-1,857	-1,401	-1,170	-1,168	-943	-795	-650	-724	-831	-671
23	-42,796	-29,285	-33,138	-39,356	-25,066	-28,096	-24,387	-20,548	-19,028	-17,999	-14,785	-10,203	-9,040	-8,001	-8,159	-3,562	-2,909	-2,822	-2,573
24	-2,687	-2,623	-2,560	-2,255	-2,116	-2,255	-2,116	-1,871	-1,919	-1,893	-1,686	-1,686	-1,534	-1,287	-1,460	-1,287	-1,214	-1,229	-1,214
25	-203,577	-190,072	-144,787	-110,176	-107,836	-121,159	-139,402	-138,639	-115,722	-91,332	-79,095	-73,087	-74,036	-53,700	-66,412	-63,626	-42,532	-32,961	-21,680
26	-32,132	-30,345	-20,154	-6,574	-302	3,433	-2,671	-6,507	-11,693	-7,425	-7,058	-7,213	-8,723	-4,206	-1,943	-6,898	-8,635	-6,357	-4,211
27	-100,103	-98,448	-77,614	-63,041	-67,054	-83,063	-95,499	-93,766	-72,314	-57,659	-47,412	-42,745	-44,158	-30,501	-35,187	-29,415	-21,214	-15,491	-8,795
28	-71,342	-61,279	-47,019	-41,561	-40,480	-41,529	-41,042	-38,364	-31,715	-26,218	-24,625	-23,129	-21,155	-18,993	-19,282	-17,313	-12,694	-11,122	-8,674
29	-39,968	-34,048	-38,845	-38,137	-35,192	5,122	-34,588	-26,063	-25,988	-23,900	-24,679	-22,700	-20,598	-17,718	-17,075	-11,702	-8,349	-6,593	-6,788
30	-14,833	-11,096	-15,671	-16,821	-15,826	24,160	-17,433	-10,911	-10,537	-10,309	-11,883	-11,268	-8,696	-6,469	-6,087	-5,145	-5,486	-4,015	-3,612
31	-4,331	-3,420	-4,544	-4,081	-1,018	-3,730	-3,184	-2,744	-2,709	-2,409	-2,372	-2,138	-2,159	-2,207	-2,251	-2,041	-1,818	-1,658	-1,532
32	-20,704	-19,530	-18,630	-17,235	-15,348	-15,309	-13,972	-13,308	-12,742	-11,192	-10,424	-9,295	-9,742	-9,043	-8,738	-4,516	-1,044	-920	-844

Line	C1	C2	C3	C4	C5	C6	C7	C8	C9	C10	C11	C12	C13	C14	C15	C16	C17	C18	C19
33	-352,444	-307,207	-160,516	-194,537	-68,774	-57,881	-74,011	-168,744	-100,221	-72,817	-106,753	-90,889	-36,313	-61,573	-122,335	-114,147	-86,947	-66,054	-51,130
34	6,668	-9,742	5,346	-1,379	3,901	5,763	-2,158	-25,293	-3,912	9,149	312	-3,858	-3,131	-1,196	-4,965	-6,175	-8,155	-1,133	732
35	370	-806	441	-637	2,316	-177	-192	-635	127	-609	-246	-997	-979	-66	-1,377		-16	-65	-65
36	-1,280	-2,456	494	-44	2,692	-367	731	471	1,025	2,070	1,501	908	-995	-4,434	-2,552	-1,824	-1,667	-189	1,249
37	7,578	-6,468	5,293	-797	4,277	6,307	-2,697	-25,229	-6,064	7,588	-942	-3,869	-1,156	3,304	-1,041	-2,491	-6,472	257	4,221
38																			-4,683
39	-690	-549	-352	-342	-1,657	2,911	2,307	1,259	2,967	1,006	-2,022	-2,821	-6,489	-6,006	-6,131	-6,297	-6,162	-3,746	-4,660
40	-4,930	-1,803	-5,212	-6,299	-7,398	-12,874	-8,430	-6,590	-7,680	-6,506	-9,084	-7,657	-9,599	-9,967	-10,063	-9,674	-9,850	-7,537	-7,470
41	4,134	4,115	5,045	6,270	5,807	16,776	10,867	6,723	10,370	7,625	6,089	4,719	4,490	5,012	4,292	4,413	4,456	3,925	2,941
42	106	139	-185	-313	-66	-992	-130	125	277	-113	973	117	-379	-51	-360	164	242	25	-131
43	-358,422	-296,916	-165,510	-192,817	-71,018	-66,555	-74,160	-144,710	-99,275	-82,771	-105,044	-33,211	-27,694	-55,372	-111,239	-103,875	-73,651	-51,176	-57,202
44	-87,813	-86,737	-69,262	-277,945	-42,640	-31,369	-29,950	-36,834	-16,175	-28,355	-19,025	-14,065	-12,344	-7,728	1,991	-9,624	-19,222	-25,222	-16,056
45	-108,189	-100,074	-60,309	-146,253	-49,166	-45,673	-28,765	-22,070	-7,960	-5,251	-4,271	-7,481	-4,756	-6,762	-7,903	-6,699	-3,568	-4,726	-3,626
46	-94,234	-34,997	-31,739	766	-387	1,097	27,824	-27,646	-21,193	-1,046	-21,773	-10,342	533	-10,954	6,823	-4,377	-4,023	-5,014	-3,853
47	-98,186	-75,108	-4,200	30,615	21,175	-610	12,379	-68,160	-53,927	-2,119	-59,975	-1,323	-11,127	8,164	-111,070	-84,175	-46,838	-26,313	-33,567
48	547,555	451,224	297,337	279,671	168,776	109,841	140,992	224,390	246,065	248,383	230,211	148,383	118,032	88,780	96,418	86,232	62,612	40,852	67,038
49	122,354	110,729	40,385	71,753	40,477	17,389	33,910	8,503	39,758	45,387	35,648	-1,119	3,140	5,845	3,593	4,960	15,497	13,565	33,678
50	115,634	72,712	36,827	53,014	22,400	16,147	30,243	1,532	43,050	44,802	33,150	-1,139	4,703	6,496	5,085	6,322	11,895	21,972	24,221
51	111,253	68,977	30,750	48,952	18,454	14,846	29,576	149	41,741	43,238	34,364	-838	4,690	6,972	5,779	5,019	9,709	22,435	23,555
52	4,381	3,735	6,077	4,062	3,949	1,301	1,888	1,383	-467	-1,214	-1,214	-301	13	-476	1,303	1,303	2,187	463	2,666
53	720	744	2,366	1,313	2,191	1,367	3,385	160	-319	-2,326	2,195	844	739	602	605	-338	615	-40	5,551
54	4,722	34,008	3,665	14,841	16,571	-1,484	-1,586	4,976	-2,506	3,918	1,187	645	555	545	-1,747	-3,670	-159	7,213	1,430
55	1,278	3,265	-2,473	2,565	-688	1,359		1,835		-1,007	-884	-1,469	-2,857	-1,798	-350	2,646	3,146	1,135	33,356
56	425,201	340,505	256,952	207,918	128,299	92,253	107,082	215,887	206,307	202,996	194,563	147,501	114,692	82,934	92,826	81,272	47,115	54,516	7,897
57	76,955	67,526	45,679	48,993	17,936	22,004	47,915	67,736	57,278	58,219	35,623	20,010	24,748	10,457	112,464	25,195	16,918	11,877	135,178
58	172,878	111,848	57,674	43,281	50,531	34,226	16,265	35,518	26,029	-2,243	7,909	25,633	27,101	114,089	111,027	116,127	117,145	137,060	2,254
59	133,798	96,367	56,971	80,092	30,043	35,144	1,592	38,767	26,353	42,120	70,969	50,962	12,568	8,164	6,085	6,905	5,457	1,351	1,889
60	31,786	34,598	-7,710	10,489	13,573	-3,115	45,133	22,086	32,893	18,363	3,325	9,851	16,626	-118	-2,383	917	6,852	1,621	16,141
61	9,784	30,176	104,338	25,063	16,216	3,994	-3,824	51,160	63,744	86,537	76,737	41,045	33,849	50,242	65,633	42,128	10,743	32,607	9,236
62	-46,927	-14,931	-3,283	5,037	-43,619	-48,103	24,911	48,585	-17,600	-7,713	29,735	17,494	17,231	15,779	37,355	1,093	1,152	1,139	
63																			
64	-191,170	-173,560	-166,192	-132,609	-96,106	-74,068	-109,030	-115,245	-126,959	-159,557	-145,081	-122,173	-112,492	-67,102	-36,495	-28,023	-25,500	-27,558	-33,927
65	80,130	71,703	61,776	60,306	56,699	43,041	27,805	22,957	11,059	4,476	4,476	294	3,419	9,335	12,329	11,852	6,093	3,003	4,164
66	-111,040	-101,857	-104,416	-72,301	-39,207	-31,027	-81,225	-82,288	-115,900	-153,353	-140,605	-121,880	-109,073	-57,767	-24,156	-16,172	-19,407	-24,555	-29,763
67	2,824	6,808	9,723	19,668	18,016	20,249	23,921	15,020	13,644	9,209	12,091	20,592	30,720	31,500	29,788	32,903	30,073	30,873	20,408
68	-108,216	-85,049	-94,693	-62,634	-21,191	-10,779	-67,304	-77,268	-102,256	-144,144	-128,514	-101,288	-78,353	-26,267	5,632	16,732	10,666	6,308	-9,155
69	-39,968	-34,046	-38,845	-38,137	-35,192	5,122	-34,586	-26,963	-25,988	-23,909	-24,679	-22,700	-20,598	-17,718	-17,075	-11,702	-11,702	-6,593	-6,781
70	-148,184	-129,095	-133,538	-90,771	-56,383	-6,657	-91,892	-104,231	-128,245	-168,053	-153,193	-123,987	-98,951	-43,985	-11,443	5,020	2,317	-285	-15,143

Source: Survey of Current Business, U.S. Department of Commerce, July 1997, pp. 64–65.

Index

ABC, 175
Accounting, 20, 22, 24
Accounting equilibrium, 63
ACP, see African-Caribbean-Pacific
    Conference
Acquisition, 35
Adjustment process, 63–64
Ad-valorem taxes, 194, 195
African-Caribbean-Pacific Conference, 196,
    250
After-sales service, 30, 35
Airfreight, 88
Annuities, 60
Arm's-length concept, 86, 92, 97
ASEAN, see Association of Southeast
    Asian Nations
Assembly, 155–162
Association of Southeast Asian Nations,
    249–250
Autonomous transaction, 57, 58, 61, 63,
    64

Balance of merchandise trade, 59
Balance of payments, 55–65, 83, 259,
    281–285
    adjustment and restoring equilibrium,
        63–64
    components of, 57–61
    defined, 55–56
    importance of, 62–63
    significance of, 55
Balance sheet, 58–61
Banking, 11
Banking system, 42

financing trade, 125–136
    international, 138–139, 144
Banks, 42
    international, 87, 88, 90
Bayer, 200
Behavioral ideologies, 3–4
Benelux, 246, 247, 263
Berne Convention for the Protection of
    Literary and Artistic Works, 110, 169
Best-source purchasing, 21
Big business, 5
Bill of exchange, 130, 141, 142, 144
Bill of lading, 127–128, 135, 130
BMW, 30
Board of directors, 17, 25
Boeing, 31, 35, 174
Bonds, 37, 39, 181
BOP, see Balance of payments
Borrowing, 50
Branch office, 159, 208–209
Brand name, 34
Bretton Woods Conference, 257
Bullion, 43

C&F, 115
Capital account, 59, 60–61
Capital gains, 37, 39, 181
Capital goods insurance, 232
Capitalism, 16, 17, 25
Caribbean Common Market, 248
Carriage of Goods by Sea Act, 120
Cash against documents, 132, 141, 144
Cash in advance, 139
Central American Common Market, 249

Central banks, 43, 44, 45, 49, 53, 56, 57, 70
  coordination with IMF, 48
  monetary stability and, 46–47
Certificate of insurance, 128, 135
Certificate of origin, 128, 135
Changes, 3
Check, 130, 142
CIF, 115, 121, 194
Clean collection, 129, 130, 135, 142
Coca-Cola Company, 32, 106, 108, 157, 164
"Coins of the realm," 43
Colgate-Palmolive, 21, 31, 157
Collecting bank, 128, 129, 130, 142, 144, 147, 149
Collection, 128–131
  types of, 142
Collection process, 140, 144
Commercial invoice, 126, 135
Commodity price changes, 46
Common carrier, 87–88, 89, 120, 127
Common market, 246, 247, 264
Communications, 11, 13
Communism, 16, 25
Community, obligation to, 9–10
Compensation, 9
Compensatory transaction, 57, 64, 65
Consistency, 34
Contract-filling operation, 32, 157
Contract Loan Program, 236
Contract manufacturing, 20, 31–32, 38, 157–160, 161
Contractual safeguards, 176
Copyright, 105, 106, 107, 110, 111, 163, 164–165, 170
Corporate challenges, 12–13
Corporate responsibility, 9–10
Corporations
  international business operations, see International business operations
  organization and philosophy, 17–24
Correspondent bank, 128, 129, 147, 149
Correspondent relationship, 87
Counterfeiting, 170
Crate & Barrel, 184
Credit, 11, 50, 138
Credit risk, 231
Cross-border currency prices, 67, 68
Cross rates, 76

Currency, 42, 49, 52, 53, 262
  changes, 212
  convertibility, 138
  defined, 67–73
  devaluation, 63
  price changes, 46
  reserves, 72, 76
  stability, 259
Currency futures, 72, 76
Currency of ultimate redemption, 48
Current account, 59–60, 259
Customs, 126, 212
Customs broker, 86–87, 88, 89
Customs union, 247, 263

Data verification, 140–141
Dealer, 30, 31, 38, 101
Debt, 56
Deficit, 57, 62–63
Delivered at frontier, 116
Delivered duty paid, 117
Democracy, building, 239, 240
Demographics, 3, 6–8
Design patent, 108, 164
Developed country, 13
Developing country, 8, 10, 11, 12, 13
Direct exporting, 29–30, 38
Direct financing, 229
Direct loans, 226
DISC, see Domestic international sales corporation
Disclaimer, warranty, 99–101
Disney, 108, 175
Distribution, 35
Distributor, 20, 31–31, 38
  import, 96, 97
  warranty and, 101
Distributorship
  agreement, 175
  international, 93–94
Dividends, 37, 39, 181, 202, 221
Documentary collection, 129, 130, 135, 142
Documentary draft, 132
Documentation, 125–128, 130, 135, 140, 152, 148
Documents against acceptance, 132, 144
Documents against payment, 132, 141, 144
Dollar, U.S., see U.S. dollar
Domestic international sales corporation, 217–218, 222

Double-column tariff, 195
Double taxation, 209, 223
Draft, 126, 130, 131–134, 136, 141, 142, 144, 152
Drawee, 129, 132
Drawer, 129
Duty drawbacks, 215
Duty-free customs areas, 212

Earnings distribution, 184
Eastman Kodak, 165
Economic cooperation agreements, 247
Economic development, 239, 240–241
Economic growth, 4, 7, 11, 16
Economic integration, 246–248, 263–264
Economic regionalism, 248–250
Economic transactions, 57–58
ECSC, see European Coal and Steel Community
Education, 10, 13
Employees, obligation to, 9
Employment, 11, 13
Energy, 10, 13
Engels, Friedrich, 16
Entrepreneurs, 4
Environmental responsibility, 9–10, 12, 15, 239, 240
Equilibrium, 57, 63–64, 76, 259
Equity distribution, 183
ETC, see Export trading company
Ethnocentric corporation, 17–20, 25
EU, see European Union
EURATOM, see European Atomic Energy Community
European Atomic Energy Community, 247
European Coal and Steel Community, 247
European Common Market, 246, 247
European Economic Community, 246, 247
European Monetary System, 52
European Monetary Union, 52
European terms, 75
European Union, 107, 110, 158, 167, 195, 196, 197, 201, 246, 248, 250
Exchange control authority, 45
Exchange rate, 74
Excise tax, 211
Exclusivity, 106
Expatriates, 18
Experience curve, 28, 33, 168
Explicit warranty, 99, 101

Export credit insurance, 229, 231–232
Export Declaration, 126, 136
Exporter, 84–85, 89, 94, 127
  agreement to follow prescribed rules, 117–118
  collection problems, 131, 142–143
  contract manufacturing, 158–159
  drafts and, 133–134
  insurance, 119
  loan guarantees for, 235
  payment terms, 139–140
Export financing, 229
Export-Import Bank of the United States, 142, 210, 222–223, 228–234, 243, 255
  Small Business Administration and, 234–235
Exporting, 28–31, 38, 59, 83
  direct, 29–30, 38
  restrictions, 191–193
Export letter of credit, 152–153
Export quotas, 191, 192–193, 197–198
Export support, 229
Export taxes, 191, 193, 198
Export trading company, 29, 39, 85
Export Working Capital Program, 236–237
Express warranty, 100
Expropriation, 200, 205
Ex quay, 115
Ex ship, 115
Ex works, 114–115

FAS, 115
  dock, 88
FCIA, see Foreign Credit Insurance Association
FCPA, see Foreign Corrupt Practices Act
FDI, see Foreign direct investment
Federal Reserve, 43, 138, 144, 257
Finance, 11, 20, 22, 24
Financial assistance, 230
Financial institutions, 5
Fixed exchange rate, 44–47, 52
  variable, 47–48
Fixed foreign exchange rates, 49
Fixed-rate import tax, 194, 195
Flagler, Henry, 9
Floating exchange rates, 53, 70
Floating rate system, 48–50, 261
FOB, 115
  airport, 117

carrier, 117
factory, 88
vessel, 88, 194
Food, 10, 13
FOR/FOT, 115
Foreign branch office, 159
    taxation of, 208–209
Foreign Corrupt Practices Act, 204
Foreign Credit Insurance Association, 231
Foreign currency, 42
Foreign direct investment (FDI), 35–37,
    39, 60, 65, 181–183, 187, 199
Foreign-earned income, taxation of, 22
Foreign exchange, 42, 51–52, 67–68, 262
    defined, 67–73
    purchasing power parity theory, 73–74
    rate quotations and terminology, 75–76
Foreign exchange markets, 70, 74–76
Foreign exchange rates, 45–46, 47, 48,
    52, 67, 68–70, 75, 77
Foreign exchange reserves, 50, 52, 53,
    72, 77
Foreign import agent, 31, 38
Foreign import distributor, 30–31, 38
Foreign Investment Advisory Services, 255
Foreign investments, 181–188
Foreign portfolio investment (FPI), 37, 39,
    60, 65, 181, 187, 199
Foreign sales corporation, 216–222
Foreign Sales Corporation Act of 1983,
    210, 216–222, 223
Foreign-source income, 20, 22, 211
Foreign sourcing, 160
Foreign subsidiary, 182–183, 186, 209
Foreign tax havens, 211–212, 223
Foreign Trade Zones Act, 214
Forward contract, 71–72, 77
Forward exchange rate, 69
Forward rate, 69–70, 74, 78
Forward swap, 69, 77
Forward transaction, 69–70
FPI, see Foreign portfolio investment
Franchising, 5, 34, 39, 163, 168, 170
Free trade association, 247, 248, 249, 264
Free trade zone, 31, 95, 212–216, 223
Freight/carriage and insurance, 116
Freight/carriage paid, 116
Freight forwarder, 86, 88, 89, 129
"Friendly high-risk" countries, 200–201
"Friendly low-risk" countries, 201

FSC, see Foreign sales corporation
FTZ, see Free trade zone

GATT, see General Agreement on Tariffs
    and Trade
General Accepted Accounting Procedures,
    20
General Agreement on Tariffs and Trade,
    110, 169, 197, 215, 218
General Analine & Film Corporation, 200
General average, 120
Geocentric corporation, 22–24, 25
Gifts, 60
Global challenges, 9–13
Globalization, 13–14, 83
Global sourcing, 5, 21
Global vision, 4, 5–6
Gold, 43, 45, 47, 49, 50, 262
    monetary, 51, 52
    reserves, 72, 73, 77
Gold exchange standard, 47–48, 49, 53
Gold standard, 43–47, 53
Goods, 59, 83, 90
Goodwill, 109–110, 111, 163, 164, 170,
    176
Government responsibility, 5, 17
Grants, 60
Green Line Program, 238
Group insurance, 121
Growth, 5–6, 7, 11, 16

Handicapped Assistance Loan Program,
    238
Hard currency, 49, 53, 68, 77
Harmonization, 177
Hawley-Smoot Tariff of 1932, 203
Healthcare, 10–11
Hewlett-Packard, 108
High-income countries, 202
Hilton International, 34, 39
Hoffman LaRoche, 58, 92, 208
Home country nationals, 23
Horizontal integration, 34–35, 39, 174, 178
Host country, 182–183
Host country nationals, 21, 23
Humanitarian assistance, 239, 241
Human resources
    development and management of, 18,
    21, 22–23
    obligation to, 9

IBM, 35, 108, 174
IBRD, see International Bank for
    Reconstruction and Development
ICSID, see International Commission for
    Settlement of Investment Disputes
IDA, see International Development
    Association
IFC, see International Finance Corporation
IMF, see International Monetary Fund
Import agent, 20, 31, 38, 94–95, 97
Import distributor, 20, 30–31, 96, 97
Importer, 85–86, 89, 94, 127
    agreement to follow prescribed rules,
        117–118
    drafts and, 133–134
    insurance, 119
Import letter of credit, 150–152
Import quotas, 193, 196–197, 198
Import restrictions, reduced, 215–216
Imports, 39, 59, 83
    restrictions, 193–197
Import taxes, 193, 194–196, 198, 213
In-bond warehouse, 215
Income, 11
Income gap, 8–9
Income statement, 58–61
Income taxes, 159, 160
Incoming investments, 201–202, 205
Incorporation abroad, 159–160
INCOTERMS, 114, 118
Infrastructure, 7, 15
Infringement, 106
Insurance, 88, 89, 118–123, 227, 229,
    231–232
Intellectual assets, 105–111, 163–165, 171,
    see also specific assets
Interbank market 75
Interest, 37, 39
Interest income, 181
Interest rates, 42
Internal Revenue Service, 209, 211
International Bank for Reconstruction and
    Development, 252–253, 254
International banking system, 138–139, 144
International banks, 87, 88, 90
International business, legal environment,
    91–98
International business operations, see also
    specific topics
    contract manufacturing, 31–32

exporting, 28–31
    foreign direct investment, 35–37
    foreign portfolio investment, 37
    franchising, 34
    licensing, 33
    strategic alliance, 34–35
    turnkey system, 32–33
International Chamber of Commerce, 143
International Commission for Settlement
    of Investment Disputes, 252, 256
International Development Association,
    252, 254–255
International distributorship, 93–94
International Finance Corporation, 252,
    253–254
International liquidity, 50–52, 53, 72–73,
    77
International Monetary Fund (IMF), 41,
    43, 49, 50, 53, 56, 70, 256–261, 264
    coordination with central banks, 48
    currency reserves, 72, 76
    deposits with, 51
    special drawing rights, see Special
        drawing rights
International monetary system, 41–43, 53,
    see also Monetary system
International payments and collection
    process, 128–131
International reserves, 50, 63
International taxation, 207–212
International trade
    logistics, 113–124
    practices, 89–90
International Trade Loan Program, 237
Investment, 11
Investment incentives, 202
Investment restrictions, 199–205
Invoice, commercial, 126, 135
Irrevocable confirmed letter of credit,
    150, 154
Irrevocable letter of credit, 148–149, 154

Joint venture, 20, 30, 35, 36, 38, 176,
    182, 183–185, 188, 211
    taxation of, 209

Keynes, John, 16
Know-how, 14, 19, 165, 171, 175
    protecting, 108–109
    transfer of, 163

Labor laws, 95
Latin American Free Trade Association, 249
Legal environment, 91–98
Lending, 50
Letter of credit, 140, 147–154
Liability, 99, 101–102
Liability insurance, 119
Licensing, 5, 20, 30, 33, 36, 38, 39, 163, 166–168
Lines of credit, 236
Liquidity, 50, 72–73, 77
Loans, 229, 235–238
    direct, 226, 230, 232–233
    guarantees, 226–227, 230, 232, 235
Location economies, 28, 33, 168
Logistics, 113–124
Logo, 164, 168, 170
Long-term deficit, 62–63
Loreal, 184
Low Documentation Loan Program, 238
Lower income countries, 202–203

Malthus, Thomas, 16
Management contract, 156
Management style, 177
Manufacturing, 33, 155–162
    contract, see Contract manufacturing
Marine risk, 121
Market access through exporting, 28–29
Market demand, 28
Marketing, 4, 20, 22, 23–24, 33
Market share, 23, 35
Marx, Karl, 16
McDonald's, 34, 39, 168
Mennen Company, 184–185
Merchandise, 59, 83, 90
MERCOSUR, 195, 197, 249
Merger, 35
Microsoft, 35, 174
MIGA, see Multilateral Investment Guarantee Agency
Mill, John Stuart, 16
Mixed economy, 16–17, 25
Monetary gold, 51, 52
    reserves, 72, 73, 77
Monetary stability, 46–47
Monetary system, 41–54
    defined, 41–43

historical background, 43–50
international liquidity, reserve assets and settlement of obligations, 50–52
Money, 11, 67, 78, see also Currency
Morgan, J.P., 44
Most favored nation status, 195
Multilateral Investment Guarantee Agency, 252, 255
Multinational corporations, 4, 14
    challenges for, 11–12
    exporting, 28
    foreign sales corporation and, 221
    international business operations, see International business operations
    organization and philosophy, 17–24
    responsibilities of, 9–12

NAFTA, see North American Free Trade Association
National Cash Register Company, 22
Nationalization, 200, 205
National security restrictions, 191, 192
Nestle, 108
North American Free Trade Association, 160, 195, 196, 197, 200, 216, 248–249, 250, 251

Ocean carrier, 120
Ocean freight, 88
Open account payment, 139
Open account shipments, 134
OPIC, see Overseas Private Investment Corporation
Outgoing investments, 200–201, 205
Overseas Private Investment Corporation, 210, 223, 225–228, 243

Paper money, 43–44, 48
Parent, 36–37, 186, 211
Paris Convention for the Protection of Industrial Property, 110, 169
Partnership, 208
Patent, 105, 106, 107–108, 110, 111, 163, 164, 165, 170, 171
Patent and Trademark Office, 107
Patent Cooperation Treaty, 169
Patent Office, 170
Payment, 128–131
Payment terms, 137–144

Pegged currency, 49–50, 53, 68, 78
Pensions, 60
Pepsi, 32, 157
Philadelphia Stock Exchange, 72, 76
Piracy, 170
Policy and Advisory Services, 255
Political relations, 199–200
Political risk insurance, 140
Political risk loss, 231
Political stability, 13
Pollution Control Loan Program, 237–238
Polycentric corporation, 20–22, 25
Population, 6–7, 239, 240
Portfolio investments, 202–203
Pratt & Whitney, 35, 174
Pre-investment services, 227
Private enterprise, 4
Private ownership, 5, 14, 25
Private sector, 17
Privatization, 5, 14, 45
Process patent, 108, 165
Procter & Gamble, 18, 31, 157
Product liability, 99, 101–102
Product patent, 108, 165
Product warranty, 99–101, 102
Production, 4, 5, 19, 21, 35
Profits, 202
Promissory note, 130, 142
Proprietorship, 208
Purchasing, 19, 21
Purchasing power parity theory, 73–74, 78

Qualified Employee Trust Program, 237
Quality control, 34

RCA Corporation, 33, 166
Regulations, 191–198
Remitting bank, 128, 129, 140, 142, 147
Research and development, 18, 21, 23
Reserve assets, 72–73, 77
Residency, 58, 65, 91–93, 98, 207–208, 223
Resources, 12–13, 19
   development and allocation, 4, 6, 7
Restrictions, 29
   investment, 199–205
   trade, 191–198
Return on investment, 9
Ricardo, David, 16
Riots and civil commotions, 122

Rockefeller, John, 9
Royal Dutch Shell, 20
Royalty, 33, 109, 163, 166, 167, 169

Sales, 20, 22, 23–24, 35
SBA, see Small Business Administration
Schumann Plan, 247
Scrip, 43
SDRs, see Special drawing rights
Seasonal Line of Credit Program, 236
Seed capital, 227
Services, 34, 59–60, 83, 90, 160
Shareholders, 221
Shelter, 11, 13
Shipper's Export Declaration, 126, 136
Shipping and selling terms, 113–118, 124
Shipping documentation, 125–131, 136
Shipping documents, 130
Shipping terms, 137
Sight draft, 129, 132, 140, 141, 142, 144
Sight letter of credit, 151
Silver, 43
Single-column tariff, 195
Small business, 184
Small Business Administration, 210, 223, 234–239, 244
Small General Contractor Loan Program, 236
Smith, Adam, 16, 70
Socialism, 16
Social services, 12
Soft currency, 49, 53, 68, 77
Sole proprietorship, 208
Sourcing, 5, 21, 160
Special drawing rights, 50, 51, 63, 78, 258, 261–263, 264
Spot rate, 69, 74, 78
Spread, 70, 78
Statistical discrepancy, 58, 65
Statistical discrepancy account, 61
Stockholders, 5, 17, 25, 181
   obligation to, 9
Stocks, 37, 39, 181
Strategic alliance, 34–35, 36, 39, 173–179
Subsidiary, 35, 36–37, 167, 182, 186, 211
   taxation of, 209
   wholly owned, see Wholly owned subsidiary
SWIFT, 131, 143

"Tariff of Abominations," 203
Taxation, 159, 160
  foreign sales corporation, 219–222
  U.S. policies, see U.S. policies
Tax havens, 211–212, 223
Tax holidays, 210
Tax incentive programs, 210
Tax treaties, 209–210, 211, 223
Technical restrictions, 197
Technology, 4, 11, 12–13, 14, 18, 19, 21, 23, 37
  foreign exchange and, 70
  protecting, 108–109
  transfer of, 163
Telephone transfer, 74
Three-cornered hat concept, 9–10, 14
Time draft, 129, 132, 140, 141–142, 144
Time letter of credit, 151, 152
Title, 94, 137
Trade acceptance, 142, 144
Trade blocs, 245–251, 264
Trade deficit, 57, 62–63
Trademark, 105, 106–107, 110, 111, 163, 164, 170
Trade name, 105, 106, 111, 163, 164
Trade practices, 83–90
Trade regulation and restrictions, 29, 191–198
Trade retaliation laws, 203–204
"Trading with the enemy," 203
Transportation, 11, 13, see also Logistics
Transport costs, 29
Transport documents, 130, see also Documentation
Triple-column tariff, 195
Turnkey system, 32–33, 40, 155–156, 160–161, 162

Unemployment, 11, 13
"Unfriendly high-risk" countries, 201
"Unfriendly low-risk" countries, 201
Uniform Rules for Collections, 143
Unilateral transfers, 60
Unilever, 20, 31
United Nations, 41, 256
United States Agency for International Development, 210, 223–230, 239–243, 244

United Technologies, 35, 174
USAID, see United States Agency for International Development
Usance draft, see Time draft
U.S. balance of payments, 281–285
U.S. Customs, 126
U.S. dollar, 48, 67
U.S. policies, taxation and related programs, 207–223
  Foreign Sales Corporation Act, 216–222
  free trade zones and duty-free customs areas, 212–216
  international taxation, 207–212
U.S. terms, 75
U.S. worldwide income rule, 208, 223
Use tax, 211

Value-added tax, 116, 194
Variable fixed-exchange rate, 47–48, 49, 54
VAT, see Value-added tax
Vertical integration, 34–35, 39, 173–174, 179
Vietnam-Era and Disabled Veterans Loan Program, 238
VOLs, see Voluntary restraints
Voluntary restraints, 193

Warranty, 99–101, 102
Warranty breach, 100
Warranty disclaimer, 99–101
Welfare, 12
Western hemisphere trading corporation, 217
Westinghouse, 108
Wholly owned subsidiary, 20, 30, 35, 36–37, 38, 92, 167, 182, 185–187, 188
Williamson, Gilbert, 22
Women's Loan Program, 238
Working Capital Guarantee Program, 229, 230–231, 234
World Bank, 41, 230, 251–256, 264
World population, 6–7, 239, 240
World Trade Organization, 110, 169, 197, 203, 215, 222
Worldwide income rule, 208, 223
WTO, see World Trade Organization